HEBREW THOUGHT COMPARED
WITH GREEK

HEBREW THOUGHT
COMPARED
WITH GREEK

THORLEIF BOMAN

W · W · NORTON & COMPANY

New York · London

Translated by Jules L. Moreau, M.A., S.T.M., from the German
Das hebräische Denken im Vergleich mit dem Griechischen
(2nd edition), published 1954 by Vandenhoeck & Ruprecht, Göttingen,
with the author's revisions to January 1960

W. W. Norton & Company, Inc., 500 Fifth Avenue, New York, N.Y. 10110
W. W. Norton & Company Ltd., 10 Coptic Street, London WC1A 1PU

ISBN 0-393-00534-8

PRINTED IN THE UNITED STATES OF AMERICA

9 0

CONTENTS

INTRODUCTION: THE PROBLEM

The problem of the peculiarity of Hebraic thinking in comparison with Greek thinking is epistemological, but it has eminent theological meaning because on it depends the question of the essence of Christianity. Harnack saw the problem rightly but misjudged it. Later attempts to solve the problem

I · DYNAMIC AND STATIC THINKING

In the ancient Orient the divine Word belongs more to the physical realm, in Assyria and Babylonia as dreadful power, in Egypt as material emanation

In the Old Testament the Word of God appears as moral act; apparent exceptions. The creative word in Israel and in the rest of the Orient. Words bear the same character as their author

II · IMPRESSION AND APPEARANCE

SUMMARY AND PSYCHOLOGICAL FOUNDATION OF THE DIFFERENCES

TRANSLATOR'S PREFACE

THE WORK here translated has already been published in a Japanese translation by Professor Shigeo Ueda under the title *Heburai-jin to Girisha-jin no shii* (Shinkyo Shuppansha, Tokyo, 1957). It deserves the attention of English-speaking scholars for at least two reasons. On its own merits it is a responsible contribution to an understanding of the unique kind of thinking represented by the Old Testament; further, it deals penetratingly with one of the basic questions currently facing biblical scholars and systematic theologians alike.

The translation is made from the second German edition further revised by the author himself. In addition to classifying the bibliography, the translator has completed bibliographical data where this was necessary to comply with English and American style. Unless otherwise noted, biblical quotations in the translation are from the *Revised Standard Version* (New York: Thomas Nelson & Sons, 1952); the author regularly quoted from E. Kautzsch's German translation which formed the basis of the two-volume commentary, *Die Heilige Schrift des Alten Testaments* (4th ed., Tübingen: J. C. B. Mohr, 1922–23), and where the sense required it, the translator has rendered the German of this version indicating it appropriately (e.g. Eccles 1.1 Kautzsch). Less frequently the author employed a rendering of Mowinckel's translation which served as the text for a work similar to that of Kautzsch's, edited jointly by Mowinckel, S. Michelet, and N. Messel (*see* Bibliography); where it was fundamental to the meaning, the translator compared Mowinckel's Norwegian rendering with the author's German rendering of Mowinckel and translated as literally as possible citing in the notes Mowinckel's translation (M.M.M.).

A few expansions of the notes have been made for English and American readers, and these have been marked with the abbreviation [tr.].

Evanston, Illinois   J. L. M.
June 1958

PREFACE TO ENGLISH EDITION

THREE GERMAN and two Japanese editions of this monograph have already appeared, and careful attention has been given in this edition to critical remarks that have been made in reviews of the first two German editions; since the criticisms have not been directed at the essay's main thesis, it can be judged, therefore, to have been established on the whole.

Within the restricted boundaries that I have set for this essay, many important problems are only touched upon; however, since the majority of reviewers felt especially keenly the lack of some clarification of the problems of history and the biblical notion of creation, I have briefly entered into these problems in this edition. A brief presentation of Hebraic ideas of cosmology, often erroneously referred to as cosmogony, is included here (Section E of Chapter Three). With reference to this point, however, I should say that I feel constrained to protest against the theologians' customary conception that only the Israelites had any knowledge of what history is. Whether or not a nation attains a real understanding of history rests not upon their being gifted psychologically but rather upon their making principled decisions during fateful periods whereby the nation experiences or even makes history. Consequently, not only the Israelites but also the Greeks, in distinction from all their neighbours, attained a true understanding of history. The difference lies in the way in which the historical consciousness took shape; here the national peculiarity is effective. Put succinctly, it can be said that the Israelites gave the world historical religion and the Greeks gave it historical science.

The relation between the Old Testament belief in creation and that of Plato deserves closer examination. The vagueness and difficulty in stating the problem dogmatically, felt even by Karl Barth (*Kirchliche Dogmatik*, III, i, Vorwort), is connected partly at any rate with the fact that Christian belief contains both conceptions of creation, which are, however, basically different and incommensurable, a fact to which sufficient attention has not been given. Someone should clear up in all directions the inner relation existing between (Greek) belief in the beyond (*Jenseitsglaube*) and (biblical) eschatology, since both represent indispensable elements in our Christian faith; this is suggested in the excursus to Section C of Chapter Three.

The Hebrew (Semitic) and the Greek (Indo-European) kinds of

thinking are sharply distinguished in this essay; therefore, no Greek author after Aristotle is cited. From the days of Alexander the Great onward, the history of European civilization manifests only mixtures and syntheses of the two ways of thinking, in which now one and now the other prevails; the most important of these are Hellenism (in which are included Stoicism, Neoplatonism, and the Jewish Diaspora under which are subsumed both the Septuagint and Philo), Christian religion and culture, Islamic culture, and the Renaissance. Should my analysis of these two homogeneous kinds of thinking have, in the main, hit the right note, we have thereby found a means also of understanding these mixed cultures more fundamentally. Oswald Spengler, who in *The Decline of the West* brilliantly analyses the peculiarity of classical Greek thinking, founders in his attempt to represent the Semitic kind of thinking because he is building upon an analysis of Islamic culture as a foundation.

A fundamental examination of the way in which Hebrew thought-forms are related in the New Testament to the Greek forms would be extremely valuable. Canon Quick has made a beginning on this.

In Church history and in the history of dogma both kinds of thinking are encountered, sometimes in harmony, as in the leading personages of the ancient Church, chiefly Augustine, and sometimes in disharmony and opposition, as in the conflict between Realism and Nominalism in the Middle Ages.

It becomes evident that the Renaissance contains a Semitic element when, for example, Michaelangelo's dynamic sculpture is compared with the harmonious classical Greek sculpture or when Galileo's physics is compared with Aristotelian physics.

It is easy to establish that in contrast to the visual, contemplative piety of the Catholic Church Luther's thought and religion are expressed in a dynamic-auditive way and that the Lutheran Church has preserved this peculiarity. It helps to a considerable extent to understand the content of the Bible immediately and to appropriate it, but in itself it has nothing to do with the genuineness of Christianity. Our inquiry should contribute to a better understanding and a fairer estimate of the Eastern Orthodox Church. As no other church body the Orthodox Church has preserved the Greek heritage, and with sure instinct it has given preference in the New Testament to the Johannine literature as that which corresponds most closely to its spirit, while the Evangelical Church has more the Pauline characteristic and the Catholic Church the Petrine. In the Ecumenical Movement today there is much said about non-theological factors that have contributed to divisions in the Church; one of the most important, until now little noticed, among these factors is the different psychology of religious life and thought.

The problem analysed in this essay is, so to speak, in the air in our day. Johannes Hessen in his book *Platonismus und Prophetismus* and Claude Tresmontant in his *Essai sur la pensée hebraïque* investigate the problem from an abstractly philosophical viewpoint. In his book *The Fulness of Time*, John Marsh has undertaken a thorough philological and theological analysis of the Hebraic understanding of time, and he has arrived independently at a result similar to that achieved in this book.

In a single monograph it is obviously impossible to master the exceedingly rich subject here undertaken. Indeed at the present time it is quite impossible for a single scholar to master completely in a scientific way all the fields that are relevant. For this reason I invite all interested scholars to examine this problem area from their own standpoints; they will surely earn a rich reward for their effort.

I should like to take this opportunity of expressing my thanks to those whose interest and help have led to this English edition—the publishers in Britain and America, and especially the translator, Professor Moreau, who not only urged that the translation be made but also kindly offered to undertake the task.

Oslo, January 1960   THORLEIF BOMAN

ABBREVIATIONS

Ges.-K.   *Genius' Hebrew Grammar*. ed. E. Kautzsch. Translated by A. E. Cowley (*see* Bibliography—Kautzsch).

Kautzsch *Die Heilige Schrift des Alten Testaments*. Trans. and ed. E. Kautzsch (*see* Bibliography—Kautzsch).

M.M.M.   *Det gamle testamente oversatt av* S. Michelet, S. Mowinckel, og N. Messel, I–III (*see* Bibliography—Michelet, S.).

RGG¹   ⎱ *Religion in Geschichte und Gegenwart*. 1st and 2nd editions
RGG²   ⎰ (*see* Bibliography—*Religion*).

NTT   *Norsk Teologisk Tidsskrift*. Periodical published at Oslo.

ZAW   *Zeitschrift für die alttestamentliche Wissenschaft*. Periodical published since 1924, first at Giessen and then at Berlin.

TRANSCRIPTION OF HEBREW LETTERS

A. Consonants are transcribed as follows:

'Begadkepat' letters are transcribed with 'h' when fricative, and without when plosive.

א — '	מ — m
ה — h	נ — n
ו — w	ס — ṣ
ז — z	ע — '
ח — ḥ	צ — ts
ט — ṭ	ק — q
י — y	ר — r
י — ê or î (when vocalic)	שׂ — s
ל — l	שׁ — sh

B. Vowels are transcribed as follows:

Pathaḥ — a	Seghol — e
Qamets — a	Qibbuts — u
Ḥireq — i	Ḥolem — o
Tsere — e	Shewa — e
	Shewa compound — a, e, o

INTRODUCTION
The Problem

CHRISTIANITY arose on Jewish soil; Jesus and the Apostles spoke Aramaic, a language related to Hebrew, unless Harris Birkeland should prove to be right in his hypothesis that Jesus and the Apostles spoke a folk dialect of Hebrew.[1] As the New Testament writings show, they were firmly rooted in the Old Testament and lived in its world of images. Shortly after the death of the Founder, however, the new religious community's centre of gravity shifted into the Greek-speaking Hellenistic world, and after the year 70, the community was severed finally from its motherland: Christianity has been the religion of Europeans ever since. It is significant, however, that despite their absolute authority the words of Jesus were preserved by the Church only in the Greek language. Not only are these two languages essentially different, but so too are the kinds of images and thinking involved in them. This distinction goes very deeply into the psychic life; the Jews themselves defined their spiritual predisposition as anti-Hellenic.[2] Once this point is properly understood, it must be granted completely.

The peculiar character of the Hebrew language and its manner of expression must have been obvious to every European who has read the Old Testament in Hebrew; Luther made occasional reference to it, and Herder described the distinctive traits of Old Testament poetic art.[3] The question of the formal and real relationship between Israelite-Jewish and Greek-Hellenistic thinking became for Christianity and the Church a live problem, and the occasion of penetrating theological investigations,

[1] Harris Birkeland, *Språk og religion hos jöder og arabere*.

[2] 'Kunst', *Jüdisches Lexikon*, III, 934: 'One of the reasons that the Jews produced no significant art of their own is the particular mental attitude of the Jewish people, the "anti-Hellenic" in them. The genius of this people was directed not toward the fashioning of form, nor toward a harmonious experience of the surrounding world, but toward the legitimacy of moral activity. The Second Commandment's prohibition of images results mainly from this orientation; this commandment would never have consistently been observed had not this mental attitude existed.'

[3] J. G. Herder, *Vom Geist der ebräischen Poesie* (*Sämmtliche Werke*, ed. B. Suphan [1877–1913], vol. XI).

only after Adolf Harnack had called attention to its great importance for the development of dogma in the early Christian Church, a Church endowed with Greek thinking and mental life, and after he had maintained that the Gospel was hellenized and that dogma was a product of the Greek intellect in the soil of the Gospel.[1] We cannot concern ourselves with a discussion of the controversies that followed the publication of Harnack's work; in any case, they caused first one, and then another theologian to become aware of the uncommon relation between Israelite-Jewish and Greek modes of conception and thought-forms and to reflect more deeply upon it. At first the full significance of this relationship for an understanding of Christianity was understood slowly, and even after the discovery of the importance of the distinction there was no unanimity in evaluating it.

The English Platonist, Canon Oliver C. Quick, recognized most clearly the bearing and the significance of the distinction. In a distinguished study[2] he tried from a definite standpoint to grasp the Greek and Hebrew kinds of thinking as one closed yet complete unity, which would require a corresponding exposition of Christianity. Since the difference in development is merely formal, he can value the Greek form as highly as the Hebrew. He also points out both types in the New Testament and in the history of the Church until twentieth-century English church life.

From another viewpoint and on a much narrower base, Anders Nygren analyses with impressive profundity the Hebrew and Greek types of Christianity in a carefully planned work wherein he conceives love as a basic motif defining the whole conception of Christianity.[3] It is quite correct and meritorious that Nygren regards the Platonic understanding of love, *Eros*, as the only possible basis for a comparison with the biblical-Hebraic idea of love, *Agapé*. Platonism represents the acme of Greek intellectual life, as Nygren also thinks, and because it is religious in nature, it is quite comparable with Israelite thinking which is religious through and through. In this monograph, too, Greek thinking will be represented principally by Plato. Nygren maintains that Agapé is the free and unmerited love that comes from God and flows toward man; Eros, he says, is the love that stems from man and strives toward God. That may be quite correct, even though Nygren presents his interpretation too

---

[1] A. Harnack, *History of Dogma*. Since ancient times many theologians have been aware of the inner relationship between Christianity and Greek, especially Platonic, philosophy as noted by F. C. Baur, *Drei Abhandlungen zur Geschichte der alten Philosophie und ihres Verhältnisses zum Christentum*. Harnack, on the contrary, feels that this relationship is an opposition.

[2] Oliver C. Quick, *The Gospel of Divine Action*.

[3] Anders Nygren, *Agape and Eros*.

schematically. Apart from this, serious objections have been raised to his analysis. Hans Ording in an article[1] points out how biased a comparison between Eros and Agapé must become because they both represent quite heterogeneous complexes in which Agapé is the divine factor and Eros the human factor in relation to God. As F. C. Baur has convincingly demonstrated,[2] faith in the Christian sense corresponds to the Platonic Eros. Just as there is a human factor at work in the Christian relationship with God, so in the Platonic there is a divine factor; Plato's God is in part represented impersonally as the Idea of the Good with the sun as a symbol[3]—which is surely not ineffective but life-bestowing, glorious, and attractive—and in part personally when God is called the good creator and father.[4] For other details, the reader is referred to my criticism of Nygren's book.[5] Along with Rudberg and many others I contend that Platonism and Christianity are related essentially and that they support joint values just as they earlier did jointly. The decisive and self-evident fact is not the antithesis but the unity, the cohesion. It is blindness or dishonesty, says Rudberg, to believe or allege to believe that an eradication of the 'Platonic man' in the West would mean the triumph of the Gospel.[6]

Plato plays a much greater rôle in English intellectual life than in the German. This is certainly related to the fact that for centuries in English universities there has been a living Platonic philosophical tradition which has also had a great influence upon English theology, while in Germany a peculiarly German brand of idealist philosophy has repressed Platonism and to a considerable extent replaced it. There is, however, a great difference between these two, i.e. Platonism and German Idealism. Platonism is the doctrine of what really *is*; idealist philosophy is the doctrine of the shaping of the human mind. So far as the theologian uses philosophy, John Marsh is right in his assertion: 'It would seem to be as characteristic for the reformed theologian to follow Plato as for the catholic to be Aristotelian.'[7]

It can surely be regarded as generally recognized that Hebrew thinking is dynamic and Greek static, but this must be understood in its total bearing and more fully substantiated. In a much-quoted article, to which

---

[1] Hans Ording, 'Frelsesoppfatningen hos Platon og i kristendommen', *Norsk teologisk tidsskrift*, XXXIII (1932), 261 ff. In a reply, Nygren has maintained his position. *Filosofi och motivforskning*, pp. 90 ff.

[2] Baur, *op. cit.*, pp. 276 f.

[3] Plato *Republic* vi, pp. 508a ff. [citations of Plato's works follow Stephanus pagination].

[4] Plato *Timaeus*, pp. 28 ff.; *Statesman*, p. 274.

[5] Thorleif Boman, 'Israelittiske og greske tankeformer i den eldste kristendom,' NTT, XLVIII (1947), 66 ff.

[6] Gunnar Rudberg, *Platon*, pp. 229 ff.

[7] John Marsh, *The Fulness of Time*, p. 17.

we shall later return, von Dobschütz thinks he can establish that the thinking of the Greeks is spatial and that of the Hebrews is temporal.[1] In itself this thesis is correct, but it must be otherwise argued and substantiated. If time is considered by itself, it is not hard to discover that Greek and Israelite-Jewish interpretations of time are entirely different, as Oscar Cullmann, among others, has tried to establish more fully.[2] We, too, are of the opinion that the two peoples' understanding of time is different, even though the difference, in our opinion, is of another sort.

For a long time theological scholarship has been aware of the peculiar relationship between Greek and Hebrew thinking; yet this relationship has been differently interpreted and evaluated. Further, all these scholars have seen but one side of the problem, or at least have analysed but one side. Moreover, none of them, with the possible exception of Canon Quick, has distinguished clearly between the formal and the material sides of the problem. If the rethinking of early Christianity in Greek thought-forms is to be assessed correctly, the nature as well as the significance of the formal distinction must first be established; without doubt, it is an important task to analyse and illuminate from all sides the formal distinction between Greek and Hebrew thinking. Only then is it possible to see and to judge whether and to what extent the *content* of Christianity has been affected by the rethinking. For this reason, we have confined our inquiry to *a comparison of the intellectual world of the Old Testament with the intellectual world of the Greek, principally that of the philosophers, and particularly that of Plato.*

According to the view of Walter F. Otto, we could just as well have chosen Homer as representative of Greek thought. In his book *The Homeric Gods*, Otto first describes the peculiarity of the Greeks quite as we have done: 'First and highest is not the power that acts, but the being that is manifested in the form of the act.' Then he continues: 'This concept of the world which we call specifically Greek found its first and greatest expression in the age whose monuments are the Homeric poems (p. 9). . . . The most significant event in the life of a people . . . is the emergence of a mode of thought that is peculiar to it, as if designed for it from the beginning of time, by which it is henceforward distinguishable in the world's history. This process took place when the prehistoric view was transformed into the view which we first find in Homer and which

---

[1] E. von Dobschütz, 'Zeit und Raum', *Journal of Biblical Literature*, XLI (1922), 212 ff.

[2] O. Cullmann, *Christ and Time*; cf. Gerhard Delling, *Das Zeitverständnis des Neuen Testaments.*

we never thereafter encounter with comparable clarity and grandeur (p. 10).'[1]

I believe that the results to which I have come are enduring; in principle and on the whole they are the same as I published in my first scholarly article.[2] For twenty years I have reflected on the problems discussed here, and I have tried to discover what others thought about them in order to study their views without prejudice. I am forced to confess that in this undertaking my original and basic interpretation was only deepened and strengthened. It was a special joy to discover that studies by famous scholars about which I knew nothing at the time or which had not yet been published confirmed important details of my own solution to the problem. Perhaps it is right to mention here an objection which a couple of reviewers made, since their interpretation occurs frequently among modern theologians. According to this view, the thinking of the Old Testament is *primitive* and hence can be compared only with the thinking of other primitive peoples and not with thinking as advanced as Plato's or Bergson's. It is not to be denied that a great deal can be learned from a comparison between the thinking of Ancient Israel and that of other peoples at the same stage of development;[3] but the correctness of one viewpoint of an inquiry surely does not rule out the validity of a totally different viewpoint. Moreover, the term 'primitive' is as unclear as it is ambiguous. W. F. Albright thinks that the logical epoch of humanity begins first among the Greeks in the fifth century B.C., but that since then no real advance in human thinking has taken place. In the fifth century B.C., he thinks, the mental-spiritual life of Israel achieved its zenith with the pure ethical monotheism of Deutero-Isaiah and Job, nor did monotheism later advance any further.[4] According to Johannes Pedersen, the thinking of the book of Job is typically Israelite and therefore primitive, although it stems from a relatively late period.[5] Thus it is seen that a stage of mental-spiritual development which represents for Albright an absolute zenith of its kind is on the whole for Pedersen a primitive stage. If Pedersen means, however, that the author himself no longer belongs to the primitive stage, then the poet must have been able to put himself so completely

[1] Walter F. Otto, *The Homeric Gods: The Spiritual Significance of Greek Religion*, pp. 9 f.
[2] Thorleif Boman, 'Den semittiske tenknings egenart', NTT, XXXIV (1933), 1-34.
[3] This is sufficiently demonstrated in the first volume of Johannes Pedersen's excellent work, *Israel: its Life and Culture I-II, III-IV* (2 vols.; London, 1926-47).
[4] W. F. Albright, *From the Stone Age to Christianity*, 1940, p. 83.
[5] 'That which lends its peculiar character to the Book of Job is that it rests entirely on the Old Israelitic conception of life. The speech in which Job describes his lost happiness (chap. 29) is a classical description of an old Israelitic community.' Pedersen, *Israel I-II*, p. 364.

into the ancient way of thinking that he could reproduce it correctly. But this presupposes that his readers were completely familiar with the ancient sort of thinking; then the distinction between 'primitive' and highly developed kinds of thinking in Israel cannot have been great. We ought to be able, then, to consider the two stages as a unity at least from our standpoint and for our purposes. It is possible, however, that Pedersen means by 'primitive' approximately what Lévy-Bruhl means by 'pre-logical';[1] yet this stage of development had already been transcended in Asia Minor in the third millennium B.C.,[2] a millennium and a half before Moses! Apparently by 'primitive' Pedersen means only the same thing as Vilhelm Grönbech does when he calls the thinking of the ancient Norwegians and Icelanders primitive,[3] or as Bruno Snell does when he establishes a similar distinction between Homer's thought-world and that of the philosophical age of Greece.[4] Still, Snell speaks correctly not of 'primitive' Hellenism, but of 'early' Hellenism.[5] A similar expression ought to be used when speaking of the Pentateuch and of Old Nordic literature, for under the heading 'primitive' we ordinarily think first of all of Australian Aborigines, Bushmen, and peoples who are on the same plane or even lower. If we are so willing to recognize that Homer as well

---

[1] Pedersen's reference (*ibid.*, p. 132) to Lévy-Bruhl, *Les fonctions mentales dans les sociétés inférieures*, could point in that direction. Yet it is interesting that Lévy-Bruhl found a similarity between primitive thinking and that of Bergson; of the primitive representation of time, he says, 'Elle se rapproche plutôt d'un sentiment subjectif de la durée, non sans quelque analogie avec celui qui a été décrit par M. Bergson. Elle est à peine une représentation' (p. 90). Bergson's thinking cannot be designated as primitive or pre-logical; Lévy-Bruhl's observation contains much that is correct, only it must be interpreted otherwise. Bergson's thinking is related to Israelite thinking, a point which had already occurred to Nathan Söderblom (*Uppenbarelsreligionen*, p. 163, n.; cf. *The Living God* [London: Oxford University Press, 1933], pp. 310 ff.). Israelite (as well as Bergsonian) thinking is similar to primitive thinking in that both are non-European, 'anti-Hellenic'; yet they are quite different from one another. Lévy-Bruhl has misinterpreted the similarity between the primitive and Bergsonian conceptions of time. Aubrey R. Johnson (*The Vitality of the Individual in the Thought of Ancient Israel*, pp. 1 f.) rejects Lévy-Bruhl's theory of a pre-logical mentality among primitive peoples and refers at this point to O. Leroy (*La raison primitive. Essai de réfutation de la théorie du prélogisme*, pp. 16 ff.) and P. Radin (*Primitive Man as a Philosopher*, pp. 27 ff., 229 ff.).

[2] Albright, *op. cit.*, p. 84.

[3] Vilhelm Grönbech (*Primitiv religion*, p. 1) speaks of the 'close agreement between the morals and the philosophy of the savage on the one side, and between the cultus and the faith of the Greeks and Germans on the other'. He worked this relation out more closely in *Vor folkeaet i oldtiden* 1–4, and *Hellas. Kultur og religion*, 1–4. However, he strongly emphasizes the other side, that 'it is important to recognize that every culture and religion is a whole which has absolute value in itself. (*Primitiv religion*, p. 3.)

[4] Bruno Snell, *Die Entdeckung des Geistes*. Grönbech distinguishes between two clearly defined epochs, the age of the nobles (Homer, Pindar) and the age of the commoner; between them, he asserts, there lies a revolution of eminent historical significance, which corresponds to the no less fateful upheaval that separated ancient Israel from post-Exilic Judaism (*Hellas. Kultur og religion, 1*, p. 9).

[5] Snell, *op. cit.*, pp. 7 ff.

as the Jahvist belongs to an earlier stage of development which has certain
features in common, then we must maintain decisively that it is more
characteristic that Homer was a Greek and the Jahvist an Israelite, that is
to say, what in each of the two peoples remained identical with itself
during the people's entire mental-spiritual history was more essential
than the later alterations and transformations. Therein lies the possibility
of our inquiry, a possibility which it is to be hoped will find realization in
the following monograph.[1]

The 'profane' sciences, such as ethno-psychology, psychology of
language, philosophy of language, logic of language, semantics, and comparative linguistics, of which we should have expected that they would
find interest in the problem of the peculiarity of Hebrew (Semitic)
thinking, have not yet discovered the problem, from all appearances.[2] A
psychologist of language of Bühler's rank[3] and the old master of ethno-
psychology, W. Wundt,[4] occasionally do mention details from the Hebrew

---

[1] Johannes Pedersen has recently communicated with the author to the effect that
he is not particularly satisfied with the word 'primitive', partly because it is too indefinite
and partly because it is often misleading, but he has found no better word. When he
used this word, he had in mind peoples who live in direct dependence upon nature, but
a sharp demarcation cannot be made. He also thinks it perfectly correct that there is
something in Israelite thinking which remains identical with itself through its entire
history and that it is an important task to examine the relation between Hebrew and
Greek thinking. If the view set forth here is correct, an objection raised by Rudolf
Bultmann, in his review of my work, vanishes: 'It may be asked whether or not it is
possible, by means of this comparison (of the Old Testament with the thought world of
the Greeks during their philosophical period), to acquire a correct picture. (*Gnomon*,
XXVII [1955], 551 f.). But Bultmann rightly commends Erich Auerbach's essay
('Odysseus' Scar', *Mimesis*, pp. 3–23) in which the Old Testament account of the sacrifice
of Isaac is compared in a highly instructive way with the Homeric account of the scar on
Odysseus' thigh. Auerbach's comparison between the Old Testament art of narration and
the Greek coincides with the viewpoint of the present work so well that it could have been
included as a chapter in this book almost without alteration. It is very interesting, however, that other reviewers have raised the same objection to Auerbach's essay, which
has become famous in the meantime, as Bultmann raises against my work. Otto Regenbogen writes, 'It would be justifiable to raise at the beginning the fundamental question
as to whether or not things generally comparable are here being compared. Should both
texts be dealt with as *epic*, which is what the author is expressly doing? That the Homeric
text is epic is self-evident; the Old Testament material belongs, however, with prehistoric saga or tales, and it is constructed in a historically supra-historical, or if you will,
in a metaphysical context. On the basis of such observation, the Greek parallel that
appears to me to be alone commensurable results automatically: it is the *logoi* of early
Greek prose, chiefly those to be found in Herodotus' works' (O. Regenbogen, '*Mimesis*:
Eine Rezension' *Motala* [1949], pp. 11 ff.). For all that, Regenbogen agrees in the rest of
his review with Auerbach's comparison but finds in Homer numerous parallels to almost
all the peculiarities of style (cf. Bultmann!) which Auerbach had found in the Old
Testament account.
[2] By way of example we cite: Friedrich Kainz, *Psychologie der Sprache I-II*; Julius
Stenzel, *Philosophie der Sprache* (Munich, 1934); Richard Hönigswald, *Philosophie und
Sprache : Problemkritik und System*; Edward L. Thorndike, *Studies in the Psychology
of Language* ('Archives of Psychology', 33 [New York, 1938]).
[3] Karl Bühler, *Sprachtheorie* (Jena, 1934).
[4] W. Wundt, *Völkerpsychologie*, Bd. I, *Die Sprache* (3te Aufl.; Leipzig, 1911–12).

language but never anything essential for Hebrew thinking. Modern linguistic philosophy, the founder of which is taken to be W. Humboldt (we pass over Herder because his significance as a philosopher of language is disputed),[1] is perfectly clear about the fact that languages are the expressions of thinking peculiar to peoples, even of the most primitive peoples, those closest to nature: '. . . There is a petrified philosophy in language', as Max Mueller puts it; even they have not seen the peculiarity of the Hebrew language. Humboldt and Mueller,[2] both of whom understood Hebrew, mention only superficial things; Humboldt finds it not only characteristic of Hebrew but also fatal to its higher development of thought that its word roots are *triliteral*! Still more remarkable is it that Ernst Cassirer, a Jew who knew Hebrew, whose philosophy of language is by far the most basic and versatile accomplishment in this field in our time, and who makes frequent references to Hebrew, adduces nothing specific for Hebrew thinking. Cassirer thinks as a European, more precisely as a Kantian; at one point he comes very near to discovering that there are two incommensurable concepts of time, but he finally resolves them into a unity while extolling the synthetic power of the concept of time![3] He also thinks that spatial thinking and spatial expression are original in all languages and are carried over from space to time.[4] This notion, which we are later to show as contradicted by the Hebrew language, surely stems from comparative linguistics and has been taken over by the other sciences as incontrovertible fact, even by the learned and penetrating logician W. M. Urban, who on this point also cites Bergson.[5] The thinking of Grassler is also spatially stamped; he conceives of time as a band or schema lying ready to be filled with events.[6] His expression, 'patterns of change',[7] surely contains a *contradictio in adjecto*.

The linguistic logic of the newer philosophical tendencies can be of even less assistance to us. A man belonging to the Vienna Circle like Rudolf Carnap is looking not so much for a logic of language as for a language for logic,[8] that is to say, he does not bury himself affectionately

---

[1] Cf. Wilh. Sturm, *Herders Sprachphilosophie* (Breslau, 1917).

[2] Wilhelm von Humboldt, *Die sprachphilosophischen Werke*, herausgeben und erklärt von H. Steinthal (Berlin, 1884); Friedrich Max Mueller, *Lectures on the Science of Language I-II* (London and New York, 1871–72).

[3] Ernst Cassirer, *The Philosophy of Symbolic Forms*, Vol. I, *Language*, trans. Ralph Manheim (New Haven: Yale University Press, 1953), p. 222.

[4] *Ibid.*, pp. 278 f.

[5] W. M. Urban, *Language and Reality* (London: Allen & Unwin, 1939), pp. 185 f.

[6] R. Grassler, *Der Sinn der Sprache* (Lahr, 1938), p. 8.   [7] *Ibid.*, p. 5.

[8] Rudolf Carnap, *The Logical Syntax of Language*, Eng. trans. (London: K. Paul, Trench, Trubner & Co., 1935); 'Die physicalische Sprache als Universalsprache der Wissenschaft', *Erkenntnis*, 1931, pp. 432 ff.

in the existing language to discover its inherent logic, but from his philosophical ideal of logic he criticizes actual languages as more or less unfit for his purpose and tries to form a logical sign language with the greatest possible elimination of words. When, for example, Carnap analyses the word '(to) be', he does not aim to understand the concept of being or existence inherent in the word but rather to prove that there is no such thing as being or existence because the concept is meaningless.[1] With the correct apprehension that Logical Positivism seeks something else in languages than what the various branches of linguistics have sought before, Hans Hermes calls his 'theory of the configuration of signs as a basis for the examination of formalized speech' neither semantics nor semasiology but *semiotic*.[2] In this monograph we have found no application for semiotic or linguistic analyses such as Carnap's analysis of the German word *sein* (to be).

One single method has not been followed exclusively throughout this monograph; our purpose was to present the peculiarity of Hebrew thinking in comparison with the Greek, and with this in view each time the method had to be employed which was best adapted to the material under discussion. It was especially important for the author to avoid the charge of speculation; therefore he has adduced throughout a solid, and perhaps occasionally—particularly in the beginning—too comprehensive empirical basis for his views from the Hebrew (Old Testament) and Greek languages and literature, and he has relied as much as possible on recognized scientific authorities. A deductive method, such as that employed by Johannes Hessen or Claude Tresmontant, does not, therefore, appear suitable or useful in this regard.[3] If the inquiry is limited to Hebrew thinking in its relation to Greek thinking, we are obviously not maintaining that all the lines of Old Testament thought cited as characteristic for the Hebrews are to be found only among them; details would be found among many peoples in various parts of the world. The thinking of other

[1] Rudolf Carnap, 'Überwindung der Metaphysik durch logische Analyse der Sprache', *Erkenntnis*, 1931, pp. 233 ff.

[2] H. Hermes, *Semiotik* (Leipzig, 1938). Of a similar type is Charles Morris, *Signs, Language and Behaviour* (New York: Prentice-Hall, 1946). Against the excessively logisticizing tendencies of language analysis we should like to cite a thoughtful remark made by Louis Hjelmslev: 'An ordinary language is in practice a language into which all other languages, as well as all other ordinary languages, and even all other conceivable language structures may be translated; this translatability rests upon the fact that ordinary languages and they alone are capable of giving form to any meaning whatever. In an ordinary language, indeed only in such, can the inexpressible be dealt with until such time as it is expressed' ('Omkring sprogteoriens grundlaeggelse', *University Program* [Copenhagen, 1943], p. 97).

[3] Johannes Hessen, *Platonismus und Prophetismus*; Claude Tresmontant, *Études de métaphysique biblique* and *Essai sur la pensée hébraïque*.

Semitic peoples, particularly, is of the same formal structure on the whole as the Israelite. To follow up the parallels each time among other peoples would hardly be possible lest the study become far too long; besides it is not necessary for the purposes of our inquiry. It is further to be noticed that the Israelites had to wage bitter cultural battles and controversies with their Semitic neighbours in order to assert their cultural uniqueness; that fact points to a most important independence of thought on their part even within the Semitic family of nations.

We have preferred Kautzsch's last edition of Gesenius' grammar[1] to the later revision by Bergsträsser[2] because Bergsträsser made no attempt to discover the psychological background of the Hebrew language-forms in order to understand them from the inside out. For example, he does not reckon with the possibility that the Hebrews have a radically different concept of time from ours;[3] instead he understands the Hebrew tense forms from the viewpoint of our time concept, thereby acting completely unaware of his presupposition that this concept of time possesses universal validity. Thus, in spite of its philological excellence, his edition was not as useful for our purpose as Kautzsch's. For the same reason we could find no use for either Brockelmann[4] or for Bauer and Leander.[5]

[1] E. Kautzsch (ed.), *Gesenius' Hebrew Grammar*, trans. and ed. A. E. Cowley (2nd ed.; Oxford: Clarendon Press, 1910); this edition is revised in accordance with the 28th German Edition.

[2] G. Bergsträsser, *Hebräische Grammatik: Mit Benutzung der von E. Kautzsch bearbeiteten 28. Auflage von Wilhelm Gesenius' hebräischer Grammatik, I Teil: Einleitung, Schrift- und Lautlehre* (Leipzig: F. C. W. Vogel, 1918), *II Teil: Verbum* (Leipzig: J. C. Hinrichs, 1929).

[3] Kautzsch, *op. cit.*, 47a, n. 1, recognizes this possibility as does Johannes Pedersen, *Hebraeisk Grammatik* (Copenhagen, 1926).

[4] Carl Brockelmann, *Grundriss der vergleichenden Grammatik der semitischen Sprachen* (2 vols.; Berlin: von Reuther & Reichard, 1908-13).

[5] Hans Bauer und Pontus Leander, *Historische Grammatik der hebräischen Sprache des Alten Testaments I* (Halle: Max Niemeyer, 1922).

I
Dynamic and Static Thinking

A. DYNAMIC THINKING

1. *The dynamic character of Hebrew verbs of inaction*

If Israelite thinking is to be characterized, it is obvious first to call it dynamic, vigorous, passionate, and sometimes quite explosive in kind; correspondingly Greek thinking is static, peaceful, moderate, and harmonious in kind. Ordinarily speaking, 'static' is opposed to 'dynamic' as antipodal, but the concept 'static' is unfortunate because it represents only the negative underside of the dynamic: the rigid, inflexible, and lifeless. Only when dynamic thinking is considered the ideal does Greek thinking appear static; once it is recognized that Greek thinking is fully the peer of Israelite thinking, an attempt must be made to give positive expression to the antithesis from the Greek side as well. From that viewpoint Greek mental activity appears harmonious, prudent, moderate, and peaceful; to the person to whom the Greek kind of thinking occurs plainly as ideal, Hebrew thinking and its manner of expression appear exaggerated, immoderate, discordant, and in bad taste. Putting aside the negative, the biased, and the unjust, we intend to understand both peoples positively from within. The antithesis we have mentioned cannot, then, be simply stated as 'dynamic-static', but preferably it should be designated *dynamic-harmonic* or *-resting*. The terms static-dynamic belong to the realm of mechanics and physics and are for that reason generally unsuited to express mental qualities; yet they are so well rooted in our vocabulary that they are scarcely to be avoided.

The idiosyncrasy of a nation or family of nations, a race, finds expression in the language peculiar to them. This is not least the case with culturally less developed nations and their languages in which the inner logic and its connexion with the psychology of the nation are easier to penetrate. In any case, Hebrew, a language exceptionally unusual in our experience and to our manner of thinking, betrays in many respects the idiosyncrasy of the Israelite psyche. The verbs especially, whose *basic meaning* always expresses a movement or an activity, reveal the dynamic variety of the Hebrews' thinking. When a verb is to express a position like sitting or lying, it is done by a verb which can also designate a movement. Now the question is, how is this possible logically or psychologically? Have we here to establish two distinct and, to our way of thinking, fundamentally different and contradictory meanings for the same word? Or has the word *one* basic meaning from which its various other meanings arise as nuances? If the latter is the case, that is if two opposites appear as related concepts, it must be asked how this is to be explained in connexion with the Hebrew manner of thinking. Verbs such as the following are to be taken into consideration here:

qûm—arise and stand.
natsabh—niph. (1) take one's stand; (2) stand.
'amadh—(1) alight somewhere; (2) stand.
yatsabh—hithp. (1) take a (firm) stand; (2) hold one's ground.
shakhan—(1) stretch oneself out, alight for a while, encamp; (2) dwell.
gûr—(1) settle down as a stranger; (2) dwell.
shakhabh—(1) stretch oneself out; (2) rest (of animals and men).
vashabh—(1) sit down; (2) sit; (3) dwell (almost always with a personal
      subject). Apparent exceptions to these meanings: Gen. 49.24, where
      a thing is used in place of a person as the subject of this verb; Ps. 122.5,
      'there thrones are set' (*yashabh*); Jer. 30.18c, 'and the palace shall
      stand (*yeshebh*) where it used to be' (here *yeshebh* is either to be deleted
      as materially and rhythmically superfluous [Kautzsch], or to be translated
      as 'be occupied' on the analogy of Isa. 13.20; Jer. 17.25; Ezek. 26.20;
      Zech. 9.5; 12.6, etc. [Kautzsch], or agreeing with the parallelism to
      be translated as 'be erected', or else with LXX 'people' is to be read
      for 'palace' and the passage translated 'the people will dwell'. There
      is here no question of 'dwelling' in the same sense as in Isa. 13.20;
      Jer. 50.30 [see the discussion below regarding *shakhan*]).

Originally *qûm* is a verb of movement meaning 'rise up, raise oneself, rise up in enmity'. Here and there *qûm* does have the meaning 'stand': Now your kingdom will not *stand*, i.e. have no endurance (I Sam. 13.14). For our purpose, those cases are most instructive where *qûm*, etc. are parallel to a verb of motion because in those instances the dynamic is self-evident on the principle of *parallelismus membrorum*, even though our European feeling for style requires a static concept for a complement since mere repetition is intolerable for us. A few examples will demonstrate this point:

Who shall ascend the hill of the Lord?
And who shall stand (*qûm*—take his stand) in his holy place? (Ps. 24.3).

My sheaf arose (*qûm*) and stood upright (*natsabh*—drew itself up) (Gen. 37.7).

... all the people rose up (*qûm*), and every man stood (*natsabh*) at his tent door. ... (Ex. 33.8). (This is Mowinckel's translation, but Kautzsch translates with a verb of motion: every man stepped under the door of his tent. [!])

When Moses entered the tent, the pillar of cloud would descend (*yaradh*) and stand (*'amadh*) at the door of the tent ... (Ex. 33.9).

Dathan and Abiram came out (*yatsa'*) and stood (*natsabh* [ptcp.]) at the door of their tent ... (Num. 16.27). (This is Mowinckel's translation, but again Kautzsch uses a verb of motion: and formed up. The meaning is exactly the same, but the form of the image is different.)

Thou hast established (*kûn*) the earth, and it stands fast (*'amadh*) (Ps. 119.90).

... you shall surely be king, and (that) the kingdom of Israel shall be established (*qûm*) in your hand (I Sam. 24.20).

In the negative sense:

He will not be rich, and his wealth shall not endure (*qûm*) (Job 15.29).

The Lord has taken his place (*natsabh*) to contend, he stands (*'amadh*) to judge his people (Isa. 3.13).

These examples show that motion and standing are not opposites as they are for us, but they are so closely related to one another that together they can form a unity.[1] Movement is carried through to a standstill, or seen from the other side, standing is viewed as the result of a rising or a placing. As we shall see below, this latter idea concurs with the conception of 'building'. We can also trace this line of thinking when we compare the 'standing' in a noun clause (in which the verb is omitted) with the 'standing' that we find in sentences of our own language. The 'standing' of trees in a field is a natural expression for us because we begin from a static image; from that viewpoint it must be granted that the upright position of a tree is very similar to that of a man standing. If the 'standing' is the conclusion, the end, or the result of an actual or possible rising or being placed, then no similarity exists, and the 'standing' of trees is absurd and non-existent. We also say that a word stands fast; in such an instance we are thinking of the firmness and validity of the content of the word. The Israelites did not distinguish between the spokenness of the

[1] The Hebrew words for 'stand', 'sit', 'lie', etc. have, therefore, two meanings which to our way of thinking are opposed to one another. Words of this sort are so general in Semitic languages that Arabists have developed a special term for them, *addad*. Cf. Th. Nöldeke, 'Wörter mit Gegensinn', *Neue Beiträge zur semitischen Sprachwissenschaft*, pp. 67–101. The Hebrew verbs *qûm*, etc. are not only typical examples of this phenomenon, but they also allow us to anticipate how such concepts are to be understood psychologically. Thus, for example, even 'life' and 'death' form a unified pair of concepts since death is the weakest form of life. Cf. Aubrey Johnson, *op. cit.*, pp. 94–107.

word and its content; when Jahveh has spoken, his words stand fast [*qûm*] (Isa. 40.8; Jer. 44.28; 51.29, etc.).

It is in the very nature of verbs of motion and of 'stative' verbs that their subject is a man, an animal, or a living being; Joseph's sheaf behaves like a man, and so do the sun, the moon, and the eleven stars (Gen. 37.9), likewise the sun and moon in the valley of Aijalon (Josh. 10.12 f.). Of much greater interest are those instances in which the subject is a thing, cases in which we cannot arrive at the above explanation; they require some other explanation. In the account of Solomon's throne (I Kings 10.19 f.), alongside the arm-rests stood ('*amadh* [ptcp.]) two lions, and twelve lions stood ('*amadh* [ptcp.]) on the six steps at both sides. '*amadh* here means no mere 'being' but refers to the position of the lions; they could just as well be sitting or lying down. At Josh. 11.13, none of the cities that stood ('*amadh* [ptcp.]) on mounds did Israel burn (Mowinckel translates the verb 'were put up on' and means by this that the 'standing' of the cities is for the author the consequence of their having been previously built). The standing of Jordan's waters (Josh. 3.13, 16) is easy to explain; here the standing of the waters is the end and discontinuance of flowing. On the contrary, the standing of the waters of the Red Sea like two walls (Ex. 14.22) is not told as a direct consequence of God's action since the passage of the Israelites intervenes, and it is therefore best expressed by a noun clause. In the Song of Moses, the breath of Jahveh piles up the water (Ex. 15.8), and so it says here: the floods stood upright (*natsabh*) like a heap. When the disease or the itch is not spreading, it stands ('*amadh*), or the movement stops (Lev. 13.5, 37). '*amadh* can be used to express the idea that an expected change does not take place; hence, the taste of the wine stands, i.e. does not alter (Jer. 48.11), and this is the equivalent of documents that stand, i.e. are well preserved and last (Jer. 32.14). Generations come and go, but only the earth 'stands' for ever (Eccles. 1.4); when wisdom continues to remain, it 'stands' (Eccles. 2.9). So also 'stand' may be the equivalent of 'not die' (Ex. 21.21); again, the waters cease ('*amadh*) from their raging (Jonah 1.15), and this status is one of not moving, not changing.

The verb *shakhan* usually takes as its subject men, animals, and even God. As is the case with *yashabh*, however, the subject can also be a city such as Babel (Isa. 13.20; Jer. 50.39) or Jerusalem (Jer. 33.16); in such cases it must be translated 'be inhabited'. The Hebrew image can also be the one generally accepted, that the inhabitants of the city are meant (Ps. 147.12; Isa. 3.8; Jer. 14.2). If *shakhan*, *yatsabh*, or '*amadh* designates no motion but only a standing still of the subject, that repose is the end or the result of a movement, or else it contains a latent movement. Thus, he dwells in a place who has alighted there or who can depart therefrom; consequently, *shakhan*, *yatsabh* could be used only with such subjects as have done so or can do so, respectively. 'Dwelling' for the Hebrews is related to the person who dwells, while for the Greeks and for us it is related to the residence and the household goods.

Our analysis of the Hebrew verbs that express standing, sitting, lying, etc., teaches us that motionless and fixed being is for the Hebrews a nonentity; it does not exist for them. Only 'being' which stands in inner relation with something active and moving is a reality to them. This could also be expressed: only movement (motion) has reality. To the extent that it concerned Hebrew thinking at all, static being as a predicate is a motion that has passed over into repose.

2. *The dynamic character of Hebrew verbs of condition and of quality*

In addition to the above verbs we must analyse those showing conditions or properties, verbs which to our way of thinking also express 'being'. It is characteristic of Hebrew and the other Semitic languages that all of these verbs designate first of all the 'becoming' of the conditions and qualities in question. It is really more correct to say that we are dealing here with neither a 'being' nor a 'becoming' but with a dynamic third possibility, therefore more an 'effecting' as in the case of the verb 'lighten' which means not only to be bright or become bright but also to make light effective, i.e. illuminate. In such cases our distinction between ingressive and durative meaning does not do justice to the basic idea of the concept. Several examples are cited from the lists of F. R. Blake,[1] G. R. Driver,[2] and I. Bursztyn:[3]

'aneph—become and be angry; *'ôr*—become and be bright, lighten; *'arakh*—become and be long, lengthen; *gabhar* (for *gabher*)—become and be strong, mighty; *gadhal* (for *gadhel*)—become and be great; *zaqen*—become and be old; *ḥazaq*—become and be firm, strong; *ḥaqam*—become and be wise; *ṭaher*—become and be pure, clean; *yare'*—become and be anxious, fear, be afraid; *kabhedh*—become and be heavy; *maradh*—become and be refractory, rebel; *marar*—become and be bitter; *mashal*—become and be master, rule; *qadhash*—become and be holy; *rabhabh* and *rabhah*—become and be many, great.

Blake counts 209 such verbs,[4] and even if several of them occur only

[1] Frank R. Blake, *The Socalled Intransitive Verbal Forms in the Semitic Languages*, pp. 10 ff.
[2] G. R. Driver, *Problems of the Hebrew Verbal System*, pp. 46 ff.
[3] Israel Bursztyn, *Vollständige Grammatik der alt- und neuhebräischen Sprache*, pp. 135 ff.
[4] Blake, *op. cit.*, p. 34.

as derivatives in the Old Testament, the number is still large enough
to point to something characteristic of Hebrew and the other Semitic
languages. The majority of these verbs are distinguishable externally in
that the usual form, *Qal* perfect third person singular masculine, has *e*
(*tsere*, originally *i*) in the second syllable; some few of them have *o*
(*ḥôlem*) in the second syllable. The verbs whose second vowel is *e* or *o*
(verbs *med. e* or *med. o*) are called intransitive in Hebrew grammars;[1]
generally speaking, this will hold true, but it is not always true. There are
several transitive verbs *med. e*, such as: '*ahebh*—love, *sane*'—hate,
yare'—frighten, *shamea*'—hear, *male*'—become and be full, fill.[2] We shall
return to these verbs later.

A large number of intransitive verbs are assimilated to the form *qaṭal*,
such as: '*amar*—speak, *halakh*—walk, go, *ḥaradh*—tremble, *kashal*—
stumble, *ma'al*—default, *maradh*—rebel, *mashal*—exercise dominion,
naphal—fall. Driver lists 34 such verbs which are distinguished in content from verbs *med. e* through their action; even when these verbs designate a condition (e.g. *maradh* also means 'become and be refractory',
mashal also means 'become and be master'), the condition is an active one.
Two decidedly stative verbs of condition with *a* in place of *e* are *ḥakham*
—become and be wise, and *qatsar*—become and be short; the former
appears originally, according to Driver, to have meant 'understand',
and the latter literally means 'come too short', so that even these
two are not strictly stative verbs but rather designate action in some
form.[3]

In addition to these reflections of Driver we must mention the influence
of certain consonants upon the vowels; it is generally recognized that the
guttural consonants and *resh* prefer *a*. It must also be reckoned with that
the medial *a*, which the overwhelming majority of verbs have, has through
frequent use exercised its influence upon verbs *med. e*. Even when we draw
attention to these points, Driver's observations still stand; verbs *med. e*
belong to the class of verbs of condition or of quality in which the action
scarcely appears, or perhaps not at all.

In their own ways other scholars have recognized the same thing for a
long time although not so clearly and consistently. Böttcher wanted to
exchange the terms 'transitive and intransitive verbs' for *active* and

---

[1] Ges.-K. § 43.
[2] For other verbs *med. e*, which are actually or only apparently transitive, see Driver,
op. cit., p. 66. The only verb *med. e* that is strictly transitive, according to Driver, is
hatsebh, 'hew out'; *male*' may occasionally be transitive. The former appears only at
Isa. 5.2, where Driver suspects an error in vocalization; the latter apparently had an
alternative transitive form, *mala*'. *Ibid.*, p. 52.
[3] *Ibid.*, p. 47.

stative;[1] these terms were employed later by many including Blake and Driver. Ewald distinguished between active and half-passive verbs; Rosenmüller called the latter class *absoluta*; Merx called them *descriptiva*; and Bursztyn together with Duval and Brockelmann called them *neutra* (something between active and passive).[2] All these terms designate the action contained in these verbs, whether it be condition or quality, as an objective quantity observed from the outside. P. Haupt, on the contrary, tries to define the difference psychologically by distinguishing between *verba voluntaria* (actions depending upon the will of the subject) and *verba involuntaria* (actions or states independent of the will of the subject).[3] The element of truth in the viewpoint represented by Haupt will be granted expression later in this discussion.

It follows from these brief details that the chief interest is focused upon verbs of condition and of quality, the so-called *stative* verbs. Perhaps the intricate complex of problems involving transitive and intransitive verbs can be untangled from this vantage point. First of all, it may be maintained that even the stative verbs are not static; they are called stative because they designate a condition (status) which is not fixed and dead but is in flux—it is as much a becoming as a being. The distinction between becoming and being, which is so meaningful for us and even more so for the Greeks, appears to have been irrelevant to the Hebrews or to have been experienced by them as a unity. In order to make this comprehensible psychologically, we take as our point of departure some of our own stative verbs which can also be resolved into becoming and being. As we have already stated, 'lighten' means 'become bright', as well as 'be bright'. When Jonathan ate honey after the battle, his eyes lightened, i.e. they became bright (I Sam. 14.27); afterwards henceforth they lightened, i.e. they were bright (v. 29). 'To rage' can refer to circumstances either of 'becoming angry' or of 'being angry'; so it is with all stative verbs that designate qualities or conditions: 'hush' means become silent or be silent, and 'fear' means become anxious or be anxious. In order to grasp the psychological peculiarity of Hebrew stative verbs, we need therefore to analyse only one well-known phenomenon of our own language. Why is the otherwise significant distinction between being and becoming so irrelevant for us in stative verbs? The solution to this problem lies in the observation that the stative verb expresses neither being

---

[1] Cassirer (*The Philosophy of Symbolic Forms*, Vol. I, *Language*, p. 256) also uses 'stative' to designate simple condition as such; at this point he makes reference to L. Reinisch (*Die Nuba-Sprache* [Vienna, 1879]) and to A. Hanoteau (*Grammaire kabyle* [Algiers, 1858]).

[2] Blake, *op. cit.*, p. 6; Bursztyn, *op. cit.*, p. 136.   [3] Ges.-K. § 43, n. 1.

nor becoming but asserts an action of the subject proceeding from within. 'To hush' is a conscious, wilful activity; 'to be (become) silent', on the contrary, is a visible, negative, objectively provable condition. The expected movements of lips, mouth, and throat, and the sounds proceeding therefrom are absent. When we say, 'The man is silent', we have transferred ourselves into his psychic life and think we are able to establish that his wordlessness is an expression of his will, and that it is therefore an inner activity. Inasmuch as we have before us a purely intransitive verb, it contains an activity or action which can never be repeated with a being or a becoming; the [inner] action and the nature of the corresponding quality or condition are incommensurable quantities and belong to entirely different psychological areas. The repetition of a verb by means of an adjective and an auxiliary verb is therefore a makeshift and something which implies the intention to express the activity now by a being and now by a becoming; yet it does not accomplish the task.

In our languages, we and the Greeks both have relatively few stative verbs, but conversely the Hebrews have a great many of them. We have to presuppose, therefore, that the verbal idea in Hebrew stative verbs is always living and palpable even when we are not able because of poverty of expression either to repeat it or to feel it with them. It seems particularly difficult to us to express verbally the spatial quantity; in certain connexions, however, we too can do it. Instead of saying, 'The landscape lies broad before our eyes', we can also use the verbal expression, 'The landscape stretches before our eyes'. In place of, 'The peak of the mountain is vertiginously high', we can say, 'The mountain raises its peak to a vertiginous height'. In this way the mountain and its peak become something dynamic and active, even if only through a psychological empathy or rather an intrusion.[1]

The exceedingly great number of stative verbs in Hebrew (as well as in other Semitic languages) constitutes fresh evidence for the fact that the Hebrew (and Semitic) mind is directed to the dynamic and the active. The relationship of an action to its object in Hebrew experience is apparently not of the same meaning as in our conception; plainly, it is the degree and kind of activity contained in the verb that counts more. Moreover, from this viewpoint we can understand the fact that the *Niph'al* appears as the passive of the *Pi'el* or of the *Hiph'il*, both of which have causative meaning. Actually we have to translate the *Niph'al* that way if we mean to reproduce in our own language the nuances of that form.

---

[1] Cf. Grassler, *op. cit.*, p. 5: 'Der Gestalt-Eindruck des "Hebens" kündet bei "Turm", dass er "sich erhebt", dass er "hoch" ist.'

Yet there is no ground for assuming that the Israelites themselves felt the form that way. The *Niph'al* is also a passive (or reflexive) for the *Qal* and indicates that the action inherent in the *Qal* is done to the subject as coming from the outside. Thus the *Qal* of *kabhedh* means to be (become) honoured, i.e. to come to honour, but the *Niph'al* means to be honoured in the sense of being accorded honour; examples:

His sons come to honour (*Qal*), and he does not know it (Job 14.21); but, because you are precious in my eyes, and honoured (*Niph'al*) [by me], and I love you, I give men in return for you (Isa. 43.4; 49.5).

Otherwise, the reflexive meaning of the *Niph'al* is easy to support, e.g. Hag. 1.8.

3. *Logical 'being' in Hebrew*

On the other hand, by means of the so-called noun clause the Hebrew language is much better able to express the 'static' or 'that which is' in its logical sense than the Greek and our modern languages permit with their copula and their verbs of inaction. We shall define the noun clause in agreement with Gesenius-Kautzsch,[1] in order to be able to understand the 'being' expressed in it:

Every sentence, the subject as well as the predicate of which is a noun or noun equivalent is called a noun clause, while in a verbal clause the predicate is a finite verb. This distinction is indispensable for more subtle understanding of Hebrew syntax (as of Semitics in general) because it is not merely a matter of an external, formal distinction in meaning but of one that goes to the depths of the language. The noun clause, the predicate of which is a substantive, offers something fixed, not active, in short, a 'being'; the verbal clause on the other hand asserts something moving and in flux, an event and an action.[2] The noun clause with a participial predicate can also assert something moving and in flux, except that here the event and action is fixed as something not active and enduring, as opposed to the verbal clause.[3]

For our purpose, it is not necessary to discuss all the various kinds of

---

[1] Ges.-K. § 140.

[2] A comparison with Hebrew noun clauses shows that the noun clauses mentioned by Bühler (*op. cit.*, pp. 368 f.), such as 'Ehestand-Wehestand' [marriage-woe], 'Die Gelehrten-Die Verkehrten' [scholars-fools], 'neuer Arzt-neuer Friedhof' [new doctor-new cemetery], 'lange Haare-kurzer Sinn' [long of hair-short of sense] are not true noun clauses, but they are abbreviated clauses or sentences. In the former two pairs the copula is omitted; the latter pair are abbreviated sentences. The logical content of saying 'new doctor-new cemetery' is something like this: When a new and inexperienced doctor replaces the old one, so many people will die that a new cemetery will become necessary. No reasonable man would maintain this, and so the wit in the saying (and such sayings are part of popular general wit) lies in the very abbreviation of the idea.

[3] Ges.-K. § 140.

noun clauses, and in particular not those with participial predicates which should logically be considered as verbal clauses. We shall comment more closely upon two chief types which are peculiar to the Semitic manner of expression:

(1) when the predicate consists of a substantive,
(2) when the predicate consists of an adverb or some sort of closer definition (especially those expressed with the aid of a preposition) of time, place, quality, possessor, etc., which can serve as equivalents of a nominal concept.[1]

In the first case, the clause expresses the identity of subject and predicate, because in Hebrew thinking the thing is its measure, its material, or its identity. *hammizbeah 'ets . . . weqirothaw 'ets* (Ezek. 41.22): the altar (was) wood and its walls (were) wood. In this case, the altar and its walls are identical with the material. The identity of two quantities is thus established without any kind of copula. All Jahveh's ways are *hesedh we'emeth*, i.e. are grace and truth (Ps. 25.10); that is to say, Jahveh's way of dealing is identical with grace and truth.[2] It should be asked whether it can really be a matter of identity here; it would be more correct to say that we have here a tautology since the predicate inheres in the subject. In such cases the copula would have expressed to the Hebrews an un-reality which can be overlooked, indeed must be overlooked. The case is quite different if the predicate does not inhere in the subject, e.g. *weha'arets hayetha thohû wabhohû*: the earth was without form and void (Gen. 1.2). Here *thohû wabhohû* does not inhere in *'erets*, for the latter is always the region of civilization and humanity which excludes the possibility on conceptual grounds. The predicate in this sentence could not be equated directly to the subject, for that would result in the impossible meaning that chaos and cosmos are identical concepts. The gap between subject and predicate is bridged by *hayetha*, which asserts that what in our day is cosmos, *'erets*, was at one time chaos, *thohû wabhohû*. In our experience, the difference between sentences like 'The earth was waste and void' and 'The altar was (of) wood' is not of the same fundamental sort as it is for the Hebrews, a fact that is confirmed linguistically by our use of the copula in both cases.

Our way of thinking is different from that of the Hebrews and Semites; we first of all conceive of the altar, i.e. its form, and then the material out of which it is made while presupposing that an altar formed and used in this way could as well have been made, e.g., of copper. For us, there-fore, the form and the matter of any thing are separate, and the form is

---

[1] Ges.-K. § 141b.   [2] Ges.-K. § 141b, c.

the principal consideration; for the Semites the material is the thing.[1] If an altar is wooden, then it could not possibly be copper for that would result in a totally new and different altar, namely a copper one. The same thing is true in the second example; when we say that all Jahveh's ways are grace and truth, we first of all think of Jahveh's ways and then of the kinds of ways, a thinking process which could include as a possibility that the ways of Jahveh could also be hardness and severity. But when the Israelite says, 'All Jahveh's ways (are) grace and truth', Jahveh's merciful guidance is an inseparable idea rather like our expression, 'all Jahveh's gracious and true ways'.[2]

The second type, where the predicate consists of a closer definition of place, seems more difficult to explain, for apparently in such cases the noun clause expresses a real being or that kind of being contained in the question, 'How are you?' As an example: The field of Ephron, which is in Machpelah, which is opposite Mamre, the field and the cave which (is) in it, and all the trees that (were) in the field, which (extends) throughout its whole area, was made over to Abraham (Gen. 23.17); here we have five relative noun clauses all of which are a closer definition of place. The verbs inside parentheses do not carry their literal meaning in English but are merely auxiliary verbs with the significance of copulae. The negativity of the verbs and the being inherent in them, to say nothing of any action in them, follow from the fact that in our language we could render the noun clauses by way of complements: The field of Ephron in Machpelah opposite Mamre, the field and the cave in it and all the trees in the field round about its entire border were made over to Abraham. This local 'being somewhere' of a thing is for the Israelites not a 'being' in our sense; it is only a certain belongingness of a thing to its place so that the relationship between the two can also be expressed by a genitive: the river Pishon flows around the whole land *ḥawilah 'asher sham hazza-habh uzahabh ha'arets hahi' ṭobh* = where the gold (is), and the gold of this land (is) good; the gold which is in this place is the same as the gold of this place (Gen. 2.11 f.). The distinction between the noun clause and the attributive expression has no relevance conceptually, but it is only grammatical and stylistic since in certain cases fuller expression requires a noun clause. The above-quoted definition of a noun clause (namely, that with the exception of those with participial predicates they present something fixed, not active, in short a 'being') is seen from the viewpoint

[1] Ges.-K. § 141b.
[2] We shall comment more extensively upon the Israelite conception of the *thing* and of visible objects in the next chapter.

of the Greeks and the Europeans; in Hebrew experience, noun clauses express only an attributive belongingness. What is the basic fact of 'being' for the Israelites will result from the analysis of the verb *hayah* that follows.

4. The 'being' of the verb hayah

A. The verb *hayah*: We must devote special attention to this verb not only because it occurs most frequently but also because the verbal problems discussed above are concentrated in this verb and appear in it in their most difficult form. The factual material is collected in the Gesenius-Buhl lexicon where the meanings of *hayah* are systematically arranged, and further in the excellent monograph by Ratschow, where the meanings of *hayah* are precisely analysed.[1] The most important meanings and uses of our verb 'to be' (and its equivalents in other Indo-European languages) are: (1) to express being or existence; (2) to serve as a copula. Now, as we have shown above, Hebrew and the other Semitic languages do not need a copula because of the noun clause. As a general rule, therefore, it may be said that *hayah* is not used as a copula;[2] real or supposed exceptions to this rule will be cited later.

The characteristic mark of *hayah*, in distinction from our verb 'to be', is that it is a true verb with full verbal force. The majority of formal considerations as well as the actual ones lead to this conclusion:

(i) The peculiarity of emphasizing the verbal idea by use of the infinitive absolute before finite verbs;

(ii) the occurrence of the passive form *Niph'al*;

(iii) its frequent occurrence in parallel with other verbs whose verbal force is beyond doubt; this is so frequent an occurrence that a few examples will suffice: Jahveh hurled a great wind, and a mighty tempest *was* (Jonah 1.4); God created (made, spoke) and the corresponding thing *was* (Gen. 1.3, 9, 11); its parallel use with *qûm* = 'be realized' (Isa. 7.7; 14.24);[3] the messengers of the king command the prophet

---

[1] Carl H. Ratschow, *Werden und Wirken. Eine Untersuchung des Wortes* hajah *als Beitrag zur Wirklichkeitserfassung des Alten Testaments* ('Beihefte zur ZAW', 70).

[2] *Ibid.*, p. 4. After thorough examination, Ratschow maintains that Albrecht's opinion, taken up in Ges.-K. (§ 141 i, n. 1), that *hayah* appears frequently as a copula in Deuteronomy and the P-Code, is in error (p. 5). A historical development of *hayah* within the Old Testament is not demonstrable (pp. 1 f.). It appears to me that this interpretation is not to be accepted immediately, for the use of *hayah* in the later books is still partly different from that in the earlier books, something which Ratschow himself admits later (p. 23).

[3] *Ibid.*, p. 5, where several examples are cited. It is therefore remarkable that it does not occur to the author to give attention to parallel verbs in noticing the instances in which *hayah* is combined with the preposition *'al*, 'upon', and where he suspects the meaning 'to be'. Had he done so, he would have found also in most of these cases some kind of 'coming to a place' (pp. 15 f.).

Micaiah to prophesy safety and victory, 'Let thy word *be* as the word of one of them (i.e. the prophets of good fortune)', (I Kings 22.13).

The meaning of *hayah* is apparently manifold; *hayah* has thus been considered to some extent a general word which can mean everything possible and therefore designates nothing characteristic. Closer examination reveals, however, that this is not the case. It is therefore necessary to establish the many meanings and shades of meaning of *hayah* and to find their inner connexion. We shall use first the results of Ratschow who has examined the occurrences of *hayah* in the Old Testament with a thoroughness hardly to be excelled and in whose work is to be found extensive evidence. He found three principal meanings: 'to become', 'to be', and 'to effect'; but these are related internally and form a unity. In the main this will be right, and it agrees with our understanding of Hebrew thought; we must object, however, to details.

B. Becoming and effecting:

i. *hayah* signifies *real becoming*, what is more either an arising or a passage from one condition to another. There *arose* a famine in the land (Gen. 12.10); lest the land *become* desolate (Ex. 23.29). Here too belongs 'becoming more (less)': you know what your cattle *have become* with me, i.e. how numerous they have become (Gen. 30.29).

ii. Becoming in inner reality: Ephraim *has become* a cake that is not turned (Hos. 7.8).

iii. Becoming something new by vocation: Abel *became* a herdsman, and Cain *became* a tiller of the soil (Gen. 4.2). Cf. 4.20 Jabal; 10.8 f. Cush; 21.20 Ishmael. (In these instances, the verb could as well be translated 'worked as', and then these cases could be cited under iv. A characteristic instance is provided by Esau and Jacob: Esau became [*wayehi*] a skilful hunter, while Jacob [without *hayah* since no change is involved] a quiet man [Gen. 25.27.].)

iv. *hayah* as 'effecting': Thus says Jahveh, 'I have made this water wholesome; no more shall death or miscarriage come from it', i.e. henceforth shall it *cause* death or miscarriage no more (II Kings 2.21).

C. *hayah* with prepositions:

i. *hayah le*—to become something, to work as something. The meanings of *hayah le* are the same as those discussed in section A above. The addition of the preposition *le* lends a greater definition of purpose to the sentences, which gives to the meaning of 'become' in *hayah* a particularly clear delimitation against every sort of 'being' and against everything not active.

a to become in nature and history: to become a fruitful vine (Ezek. 17.6, 8, 23); I have become two armies (Gen. 32.10).

b to become as a witness of inner reality: the people's heart melted and became as water (Josh. 7.5).

c to become meaning to serve as: brick served as building stone and bitumen as mortar (Gen. 11.3).

d to become meaning to work or to do business as: the Word of Jahveh became for Jeremiah reproach and derision (Jer. 20.8; cf. II Sam. 13.28; I Kings 2.2). When *hayah* is combined with *le*, the meaning 'effect' protrudes more.

ii. *hayah ke* :

a become like: the Israelites would be like other nations (I Sam. 8.20).

b become effective, or the occurrence *in actu* as opposed to a potential shown in the word: as the servant said, so it happened (II Sam. 13.35).

c act as: you shall not act as a creditor to my people (Ex. 22.24).

d the inner reality: that Jahveh's congregation be not like sheep that have no shepherd (Num. 27.17; Isa. 1.18).

e pass for, be as though: the stranger shall be as a native of the land (Ex. 12.48).

f appear as: Lot seemed to his sons-in-law to be jesting (Gen. 19.14).

g It is certainly incorrect, however, to assume the meaning 'attributed being', or a simple 'being thus'.[1]

---

[1] I Kings, 7.8, *hayah ke* means 'be built like this'; *vide infra* Isa. 1.9, where *hayah ke* means not a 'being like' Sodom but a hypothetical 'having become': Except Jahveh of Hosts had left unto us a remnant, it would have become (i.e. come within an ace of happening) to us as it did to Sodom, we should have become like Gomorrah. Deut. 28.62 does not mean that the people 'is' like the stars in number but that *once* they were as numerous; *hayah* is required here to indicate the past time; *vide infra* Gen. 3.5, 22, where the meaning 'become as' is unambiguously clear. In Gen. 27.23, *hayah* expresses the refinement that Jacob's hands were not actually hairy but that they were made so. The 'not-being' in II Sam. 14.25 means that wherever one looked in the land, as fair a man as Absalom was not to be found and when his figure was examined from head to toe, no flaw was found in him; therefore, it is no simple 'being thus'. In I Kings 22.13, the meaning of 'Let thy word *become* like the word of one of them' is determined from the second half of the verse, 'and speak what is good'. If the attempt be made to strike out *'eheyeh* in Ruth 2.13, it will be discovered that the sense is altered; what remains is an actual 'being thus': I am not like one of your handmaidens. However, the meaning lies in the *'eheyeh*: I have not come so high as one of your handmaidens, something that we can express more simply by an inserted 'now': I am not now like ... (Zech. 9.7); in Num. 23.10, the meaning 'become like' is clear. At Ezek. 40.21, *hayah* is to be stricken out with the Vulgate. At II Chron. 30.7, *'al tiheyu ka'abhôthekhem* means, as the explanatory relative clause indicates, 'don't behave as your fathers did!' *lo' hayah* (Ezek. 31.8b) is to be omitted as a redundant and prosaic passage destructive of the rhythm. In spite of the many citations made by Ratschow, the meaning 'be thus' or 'attributed being' for *hayah le* is not demonstrated.

iii. *hayah 'al* :

a the combination at first sight seems to mean 'being at'; this hardly gets at the real meaning: *'al* certainly designates something local, but not a local *being*, rather an *arrival*.[1]

b the meaning 'act upon' is more to be preferred, even if the examples cited are not overwhelmingly convincing; thus the obvious translation of *hayah* as 'come' (Lev. 15.17, 24). It is a general characteristic of *hayah* and not least of *hayah 'al* that several translations seem equally good; thus Kautzsch translates Gen. 9.2, 'Fear and dread of you shall come upon every beast', but Michelet translates it 'shall lie'. Both renderings are in the Hebrew verb, or perhaps better, what is inherent in *hayah* corresponds to none of our verbs and can therefore be rendered in a variety of ways but never quite accurately.

c the meaning 'act upon' is clearer in those cases where it is a matter of ruling (Gen. 41.40; I Sam. 8.19; I Kings 8.16); here the distinction between 'being' and 'becoming' is clearly irrelevant, but, as we have seen, it is actually false when Ratschow (p. 16) says that in the combination *hayah 'al* only the meanings 'be' and 'effect' and not the meaning 'become' stand next to one another. The meanings 'become', 'arrive', etc. also frequently occur.

iv. *hayah be* :

a it used to be assumed that a local existence was implied in the combination *hayah be*, a 'being in'; it is to be noted, however, that the subject is most frequently a person so that it can be translated just as well

---

[1] Ratschow offers the following citations: the bread shall be on the table (Num. 4.7); as the context shows, however, this is not a question of 'being at rest' or of 'lying' but of an 'arrival'. The whole section (Num. 4.5–15) deals with what is to be done when the camp is to set out. Then v. 7 means: over the show-bread table they are to spread a cloth of blue material, and on it the dishes, spoons, and bowls, as well as the vessels for the drink offering are to be set (*nathenu 'alaw*); after that it is quite natural to continue: 'and the continual bread shall be laid thereon (*yiheyeh*)`, if, however, the *'alaw* is to be construed with *lehem hattamid*, the meaning is: 'the continual bread shall be taken along on it'.

At Ex. 10.6, *miyyom heyotham* obviously denotes a beginning and means either 'from the day when they came into the land' or 'from the day when they originated on the earth'.

II Sam. 12.30 deals with an arrival.

At Num. 9.20 *yiheyeh . . . 'al* is synonymous with *yaḥanu'al* (v. 18) and with *beha-'arikh'al* (v. 19).

Num. 36.12 also does not speak of a local existence at a place but of the abiding in a family.

In Judg. 6.37, 39, arrival is also very clear.

The text of I Sam. 14.25 is corrupt, but the possible 'being' of the honey is illuminated by the next verse where the 'flowing' of the honey is reported.

At Jer. 46.2, *hayah* means 'to abide'.

I Chron. 29.25 and II Chron. 26.15 belong under point *b* following.

In both Ex. 34.1 and Jer. 36.28, *hayah* is synonymous with *kathabh*: new letters shall be inscribed (written) in place of the letters which were written before (*vide infra*, chap. II, on the Israelite conception of buildings).

The meaning 'local existence of a thing in some place' is thus more than merely doubtful.

either by 'abide' (Gen. 4.8) or by 'be operative, live' (Gen. 6.4). The subject can also be a thing, but it is then a power-laden thing, such as the death- and destruction-dealing ark (I Sam. 6.1; cf. 5.3–12), or the temple in Shiloh (Judg. 18.31), or the quite living, spirit-filled, seeing wheel that Ezekiel saw (Ezek. 1.16; 10.10).

The end result of the investigation contained in paragraphs i–iv is, therefore, that the prepositions exercise no real influence upon the inherent meaning of *hayah*; this is also true of the prepositions *'aḥar*— 'after', *'eth*—'beside', *'im*—'with', and *liphne*—'before'.[1]

D. The ostensibly static uses of *hayah*:

i. Being: in a separate paragraph Ratschow deals with the places where *hayah* should mean 'to be'; his arguments are not very convincing. The majority of the cases could have been subsumed under the preceding paragraphs. To be sure, it is obvious and natural for us to translate *hayah* at Isa. 51.6 by 'endure' or some similar word: my salvation will be for ever. Yet an important part of the notion of salvation is that it is not a static thing; we get the prophet's idea much better, therefore, with a dynamic expression: my salvation will live unto eternity effectively or will eternally go on working. An exact parallel to this verse is found earlier in the same book: . . . the word of God will continue living and effective for ever (Isa. 40.8), where *qûm* means not standing at rest, but has inherent in it an inner activity which says that the power of the working of God's word will always be the same.

ii. Time designation: Here and there *hayah* is necessary to designate 'time', e.g. the earth was (*hayethah*) once upon a time waste and void, i.e. chaos (Gen. 1.2); *hayethah* could not be omitted for that would give the impossible meaning that the area of civilization was identical with chaos (cf. pp. 35 ff., above). Again, Nineveh was (once upon a time) an exceedingly great city (Jonah 3.3); to complete the sentence it is necessary to say that Nineveh is no more. Or again, Joseph was (already) in Egypt (Ex. 1.5). The same use of *hayah* is surely to be found in: they were both naked (grown people no longer appear naked) (Gen. 2.25). Or, the serpent was more subtle than all the other beasts of the field (Gen. 3.1; cf. Gesenius-Kautzsch, 141, i), i.e. it is no longer so prudent as it was at that time. Likewise, the whole earth (humanity) had (once upon a time) one language (Gen. 11.1). In these latter instances *hayah* could be translated dynamically as well: Joseph was (already) active in Egypt; man and

---

[1] In places like 'you shall go to the priest who *will be* in that day' (Deut. 26.3), Ratschow (*ibid*. n. 83) finds it difficult to decide whether 'live' or 'hold office' is meant. The difficulty is not great, for both are meant.

woman went about (then) naked; the serpent acted (at that time supernaturally) subtly; Nineveh had become (at that time) an exceedingly great city; the whole earth at that time spoke one language. Apparently in these sentences the dynamic motif is operative quite as much as the motif of transposition into past time. Pure noun clauses could not have been used here; the *hayah* has a necessary function to fulfil and, consequently, is not a mere copula as Ratschow thinks.

iii. Stylistic use—'to be beautiful': The placing of *hayah* before most of the genealogical name-lists is, on the contrary, meaningless for any material purpose, and it is surely done on stylistic grounds (Gen. 9.18 [P]; 25.3 [J]). Lund sees this as a formula peculiar to the Priest.[1] We accept Ratschow's opinion that *hayah* is here only for the purpose of joining these lists to the context of a narrative complex.[2] *hayah* has more verbal force when it is used with numerals and means 'amount to, add up to' (Lev. 15.15; 23.17).

'To be beautiful' can be construed with *hayah* (Gen. 29.17; 39.6b; cf. II Sam. 14.27). Leah's eyes (were) weak, but Rachel was (*hayethah*) beautiful in form and beautiful in face (Gen. 29.17); the same construction is employed at 39.6b. *hayethah* means that the whole person acted gracefully in quality and deportment. Thus it is also said of the daughter of Absalom: she (Tamar) was (*hayethah*) a woman of beautiful countenance (II Sam. 14.27); compare also the treatment of beauty below in the descriptive lyrics of the Song of Solomon.

A thing's 'being foursquare' is, as the context shows, its 'being made foursquare' (Ex. 27.1; 28.16; 30.2): you shall make the altar of acacia wood, five cubits long and five cubits wide—the altar shall be made square.

iv. *hayah* with participle: *hayah* is used with the participle to designate an action as durative or oft-repeated: Hiram was supplying (i.e. Hiram gave) Solomon cedar and cypress trees, as often and as many as he asked (I Kings 5.10 [MT 5.24]); Esther used to find favour (found favour) with all who saw her, or as often as she saw anyone (Esth. 2.15). Or again, 'I went out (imperfect consecutive) by night by the Valley Gate to the Jackal's Well and to the Dung Gate, and I inspected (*hayah* with participle) the walls of Jerusalem . . . then I went on (imperf. cons.) to the Fountain Gate and to the King's Pool; . . . then I went up (*hayah* with participle) in the night by the valley and inspected (*hayah* with

---

[1] E. Lund, 'Ein Knotenpunkt in der Urgeschichte: Die Quellenfrage Genesis 9.18–19', ZAW, XV (1938), 34–43.
[2] Ratschow, *op. cit.*, pp. 22–23.

participle) the wall; and I turned back (imperf. cons.) and entered (imperf. cons.) by the Valley Gate' (Neh. 2.13–15); the detailed inspection and the difficult nocturnal ascent are portrayed by *hayah* with the participle. Again, the cherubim arĕ to spread out their wings above (*hayah* with participle) (Ex. 25.20); also, your children shall be shepherds in the wilderness for forty years (*hayah* with participle) (Num. 14.33). Jahveh tells Moses that the people are to be ready (*hayah* with participle) on the third day (Ex. 19.11, 15; 34.2; Josh. 8.4). The Second Isaiah proclaims, your iniquities have made a separation between you and your God, i.e. they separate you continually from your God (Isa. 59.2).

The passive participle of the *Qal* is construed with *hayah*: you shall only be oppressed and crushed continually (Deut. 28.33), you shall be driven mad (28.34), your life shall be hung before you (i.e. be in constant jeopardy [28.66]). Again, all the people who came out had been circumcised (passive participle *Qal* [Josh. 5.5]); as an act circumcision is instantaneous, but it gives to the one circumcised an indelible character which makes of being circumcised an enduring thing. Or again, they remained hanging on the trees until evening (Josh. 10.26); they (ten concubines) were shut up (*hayah* with passive participle *Qal*) until the day of their death, i.e. they lived as people shut up (II Sam. 20.3). Jeremiah was imprisoned in the court of the guard, i.e. he sat as a prisoner, or he lay imprisoned (Jer. 32.2). Likewise, the side chambers are not to be interlocking into the wall of the house, i.e. they are not to intermember with the wall of the house (Ezek. 41.6); Ezekiel is told, this gate shall remain shut (44.2a, b; 46.1; cf. Zeph. 2.4; Zech. 3.3; Job 11.15; II Chron. 7.15). In general, the action is represented as durative or durative in its effect, and it is thus distinct as much from a property as from an instantaneous action.

The *Niph'al* participle is also construed with *hayah* to designate a durative action: David's servants were greatly ashamed, i.e. the shame was pressing upon them (II Sam. 10.5, etc.).

v. *hayah* in the protasis: There are a great number of instances in which *hayah* stands in the protasis in order to strengthen and emphasize another verb in the apodosis, somewhat on this order: and it shall come to pass (it comes to pass) that . . . And it shall come to pass that the rod of the man whom I choose shall send forth shoots (Num. 17.5 [MT 17. 20]; other examples include Gen. 15.7a; 24.14, 43; Num. 10.32; 21.8, etc.). *hayah* has the same function when the succeeding verb is in the infinitive: (and it came to pass) when the sun went down, a deep sleep fell upon Abram (Gen. 15.12; also 35.16; Ex. 30.4, 16; Num. 7.5; 8.11, etc.). It could be contested whether in these cases *hayah* has a peculiar *meaning*, but in such cases *hayah* has incontestably the important verbal *function* of preparing for a verb that is coming and drawing attention to it. Predominantly in such cases *hayah* introduces complete sentences which contain the entry of a future event (Ex. 1.10), lays stress thereon (Gen. 27.40), or represents the preceding event as surprising, sudden or miraculous (Gen. 38.39a; I Sam. 13.10; Gen. 19.29). For the purposes of our investigation we need not enter into these cases in any greater detail since the *dynamic* character of *hayah* is generally clear.

vi. The formal character of being: As a result of his arduous investigations Ratschow establishes that the meaning of *hayah* is as much 'become' as 'be', sometimes one and sometimes the other. Sometimes it fluctuates between them, and at other times it encompasses both 'becoming' and 'being' and contains yet a third active motif; in this motif of *effecting* is apparently to be sought the arch that spans the gap between 'becoming' and 'being'.[1]

This kind of a verb is nothing new to us; we have already seen that all stative verbs or internally active verbs in Hebrew bear this character, and *hayah* takes its place very neatly in the ranks of these verbs. The inner activity, which is expressed in the various internally active verbs in particular form and manner, is gathered up in *hayah* in a general, as it were, abstract form which represents what we have called inner activity as purely as that is possible in a single word. Ratschow's attempt to understand the Old Testament's perception of reality from the concept of *hayah* is therefore a fortunate stroke. From *hayah* we can understand what 'being' was consciously or unconsciously for the Israelite; 'being' is not something objective as it is for us and particularly for the Greeks, a datum at rest in itself. It is, however, quite erroneous to conclude from this that 'being' is something subjective, evanescent and dependent upon us. The Israelites like all other ancient peoples were 'outer-directed' and did not dissect their psychic life as modern man does. In that sense, even to the Hebrew, 'being' was something objective which existed independently of him and stood fast. The 'being' of things and of the world as the totality of things was to him something living, active, and effective, a notion which, however, has nothing at all to do with primitive panpsychism. It is correct to say in the case of the Hebrew that 'being' (e.g. the being contained in stative verbs) represents an inner activity which is best to be grasped by means of psychological analogies with human

---

[1] *Ibid.*, p. 29. Similar to this is S. Mowinckel, *He That Cometh*, p. 77, n. 6.

psychic life; with that we come to the heart of the matter. In the full Old Testament sense 'being' is pre-eminently *personal being* (*Person-Sein*). What does it mean that a person *is*? If we try to define that by means of the concepts of impersonal and objective thought, we have to grasp for 'becoming' as well as for 'being' and still fall far short of the objective. The person, on the other hand, is in movement and activity, which encompasses 'being' as well as 'becoming' and 'acting', i.e. he *lives*; an inner, outgoing, objectively demonstrable activity of the organs and of consciousness is characteristic of the person. Personal being is a being *sui generis* which is incommensurable with the 'being of things' (*dingliche Sein*), and therefore cannot be expressed in terms which are grounded in impersonal and objective thinking. A system of thought in categories that stem from personal being, *mutatis mutandis*, does not do justice to objective and inanimate reality. Where personal thinking was essentially precise and measured, as is the case especially in the ethical and religious field, the Hebrew (Semitic) mind achieved the acme in human history.

E. Divine being: We have found that *hayah* contains a unity of 'being', 'becoming', and 'effecting', that it dovetails neatly into the group of internally active (stative) verbs, and that it is best understood by us in the 'being' of an active person. If the essence of *hayah* best achieves expression in the being of a person, the next question involves this *being's* intrinsic value since this is determined by the subject. It is natural, then, to concentrate the inquiry upon the most important 'being' that Israelite thought knows: the 'being' of its god, the universal author. It is to be recalled first of all that analytic judgments about God, as well as about other objects, that is judgments where for the Israelite the predicate inheres in the subject, are not expressed by *hayah* but by noun clauses. 'If Jahveh (is) (true) God, follow him, but if Baal (is), then follow him' (I Kings, 18.21, 24, 27, 36, 37, 39). 'Hear, O Israel, Jahveh (is) our God, Jahveh (is) one' (Deut. 6.4). It is characteristic of God's *hayah* that it seems to refer directly to the people's *hayah*: 'Obey my command; thus I will be your God and you shall be my people' (Jer. 7.23; cf. 11.4). 'They shall be my people and I will be their God' (Ezek. 11.20; cf. 14.11). 'For I (am) Jahveh who brought you up out of the land of Egypt, to be your God; you shall therefore be holy, for I (am) holy' (Lev. 11.45). 'I (am) Jahveh who sanctify you, who brought you out of the land of Egypt to be your God: I, Jahveh' (Lev. 22.32b–33; Num. 15.41; Deut. 26.17; 29.12). 'I will put my law within them, and I will write it upon their hearts, and I will be their God, and they shall be my people' (Jer. 31.33; Ezek. 36.28).

The *hayah* of God is to act as God, to deal as God, and to carry into effect as God. Since he did this to a particular degree in leading the nation out of Egypt, Jahveh's being God is tied up with this manifestation of grace and power—'I, Jahveh, your God, who brought you forth out of the land of Egypt to give you the land of Canaan, and to be your God' (Lev. 25.37; 11.45; 22.33; 26.45; Num. 15.41). The *hayah* of God is not given once for all in the great act of the Exodus, but is only revealed in that act with particular clarity. Continuously he shows himself in manifestation of grace and mighty acts as the God of Israel. The *hayah* of the nation is not created with the deliverance from Egypt, but it shows itself in obedience to Jahveh's command. To the gracious dealing of Jahveh corresponds an energetic and obedient response by Israel. In the patriarchal stories and later in the history of the nation, God's miraculous leading and help is expressed through his *hayah*: 'I will be with you' (Gen. 26.3; 28.20; 31.3, 5; 35.3; Ex. 3.12; 4.12, etc.). So also in prayers: Jahveh, be my helper = come to my aid (Ps. 30.10); thou hast been my help (Ps. 63.7; said otherwise in Ps. 25.10, without *hayah*; cf. pp. 35 ff., above).

The *hayah* of the word of God is worth noting for our manner of thinking; we translate it by 'came' or 'came forth': After these things the word of Jahveh *came* to Abram in a vision (Gen. 15.1); the word of Jahveh *came* to Samuel (I Sam. 15.10); in the same night the word of Jahveh *came* to Nathan while he was carrying out the command of Jahveh (II Sam. 7.4); the word of Jahveh *came* to Elijah (I Kings 18.1, 31), to Isaiah (II Kings 20.4; Isa. 38.4), and to Jeremiah (Jer. 36.1; 37.6). The *hayah* of Jahveh's word, according to the Second Isaiah, is like the coming down of the fruitful rain from heaven; it will not return until it has accomplished the purpose for which Jahveh sent it (Isa. 55.11).

The hand of Jahveh is frequently associated with his *hayah*; as will later be shown in detail, a part of a person's body can take the place of a property. The hand of Jahveh renders the mighty power of God; the *hayah* of Jahveh's hand therefore means the coming of the mighty power of Jahveh. When the Philistines had brought the ark of Jahveh to Gath, the mighty power of Jahveh came upon the city (i.e. a great panic), and he smote the men of the city, young and old alike (I Sam. 5.9). The *hayah* of God's hand therefore is the same as *kabhedhah yadh ha'elohîm sham*, God's hand was very heavy there (5.11). The hand of God is upon the Philistines as long as Samuel lives, i.e. the mighty power of God subdues

the Philistines (7.13). Thus in this and similar cases, the *hayah* of Jahveh's hand means God's invasion into history. The prophetic seizure is
described as the *hayah* of the hand of God to or upon the prophet, i.e.
as the coming of Jahveh's power; thus it is in Elijah's run from Carmel
to Jezreel (I Kings 18.46), so also it is upon Elisha as the minstrel plays
(II Kings 3.15) and upon Ezekiel (Ezek. 1.3; 3.22).

Even the *hayah* of the spirit of God is its *effect*: and then the spirit of
Jahveh came (*wattehi*) upon Jephthah, and he went through Gilead and
Manasseh against the Ammonites (Judg. 11.29); and then the spirit of
God came upon Saul's messengers, so that they also spoke in ecstasy
(I Sam. 19.20). The coming of the spirit of God upon Balaam as well as
the coming of the evil spirit upon Saul is expressed by *hayah* (Num. 24.2;
I Sam. 16.23). For an understanding of the concept of *hayah* the rendering 'come' or 'come upon' is misleading, for *hayah* does not express
movement from one place to another but gives expression to the idea that
the spirit is powerful and effective suddenly upon and in the man in
question.

Like the spirit of God, the terror of God and the fear of Jahveh are
full of power and effectiveness: a terror of God came (*wayehi ḥittath
'elohîm*) upon the cities in that region, so that they did not pursue Jacob's
sons (Gen. 35.5). When measured against our experience the following
is paradoxical: And Moses said to the people, 'Do not fear; for God has
come to prove you, and that the fear of him may *be* before your eyes,
that you may not sin' (Ex. 20.20); hence the fear of God is no anxiety
(*Angst*), but it is an effective and positive power. The same thing is true
of the blessing of Jahveh which *was* upon everything that belonged to
Potiphar for Joseph's sake, i.e. the blessing showed itself effective (Gen.
39.5). Along the same line lies the effective *being* of Jahveh's name in the
Temple at Jerusalem (I Kings 8.16, 29; II Kings 23.27; II Chron. 6.6;
7.16).

The *hayah* designates existence; only that to which one can attribute
a *hayah* is effective. We have seen time and again that the effective expresses itself in activity, and so existence is identical with effectiveness:
it is not at rest but is dynamic. This becomes especially clear in the existence of God. When the godless says in his folly or pride that there is no
God (Pss. 10.4; 14.1), he is not expressing theoretical atheism but doubts
only God's prosecution as a judge; 'he does not punish', as the parallel
(10.5) indicates. As previously pointed out, this practical atheism actually
emphasizes God's *being active*. Even practical atheism is infrequent; it is
ascribed only to the foolish and frivolous. The Israelite knows that above

all others Jahveh *is*; he is the sum of all dynamic existence and the source and creator of it. This lies in the embattled verse: *'eheyeh 'asher 'eheyeh*— I am who I am (Ex. 3.14). For our purpose we need not enter particularly into the many controversies engendered by this verse. The divine name Jahveh or its probable roots *yah*, *yahu* are demonstrably older than Moses; the content of the revelation imparted therein does not lie in the mediation of a few sounds but was only joined inseparably with them. Eichrodt's opinion that the expansion of *yah* or *yahu* into *yhwh* is to be connected with the Mosaic establishment of a religion[1] is quite likely. Even if Moses were to have taken over the full name from others like the Midianites, it still remains the principal fact that the revelation of God in Mosaic religion, which inheres in the name, is on an entirely different plane from that of Midianite religion, for example. The majority of Old Testament scholars are of the opinion that Ex. 3.14 represents a clarification of the name Jahveh, which may be correct and significant or simply a folk etymology. Ratschow energetically maintains that Ex. 3.14 is no explanation of the tetragrammaton but has a particular significance in relation to the name and its being made known. His interpretation of the words: there is not a single person or thing in the world to whom *hayah* could be ascribed if it could not be ascribed to Jahveh.[2] Be that as it may, the sentence is in any case characteristic of belief in Jahveh; to Jahveh is ascribed an unalterable (i.e. eternal) *hayah*, and this *hayah* is a dynamic, energetic, effective, personal being 'who carries out his will and achieves his purpose, and who thereby advances the good fortune and salvation of his people',[3] the obedience of the people being naturally presupposed. *The one who is*, i.e. the eternally effective Jahveh, *is the creator*.

With this the analysis of *hayah* is concluded; in the analysis of divine being, no new meaning of the word 'being' has been discovered. The above established unity inherent in *hayah* of 'becoming', 'being', and 'effecting' is curious to us because our thinking takes its orientation from visible things. However, if thinking is oriented psychologically, the synthesis is quite comprehensible, for the person is an active being who is perpetually engaged in becoming and yet remains identical with himself.

5. *The dynamic character of the world*

From this viewpoint we can also better understand one side of the Israelite conception of the world. Things do not have the immovable

---

[1] W. Eichrodt, *Theologie des Alten Testaments*, I, 92.
[2] Ratschow, *op. cit.*, p. 81.   [3] Mowinckel, *loc. cit.*

fixity and inflexibility that they have for us, but they are changeable and
in motion. So speaks Jahveh to Israel through the Second Isaiah:

> Behold, I will make of you a threshing sledge,
>   new, sharp, and having teeth;
> You shall thresh the mountains and crush them,
>   and you shall make the hills like chaff;
> You shall winnow them and the wind shall carry them away,
>   and the tempest shall scatter them (Isa. 41.15 f.).

Even stone and rock are movable and externally alterable:

> But the mountain falls and crumbles away,
>   and the rock is removed from its place;
> The water wears away the stones. . . .
> So thou destroyest the hope of man (Job 14.18 f.).

In comparison with Jahveh's immovability, even the fixity of the earth
is nothing at all:

> Then the earth reeled and rocked;
> The foundations of the mountains trembled and quaked,
> Because he was angry (Ps. 18.7);
> The mountains skipped like rams,
> The hills like lambs (Ps. 114.4);
> The mountains quake before him,
> The hills melt (Nahum 1.5).

Such hyperbolic images cannot be explained by natural phenomena
even if it be taken into account that earthquakes occur frequently in
Palestine (cf. Amos 1.1). This hyperbole has two familiar roots, the
Hebrews' distinctly dynamic-personal kind of thinking and their faith
in the omnipotent God:

> God is our refuge and strength,
> A very present help in trouble.
> Therefore will we not fear though the earth be moved,
> And the mountains be cast into the midst of the sea;
> Though the waters thereof rage and swell,
> And the mountains shake at the tempest of the same.
>
> . . . . .
> Jahveh of Hosts is with us,
> The God of Jacob is our fortress (Ps. 46.2 ff.);
> For the mountains may depart and the hills be removed,
> But my steadfast love shall not depart from you,
> And my covenant of peace shall not be removed,
> Says Jahveh, who has compassion on you (Isa. 54.10).

In comparison with the *hayah* of Jahveh and his salvation, the entire universe is nothing:

> For the heavens will vanish like smoke,
> The earth will wear out like a garment,—
> But my salvation will *be* for ever,
> And my deliverance will never be ended (Isa. 51.6).

The positive contrast to the image of Jahveh's destructive power over the world is the idea of creation; all *hayah*, even that of the universe, stems from Jahveh the author and creator. This image must be discussed separately. First of all, however, we shall elucidate the Hebraic dynamic-personal conception of the world and of 'being' by comparison with the diametrically opposite Greek conception of 'being', particularly in its Platonic form.

B. STATIC BEING

1. *The Eleatics and Heraclitus*

The Greek interpretation of being does not permit of being established by a linguistic analysis; however, in this case we can use a direct method since all Greek philosophers from the Ionian natural philosophers on have discussed the problem of *being* and *non-being*. We do not intend here to write a history of the problem but only to single out the three decidedly principal types, the Eleatic, the Heraclitean, and the Platonic.

While, as we have seen, the Hebraic kind of thinking was in the main dynamic, the kind of thinking employed by the Eleatic school of philo-sophers was not only diametrically opposite but contradictorily so. They considered *being* not only as the essential point, but even more, as the only one since they flatly denied the reality of motion and change. Only what is immovable and immutable exists; all becoming and passing away is mere appearance and is equivalent to what is not, about which nothing positive can be said. Our sense-impressions are deceptive. In a sense, the Greek kind of thinking appears here most distinctly and clearly; at the same time, however, when it was carried to absurdity, it denied another characteristic Greek quality: the moderate and prudent, harmony.

Yet in Heraclitus of Ephesus, Greek philosophy had an advocate of the significance of change; his thinking is governed by the impression of the changeableness of all things: 'Everything changes; war is the father of all things, and a man cannot step into the same stream twice' (cf. Plato *Cratylus*, p. 402). This high estimate of change and motion is un-Greek; Heraclitus stands alone among Greek philosophers with his doctrine.

Quite un-Greek as well is the obscurity of his diction; the responsibility
for this is not to be placed upon any deficiency in the consistency of his
thinking but to a considerable degree belongs to the Greek language
which, unlike Hebrew, was not capable of giving adequate expression to
such ideas. That Plato was fully conscious of this fact must fill one with
astonishment and admiration; in the *Theaetetus* he has Socrates say
very trenchantly after an attempt to express the doctrine of the disciples
of Heraclitus:

> The maintainers of the doctrine have as yet no words in which to ex-
> press themselves, and must get a new language. I know of no word that
> will suit them. . . .[1]

Perhaps this peculiarity in the philosophy of Heraclitus can be traced
to an indirect or unconscious oriental influence. As an indication of this
judgment it might be mentioned that Heraclitus came from Ephesus and
that his doctrine found its followers chiefly in Asia Minor.[2] The interesting and animated description that Plato gives in the *Theaetetus*[3] of the
followers of Heraclitus shows, in my opinion, that we have here to do with
Orientals or at least with men who think and act in an oriental manner.
Their impulsive, passionate, unlogical kind were mentally the contrary
of the clear and collected Plato, and he gave up the attempt to establish
the teaching of Heraclitus in debate with his followers. Then he himself
poses the problem of motion and change, but he examines it as though
he were confronted with a geometric problem. The problem becomes
even more complicated for Plato because Protagoras and the other
Sophists had adopted it, certainly not because they had a dynamic idea
of the world but because it allowed them to make everything wavering
and doubtful and thus to abolish the clear line between truth and untruth.

Heraclitus' thinking is, however, influenced, and in part, determined
by Greek thought-forms and ways of posing problems. He too seeks the
eternal law in the flux of all things and the *harmony* that reconciles all
antitheses. Also quite Greek is his image of the circular course of all
things which excludes both a creation of the world and a purpose of
history. His high estimate of matter is Greek, too, even though he makes

[1] Plato *Theaetetus*, p. 183. Bergson (*Perception du changement*, p. 22) also complains
about the intractability of the language to express his ideas; already in the first lines of
his doctoral dissertation and at many places throughout the work (Henri Bergson, *Essai
sur les données immédiates de la conscience* [Geneva, 1945], pp. 131, 170 *passim*) he does
the same. Cf. Henri Bergson, *Creative Evolution*, pp. 310–12, 320 f. The complaints of
Bacon, Locke, and Sir William Hamilton about the defectiveness of language bear in
another direction. Bergson complains only about the inability of language to express
his ideas. Cf Max Mueller, *op. cit.*, II, 671 ff.
[2] Plato *Theaetetus*, p. 180.   [3] *Ibid.*, pp. 179 f.

an 'ethereal' material like fire the point of departure for unceasing change. In spite of all this we cannot characterize Heraclitus as a typical Greek thinker, but we must consider him as an exception who still had provocative and fruitful effect upon Greek philosophy.

2. Plato

After having sketched the two extreme conceptions of the Eleatics and Heraclitus, we turn to the greatest mind of Greek philosophy, Plato, whose thinking is also oriented toward *being* without the excesses of the Eleatics. A comparison with Plato's philosophy is worthwhile, because the religious spirit inhering in it is most closely associated with the biblical spirit, and the ideas that come to expression through it are best able to be compared with the biblical ideas. It is not accidental that during the first five foundation-laying centuries of the Christian Church, Plato was its philosophical authority, and that the mental decline which clearly sets in at the beginning of the Middle Ages coincides with the rising authority of Aristotle. Even for Philo, the greatest mind of the Jewish Diaspora, Plato was the great teacher, and his attempt, resting on inner conviction, to unite Platonism and Judaism shows that even Jews saw and felt the spiritual kinship of Platonic and biblical ideas. Something rather unique is to be found here: while the external and formal similarity between Hebrew and Greek, in regard for example to etymology, is practically nil, the inner and real relationship is astonishingly great. Even in spite of all persecution, the Jews have sought their home among Europeans.

The object of Plato's thinking is the given, that which *is*, the world with its content; the goal of his thinking is to find what *truly is*. He recognizes two main levels of being which are each in turn divided into two further levels. The first main level is what is immediately given, namely what we can grasp with the senses, the sensible, ὁρατὸν γένος: men, animals, plants, things. As sensible things they possess a certain reality, a *being*, but there are too reflected or shadow images of the sensible things which also possess a certain though very limited reality. Visible things and their reflected images together form the first large main level of being—the kingdom of γένεσις. Characteristic of this level are *being born* and *passing away*; everything here is mutable and transitory, and nothing is eternal. The sun makes it possible for us to perceive things through light and through sight, which is the most valuable of all senses; but the sun is also first cause and source of all life and sensible being. It is the life-giving and reality-bestowing principle of the visible and transitory world.

The spiritual and intelligible world, νοητὸν γένος, has an essentially higher reality; here nothing alters, nothing comes into being, and nothing passes away. This is the kingdom of true being, οὐσία. This upper level of being is also divided into two subordinate levels; the lower of these levels consists of mathematical realities, especially geometric figures and numbers together with the laws that inhere in them, while the Ideas, which *truly are*, form the upper and highest level. By this formulation, Plato means to say that what we call the spirit (mind) and the spiritual (mental) world is not an appendage to the certain and everlasting material world, but quite to the contrary, the visible world is an appendage to the totally certain, everlasting, real, and eternal spiritual (mental) world. On this level the reality-bestowing principle is the Idea of the Good or God; as the sun gives life to plants and animals and reality to inorganic things, so God, the Idea of the Good, is the source of all true being. A celebrated passage in the *Republic* expresses it this way:

> . . . the good may be said to be not only the author of knowledge to all things known, but of their being and essence, and yet the good is not essence but far exceeds essence in dignity and power (δύναμις).[1]

This sentence obviously does not mean that God is to be thought of as not having being but that all other being has its cause in the being of God.

All being is therefore at rest and in harmony, and all higher being is unalterable and indestructible; there is also a certain order of rank among all existing things. The more original and spiritual a thing is, the more *being* it has and the higher is its dignity. The highest being possesses the beautiful 'in itself', the true 'in itself', and the good 'in itself'; but because the good is true and beautiful and therefore includes within it both beauty and truth, the *being* of the good, i.e. God, is the highest *being*. In the eternal and intelligible world the *rest* of the Eleatics rules; but the world of appearance, which consists partly of images of the Ideas and partly of images of the images, is perishable and transitory, and it possesses less reality, power, and value the farther removed it is from that which eternally is.

It is evident that the antithesis, *static-dynamic*, does not express clearly enough the real distinction between Greek and Hebrew thinking because the highest *being* according to the Platonic doctrine is complete power and because according to the Hebrew understanding the prodigious

[1] Plato *Republic* vi, p. 509.

dynamic of God is eternal, real, and therefore *is*.[1] The distinction lies rather in the antithesis between rest and movement.

C. NON-BEING

1. *In Greek Thought*

The analysis of the concept of 'being' in the *Theaetetus* is continued in the *Sophist* with the analysis of 'non-being'; the aim in the latter dialogue is to expose the legerdemain and logical deception in the Sophists' logomachy. Plato pursues the Sophist along his erring path and finally seizes him in his last dark and secret refuge, the area of boundless non-being,[2] τὸ μὴ ὄν. However, the philosopher, who in his thinking is always occupied with the idea of 'being', is also, on account of the suffusing light of his position, very difficult to fathom: the spiritual eyes of the great multitudes are unable to endure the sight of the divine.[3] Plato achieves a deeper understanding of the essence of being by a comparison with non-being. There are many kinds of being but an infinite amount of non-being; this is so because non-being is not only the negation of being but also encompasses all ideas that have and can have no reality. Non-being is the area of appearance, illusion, delusion, and error; here there are many dark corners where rogues and mountebanks can hide out and ply their Sophistic mischief. In order to put an end to their play, their land must be ransacked and the essence of non-being must be ascertained. Non-being is not; yet is has a certain existence—the existence of non-being. To say that something is non-being signifies merely the negation of being; however, nothing positive can be inferred from a negation. If something is not-big, we do not say thereby that it is small; it might be middling-big. To say that something is non-being means, therefore, not that it has no existence but that it does not have the existence of true being. It could be that there is something-besides-being, and this something-besides-being is precisely appearance and delusion, as shown above.

Non-being is not the opposite of being, whether or not it is now possible to form such a concept, but it is something *other* than being, something wholly other. If we take our point of departure in true being as the reality of existence, then the 'wholly other' is the arena of the Sophists and the

---

[1] This is emphasized strongly by Roman Catholic scholars, e.g. by Robert Loriaux, S.J., mentioned in a review of this book by G. Lambert, S.J. (*Nouvelle Revue Théologique*, LXXV [1953], 753), and by Cornelia J. deVogel, *Antike Seinsphilosophie und Christentum im Wandel der Jahrhunderte*, p. 15.

[2] Plato *Sophist*, p. 256e.   [3] *Ibid.*, p. 254a.

intellectual deceivers.[1] In our world, being and non-being are interwoven with one another; in our notions about things it is reality and appearance, in our thinking it is truth and error, and in our speech it is the correct and the incorrect that are interwoven with one another like light and shadow. In relation to light, shadow is not-light; i.e. not the opposite of light because it is not easy to say *what it is* except that it is something wholly other than light. Because there is light, in this world there is darkness too, although the darkness is a negative; but because darkness is the absence of light, it shares in the being of light since it is the wholly other than light.

2. *In Hebrew Thought*

It is easy to find the Israelite parallel to these profound ideas of Plato. True being for the Hebrews is the 'word', *dabhar*, which comprises all Hebraic realities: word, deed, and concrete object. Non-being, nothing (no-thing), is signified correspondingly by 'not-word', *lo-dabhar*. For the Hebrews, non-being, nothingness (no-thingness) also has a certain existence which in practical life is tangible and unsavoury. 'Mere words' (*Heb.*: words of the lip) are empty and vain and, therefore, pernicious and dangerous (II Kings 18.20; Prov. 14.23). The lying words of the false prophets are a negative quantity in content, yet they have a disastrously seductive strength. The prophet Micaiah ben Imlah had heard how the soothsaying spirit offered himself in Jahveh's council to be a lying spirit in the mouth of Ahab's prophets so that they prophesied a pure negativity (I Kings 22.21 ff.). A lie for the Hebrew is not as it is for us, a non-agreement with the truth; for example, he would not impute lying to the midwives (Ex. 1.19), something that the text abundantly confirms. For him the lie is the internal decay and destruction of the word: *sheqer* is the opposite of *tsedheq* (Ps. 52.5). That which is powerless, empty, and vain is a lie: a spring which gives no water lies (Isa. 58.11, *kazabh*). For this reason, it is just as clear that the God of Israel does not lie (I Sam. 15.29) as it is that idols are lies (Jer. 10.14). Lies and falsehood are also called *shaw* whose basic meaning is that which is empty, or which has no content and is futile, a mirage, a nullity: 'For what vanity hast

---

[1] *Ibid.*, p. 258b. K. Kerényi, in the epilogue to his book (*Die Antike Religion*, p. 234), discusses the religious idea of non-being; but he does not mean by it what Plato analyses in the *Sophist*, although he does cite this dialogue. His discussion has much more to do with Martin Heidegger (*Sein und Zeit*, I) than with Greek and especially Platonic thinking. We have not concerned ourselves especially with the concept of death, because the thinking of the Greeks and Hebrews was practically identical in this regard to the extent that both in contrast to the Egyptians denied a real life after death and gave their undivided attention and strength to life on earth.

thou created all the sons of men!' (Ps. 89.47). *hayah shaw* is equivalent to 'be reduced to nought' (Hos. 12.12).

Hebrew has many expressions for nullity; *hebhel* means 'a puff of wind, a breath', then 'a phantom, a deception, a false opinion':

> Surely men of low degree are vanity (*hebhel*),
> And men of high degree are a lie (*kazabh*):
> To be laid in the balance,
> They are altogether lighter than vanity (Ps. 62.9 AV).

hebhel occurs together with *tohû* to signify what is vain and futile (Isa. 49.4); *tohû* is paralleled with *shaw* (Isa. 59.4). Now *tohû* is the *terminus technicus* for chaos, either alone (Isa. 45.18) or together with *bohû* (Gen. 1.2; Jer. 4.23; cf. Isa. 34.11). Thus the kind of chaos is defined unequivocally; it is the vain, that which is lacking in reality and actuality just because it cannot effectively bring anything to pass.[1] It is difficult for us to insinuate ourselves into the Israelite thought-world in this area, because according to our way of thinking chaos is something quite real and effective since, at least, it contains formless matter; but for the Hebrew a material without specific properties is a mere nothing, and he may well be right in this. To find and express nothing or negativity is in itself difficult by nature, as Plato's above-mentioned laborious inquiry proves; but if it is recalled that Hebrew thinking is pictorial, unsystematic, personalistic, and warmly sensitive, and if it is possible to discount that peculiarity, it will not be hard to see that Plato and the great minds of the Old Testament were not only occupied with the same problem but arrived at analogous solutions of the problem. Just as the lie, the deception, the illusion, the error, futility, and vanity do not really exist and to that extent have no reality and must, therefore, be designated as τὸ μὴ ὄν, so for the Hebrews these same notions have no *hayah*; that is to say, they are of no effect, they have no validity and therefore no reality. Their existence is that of appearance which can, however, play a fateful and evil rôle on earth and in human life.

To become conscious of the similarity between Greek and Hebrew understanding of negativity, it is necessary only to compare it with the Buddhist way of understanding the same concept. In Buddhism, negativity and non-being are positive and good because the Buddhist takes his point of departure in the negative side of life and the world. For him the being of existence is a 'nothing'; likewise non-being is the negation of something negative and is, therefore, something positive. The Greeks

---

[1] Pedersen, *Israel I-II*, p. 413.

and the Hebrews are united in the idea that non-being is something dreadful; being, however, is a genuine reality and the true good, regardless of whether being is thought of as eternally resting conforming to the Greek kind or in eternal motion conforming to the Hebrew kind.

D. THE WORD

1. *The Word in Ancient Oriental and Hebrew Thought*

All over the ancient Orient, in Assyria and Babylonia as well as in Egypt, the word, and particularly the word of God, was not only nor even primarily an expression of thought; it was a mighty and dynamic force, as Herder had already observed.[1] The Israelite-oriental conception of the word is formally the opposite of the Greek conception, as Bultmann also maintains.[2] The Roman Catholic scholar, Lorenz Dürr, has produced a comprehensive monograph on the divine word in all its ramifications for the entire Orient up to the formation of the Logos idea in the New Testament.[3] With a few reservations, W. F. Albright concurs in his expositions.[4] On the basis of the overwhelmingly large amount of factual material in Dürr's book, we think it necessary, however, to reach another conclusion on one important point. In our opinion, the real similarity between the Hebrew and Greek conceptions with all their formal difference is greater than that between the Hebrew and other ancient Oriental conceptions, although these latter are almost identical formally.

It is at once obvious that in the ancient Orient the divine word possesses peerlessly a dynamic force; as examples of this, several predications from the great bidding prayer to Marduk-Ellil may be cited:

3   His word, which proceeds like a storm. . . .
12–13 The word which destroys the heavens above
14–15 The word which shakes the earth beneath
20–21 His word is a rushing torrent against which there is no resistance
24–25 His word destroys the mother with child like a reed
32–33 The word of Marduk is a flood that breaches the dam
34–35 His word breaks off great mesu-trees
36–37 His word is a storm bringing everything to destruction
60–61 His word, when it goes about gently, destroys the land.[5]

[1] Herder, *Vom Geist der ebräischen Poesie*.
[2] Rudolf Bultmann in *Vom Worte Gottes*, ed. E. Lohmeyer ('Deutsche Theologie,' III), pp. 14 ff.
[3] Lorenz Dürr, *Die Wertung des göttlichen Wortes im Alten Testament und im antiken Orient* ('Mitteilungen der Vorderasiatisch ägyptischen Gesellschaft', 42, 1).
[4] Albright, *op. cit.*, pp. 146, 285.   [5] Dürr, *op. cit.*, pp. 8 ff.

The remaining religious lyrics, above all the hymns to Ellil, praise the magnitude and strength of the divine word, frequently with similar images: Ellil's word is like a raging tempest, like the bursting of a dam taking place at night, like a snare set at the forest's edge, like a net that is spread over the sea from which nothing, absolutely nothing, can escape. 'Ellil's word, the heaven endures it not—Ellil's word, the earth endures it not.' His word is like 'the bellowing of the bull from Êkur' which drowns out everything. These citations can suffice for our purpose; Dürr adduces a great many others including examples of the beneficent, life-giving activity of the same word.[1] It is thus proven beyond doubt that the Assyrians and Babylonians conceived of the divine word under the image of a physical-cosmic power.

In Egypt, the power of creating and of sustaining everything was traced back to the divine word.[2] In this case, the word is clearly the ever-active, fluid or ethereal divine substance proceeding out of the mouth of the divinity. Atum, the primal god of the Heliopolitan pantheon, after self-gratification took his own seed into his mouth and spewed forth the first pair of gods, Shu and Tefnut. In the region of Memphis, Ptaḥ is the creator of the world, and the specific organ of creation is 'the mouth which named all things', in which the society of gods sat as teeth and lips and was part of Ptaḥ. Of the sun god Rê, whom the Memphitic system subordinated to Ptaḥ, it is said in a hymn to Ptaḥ: 'To him, whom thy mouth begot, whom thy hands created.'[3] Of Amun-Rê it is said: 'Thou art the one who has created everything, the only one who created what exists, out of whose eyes (tears!) man came forth and out of whose mouth the gods sprang.' The divinities of Abydos 'have come forth out of the mouth of Rê'. Of the creator-god Khnum of Esna, who is betokened in descriptions and pictorial representations, one reads how he formed creatures and especially men upon the potter's wheel: 'He formed the four-footed beasts through the breath of his mouth, he has breathed blooms and (. . .) on the fields.' Later on the word and speaking were expressly mentioned. Thus it is spoken of Thot to whom the creative activity passed: 'What springs out of his mouth, this happens, and what he speaks, this comes to pass.' An inscription from the time of Ptolemy IV preserves this sentence: 'Everything that is has come into being through his words.'[4] Without doubt the divine word is valued even in Egypt not because of its sensible content but because of its enormous power.

In Babylonia and Assyria there is no documentary support among the numerous creation texts for a cosmogony in the sense of a creation through

[1] *Ibid.*, pp. 12 ff.   [2] *Ibid.*, pp. 22 ff.   [3] *Ibid.*, p. 25.   [4] *Ibid.*, p. 28.

the divine word. Dürr thinks he can establish such an understanding by
a fortiori means,[1] but they are not overwhelmingly effective and at best
prove only a creatio secunda.

Finally we shall compare briefly the conception of the divine word in
Israel and in the rest of the ancient Orient. The formal similarity is quite
obvious; in Israel also the divine word had an express dynamic character
and possessed a tremendous power. A few citations from the Old Testament suffice to support this:

> My word, is it not like a fire,
> A hammer that shatters the rocks? (Jer. 23.29)[2]

It is particularly the voice of Jahveh that is described as a power working
itself out in nature: Jahveh roars from Zion and his voice is uttered from
Jerusalem so that the fields of shepherds mourn and the top of Mt Carmel
withers (Amos 1.2). The powerful effect of the voice of Jahveh is described in Psalm 29; it is hardly permissible, as Dürr does,[3] to identify
without further discussion the word and the voice (dabhar and qôl) of
Jahveh, for 'word' signifies the power- though sense-laden utterances of
God while the 'voice' in both these cases represents above all God's working
through the powers of nature. For the Hebrews as for us, 'voice' signifies
the sound of speech, but 'word' means the utterance or what is said itself.
The real distinction in the conception of the word is unmistakable: in the
Old Testament the word of Jahveh is never a force of nature as in Assyria
and Babylonia, but is always the function of a conscious and moral
personality. This is related to the distinction in the image of God; the
gods of the other Semitic peoples were originally personified forces of
nature. Thus already in the time of the kingdom of Ur, Anu, the god of
heaven, Bel, the earth and air, and Ea, the god of the deep waters, were
united into a triad. Later the same thing occurred in connexion with the
three highest gods, Shemesh the sun god, Sin the moon god, and Ishtar
the fertility goddess; or as in the case of the storm god and the rain god,
Adad and Ramman.[4] On the contrary, from the beginning Jahveh was a
conscious and moral personality.

The images under which these ancient civilizations conceived of the
divine word were completely different. In Assyria and Babylonia it
appeared ordinarily as a strong wind, in Egypt as a corporeal emanation,

---

[1] Ibid., pp. 32 ff.   [2] An English rendering of Mowinckel's translation (M.M.M.).
[3] Dürr, op. cit., pp. 19 ff.
[4] Tiele-Söderbloms Kompendium der Religionsgeschichte[5], ed. N. Söderblom (5th ed.,
1920), p. 83.

but in both cases something physical in principle clung to the word. In Israel the word belongs to the spiritual sphere; with all its formal similarities, it is nevertheless basically different from the divine word in the rest of the ancient Orient. As we shall see later, it stands in all formal distinctions on the same high level as the word in Greek thought. There are, however, a few places in the Old Testament which mention the divine word in a way reminiscent of the ordinary ways of thinking in the ancient Orient. As a *locus classicus*[1] Isa. 55.10 f. comes to mind:

> For as the rain . . . come(s) down from heaven,
> And return(s) not thither but water(s) the earth,
> Making it bring forth and sprout,
> Giving seed to the sower and bread to the eater,
> So shall my word be that 'goes forth' from my mouth;
> It shall not return to me empty,
> But it shall accomplish that which I purpose,
> And prosper in the thing for which I sent it.

Some think it possible, as it were, to trace the trajectory of the missile and the curve it describes,[2] and others see here a mere poetic personification.[3] If the section (vv. 6–11) is read as a unit, it is no hypostasis or remnant of a hypostasis[4] that stands in the foreground but it is Jahveh personally: Seek ye Jahveh while he may yet be found, receive in faith the incredible message of joy that Jahveh will deliver his people through Cyrus! The prophet speaks about this message with different expressions; it encompasses his plans, his ways (v. 8), and his word (v. 11). The somewhat peculiar form which v. 11 has preserved is certainly related to the image of the rain (v. 10) to which he likens it. This was easier to do in Hebrew than it is in English for the expression 'not return empty' was a common expression with wide application; thus he makes use of a strong wind which breaks forth from Jahveh and does not return until it has accomplished his intentions (Jer. 30.23 f.), and also of the sword of Saul (II Sam. 1.22; cf. Jer. 50.9), without the strong wind and the sword giving any evidence of independent motion or of hypostatic character. Yet even apart from that, the picture in v. 11 is no sharper than the images in the following verse in which the mountains and hills break forth in exultation and all the trees of the field clap their hands (!). The word that proceeds

[1] Dürr, *op. cit.*, p. 123.
[2] Oskar Grether, *Name und Wort Gottes im Alten Testament* ('Beihefte zur ZAW', 64), in agreement with Dürr, *loc. cit.*
[3] Paul Heinisch, *Personifikation und Hypostasen im Alten Testament und im alten Orient*, pp. 16–17.
[4] Dürr, *op. cit.*, p. 124.

from Jahveh's mouth is no fluid or ethereal substance, but it is an effective and spoken word. The next most important passage is:

> The Lord sent a word into Jacob,
> And it hath lighted upon Israel (Isa. 9.8 [v. 7 MT]).

Even here there is no hypostasis and no divine emanated substance, but a spoken prophetic word. The distinction from the divine, independently acting word in the Babylonian-Assyrian hymns is unmistakable, for in the following verse we hear nothing about a further working of the word, and from v. 11 (v. 10 MT) onward, Jahveh personally appears as the avenger. Dürr's interpretation of this and other passages is unclear, if not contradictory.[1] A layman carelessly reading Deut. 8.3 could certainly misapprehend that Jahveh's word is here a substance upon which man can live; however, the meaning of this passage is, as is generally recognized and as Marti[2] and Dürr[3] both translate it, that man can live 'from everything that Jahveh's command creates'. In the other places in the Old Testament where Jahveh's word appears as an independent entity in form (e.g. Deut. 32.47; I Sam. 3.19; Hos. 6.5; Isa. 11.4; 40.8; Pss. 107.20; 147.15, 18 f.), it is still clearer that the spoken word, the power of which is Jahveh himself, is being referred to in a pictorial way.

The word of creation must be mentioned particularly because of its significance for our understanding of Old Testament religion, even though we must forgo many of the details. Belief in Jahveh the creator who calls everything into existence when he speaks permeates the Old Testament. The similarity with the above-described belief in creation in ancient Egypt is therefore quite obvious; yet, here is the place to show the difference in conception. Because the word of creation in Egyptian religion is a fluid substance emanating from the mouth of the divinity, in reality there

---

[1] According to Dürr (*ibid.*, p. 51), the divine word, *dabhar*, is a 'divine product, a portion of the godhead which is, to so speak, incarnate in the "word", and as such, it participates also in the divine properties and powers'; he calls the word in Isa. 9.7, 'an energy-laden molecule whose power presses toward explosion and overcomes every opposition' (*ibid.*, p. 70). On the other hand, 'it is a matter here of the *spoken prophetic* word which is presented to the people as a finished product with the weight of an attack' (*ibid.*, p. 124. Italics Dürr's own). In our opinion there is an essential difference between the spoken, prophetic word which is a personal, moral accomplishment, and a molecule, a portion, or a ready-made product. In Hebrew usage the spiritual can be described with drastic and, according to our way of thinking, material images, without coming too near the peculiarity of the spiritual, as we shall show somewhat extensively later on. Mowinckel is surely on the right track when he remarks of Isa. 9.7 that the prophet has in mind here the effective power possessed by the expressed word of trouble (M.M.M., III, 188 f.).

[2] K. Marti, 'Das fünfte Buch Mose oder Deuteronomium', *Die Heilige Schrift des Alten Testaments*, ed. E. Kautzsch, I, 254.

[3] Dürr, *op. cit.*, p. 48.

is no creation in our sense but an emanation whereby one material is changed into another. Actually, then, the conception in the Babylonian creation epic *Enuma Elish*, in which the world arose out of water (Apsu the fresh water and Tiâmat the salt water mixed their waters), is not far removed from the Egyptian conception of creation. Here too the creation is a physical process, to be sure not an emanation, but more an evolution since out of the original material (water) not only heaven and earth but also gods and men gradually arose. On the contrary, in the Old Testament Jahveh, the personal and moral god, stands at the beginning as creator of heaven and earth. *How* Jahveh creates is not always particularized. It would be expected in the oldest account of creation, the J-narrative in Genesis (2.4b ff.), which stems from that ancient time when the cultural and political ties with Egypt were still close, that the Egyptian belief in the divine word of creation would also shine through; it is even more to be expected when it is expressly said of the creator-god Khnum of Esna, whose creation of man (according to many scholars) served as a source for the J-narrative, that he formed four-footed beasts, flowers, and other creatures by the breath of his mouth. But right at this point there is lacking any reference to a mediation of divine utterance or of his breath. Why? We would refer to a fairly contemporary, essentially parallel phenomenon: The oldest portion of the Wisdom literature (Prov. 22.17–24.22) is an almost literal rendering of the Wisdom collection of King Amen-em-ope, but every reference to the Egyptian gods and every motif which may not be reconciled with Jahvistic religion is either altered or expunged. Thus, for example, the divine retribution for human deeds in the after-life is changed into a retribution in this life.[1] It is thereby established that the Israelite theologians and Wisdom teachers were able, even in the most ancient times, to pick up foreign material, consciously to rework it, and to insert it, materially adapted, into their own religion. We have ground therefore for the assumption that *the Jahvist* knew the Egyptian belief in the emanated divine creative word, rejected it as un-Israelite, and traced the entire creation back to Jahveh himself as a conscious and moral personality. Later on when the cultural and religious influence came from the east where the word of creation is not to be supported in the religious literature and, therefore, in all circumstances played a subordinate rôle, the act of creation could be represented as a divine oracle. It is to be noticed that in Israel this is no dogma, no fixed doctrine; alongside it stand other conceptions equally legitimate. Hence

[1] Hugo Gressmann, 'Die neugefundene Lehre des Amen-em-ope und die vorexilische Spruchdichtung Israels', ZAW, I (1924), 272–96.

it is said in Gen. 1.1, 'God created the heavens and the earth', and later frequently: 'God made the firmament' (v. 7), 'God made the two great lights' (v. 16), 'God made the beasts' (v. 25), 'Let us make man' (v. 26), 'God saw everything that he had made, and behold, it was very good' (v. 31), but alongside these also: 'God created the great sea monsters' (v. 21), 'God created man' (v. 27) without any mention of God's word or utterance. It is to be noticed on the whole that in the Old Testament the word of creation never appears as *sermo operatorius*, as is the case later, for example, in the Wisdom of Solomon, 'Who madest all things by thy word' (9.1). We cannot explore the question as to whether this expression is a lapse into non-Israelite conceptions of faith or a legitimate further development of a genuinely Israelite idea. It is enough for us to establish that the Old Testament eschews the word of creation as *sermo operatorius*. The single, but only apparent, exception is:

> By the word of the Lord were the heavens made,
> And all their host by the breath of his mouth (Ps. 33.6).

The peculiar mention of Jahveh's word is demanded here, however, by the passive form; once the attempt is made to shift into the passive voice the sentence, 'Jahveh said, "Let the heaven and all its host be"', resort must be taken to an expression similar to that in the Psalm. The conception of the Psalmist in v. 6, then, is the same as in v. 9, where Jahveh's creative command in history is extolled:

> For he spoke, and it came to be;
> he commanded and it stood forth.

In another place stands simply:

> For he commanded and they (i.e. the heavens) were created (Ps. 148.5).

Deutero-Isaiah portrays Jahveh's creation of the world with ten to a dozen different verbs; he also praises the superiority of the divine word (40.8), but the word never intrudes as a connecting link between Jahveh and his creation. It is of moment to the prophets and the other great personalities of the Old Testament to trace the creation directly back to Jahveh. At this point the similarity between the two creation narratives in Genesis is undeniably great, a fact which religiously sensitive Israelites (narrator, author, 'redactor', hearer, and reader) certainly experienced and perhaps understood.

The idea that the creation is an expression not only of the power but also of the goodness of Jahveh is also genuinely Israelite. Thus in consequence of both creation narratives in Genesis, what God has created is extraordinarily good and beautiful. Hence in Deutero-Isaiah the creation of the world, the deliverance from Egypt, and the imminent miraculous redemption follow one after the other; everything is creation.[1] Faith in Jahveh the creator is the sure foundation for the life of the pious:

> I will lift up mine eyes unto the hills,
> From whence cometh my help?
> My help cometh from the Lord,
> Which made heaven and earth.
> He will not suffer thy foot to be moved:
> He that keepeth thee will not slumber (Ps. 121.1 ff. AV).

God's creative utterance in Gen. 1.1 is not to be understood, with Dürr, against the background of Egyptian and Babylonian sources and in the light of Jewish Apocrypha and Pseudepigrapha, but it must be seen in connexion with the use of language in the rest of the Old Testament: Jahveh's word belongs not to the physical but to the spiritual sphere; by it his will comes particularly to expression. Jahveh's word is his revelation which until the time of Samuel was an infrequent thing (I Sam. 3.1, 7) and which the prophets published later on (Jer. 1.4, 11; 2.1; 13.8; Ezek. 3.16; 6.1; etc.). Jahveh's word can be a command (Jer. 32.6, 8), a promise (I Kings 2.4), a threat (12.15), or his statutes (Ps. 50.17); the Ten Commandments are called the ten words (Ex. 34.28) etc., but Jahveh's word always has a spiritual content.

dabhar is dynamic both objectively and linguistically; it comes from the verb *dabhar*, ordinarily used in the *Pi'el* form, *dibber*, both forms meaning simply 'speak'. The basic meaning is 'to be behind and drive forward', hence 'to let words follow one another',[2] or even better 'to drive forward that which is behind'; the verb thus portrays somehow the function of speaking. *dabhar* means not only 'word' but also 'deed': Abraham's servant recounted to Isaac all the 'words' that he had done (Gen. 24.66); the rest of Solomon's 'words', and everything that he did, and his wisdom are recorded in the book of the 'words' of Solomon (I Kings 11.41). The *word* is the highest and noblest function of man and is, for that reason, identical with his action. 'Word' and 'deed' are thus not two different meanings of *dabhar*, but the 'deed' is the consequence of the basic meaning inhering in *dabhar*. If the Israelites do not distinguish sharply between word and deed, they still know of very promising words which did not become deeds; the failure in such instances lies not in the fact

---

[1] Cf. Mowinckel's introduction to the Deutero-Isaiah, § 5b and § 5d, M.M.M., III, 188 ff.

[2] Frants Buhl, *Wilhelm Gesenius' hebräisches und aramäisches Handwörterbuch über das Alte Testament, s.v.*

that the man produced only words and no deeds, but in the fact that he brought forth a counterfeit word, an empty word, or a lying word which did not possess the inner strength and truth for accomplishment or accomplished something evil. An Israelite would not therefore be able to burst out contemptuously like Hamlet, 'Words, words, words!' for 'word' is in itself not only sound and breath but a reality. Since the word is connected with its accomplishment, *dabhar* could be translated 'effective word' (*Tatwort*); our term 'word' is thus a poor translation for the Hebrew *dabhar*, because for us 'word' never includes the deed within it. The commentators[1] understand as a contrived witticism Goethe's translation of John 1.1, in the poodle scene in *Faust*: 'In the beginning was the deed.'[2] Actually Goethe is on solid linguistic ground because he goes back to the Hebrew (Aramaic) original and translates its deepest meaning; for if *dabhar* forms a unity of word and deed, in our thinking the deed is the higher concept in the unity.

The 'effective word' of Jahveh is just as dynamic as the word of the other ancient oriental gods, yet it is not on the physical, biological, or animal level and must be understood in analogy with the highest human function; it is the majestic word of command, sublime and meaningful, creative or destructive. The dynamic in the divine word is not peculiar to the word, but it is characteristic of everything divine and of Jahveh himself. The mere appearance of Jahveh brings forth the mighty activity of the divine word:

The sea saw it, and fled:
Jordan was driven back.
The mountains skipped like rams,
and the little hills like lambs.
What ailed thee, O thou sea, that thou fleddest?
Thou Jordan, that thou wast driven back?
Ye mountains, that ye skipped like rams;
and ye little hills, like lambs?
The earth trembles at the face of the Lord,[3]
At the presence of the God of Jacob;
Which turned the rock into a standing water,
The flint into a fountain of waters (Ps. 114.3-8 AV).

For behold, the Lord is coming forth out of his place,
And will come down and tread upon the high places of the earth.
And the mountains will melt under him,
    and the valleys will be cleft,
Like wax before the fire,
    like waters poured down a steep place (Micah 1.3 f.).

[1] Hj. Hj. Boyesen, *Ein Kommentar zu Goethes Faust* (Leipzig, 1882), p. 42.
[2] *Faust*, Part I, l. 889.   [3] An alteration of the text by Mowinckel (M.M.M.).

In *dabhar* therefore Jahveh makes his essence known; whoever has *dabhar* knows Jahveh. *dabhar* is more than a fragment, more than an emanation, or a hypostasis of the divinity; *dabhar* is a manifestation of Jahveh, and indeed the highest form of that manifestation. *dabhar* is Jahveh as he is recognizable to mortal man (cf. Rom. 1.20). We must, for this reason, return to this theme in dealing with the *imago dei* (cf. p. 109).

2. *The Word in Greek Thought*

It is not our intention to provide a complete discussion of the term 'word' in Greek thought, but to outline only those motifs which are significant for a comparison with Hebrew thought. We can at once limit the inquiry to *logos* (ὁ λόγος) for the synonyms do not require serious attention. λαλία signifies disorderly utterance, mere prattle; ῥῆμα means the definitely spoken word, a word which expresses quite neutrally the articulateness of the utterance.

Logos, word, came from λέγω, 'to speak'. The basic meaning of the root *leg-* is, without doubt, 'to gather',[1] and indeed not to gather pell-mell, but to put together in order, to *arrange*.[2] This basic meaning, which is so characteristic of the Greek mind, explains the three principal meanings of the concept which are so hard for us to reconcile: speak, reckon, and think. Only gradually did *logos* come into use as the designation of 'word'; in Homer the term is infrequent (he uses μῦθος in place of it), and it occurs only in the plural signifying 'the word not according to its external form, but with respect to the ideas attaching to the form'.[3] It is striking that *logos* originally had nothing to do with the function of speaking, like *epos*,[4] and one can understand that it was a long time before *logos* became the general term. It is as though the Greek mind groped to find the deepest meaning of this term; but when it had found it in *logos*, the term rapidly became general and from the time of Pindar, the philosophical poets, and the first historians became one of the most frequent words in the entire Greek language. The deepest level of meaning in the term 'word' is thus nothing which has to do with the function of speaking—neither dynamic spokenness, as was the case in the entire Orient, nor the articulateness of utterance—but the meaning, the ordered and reasonable content. The term was generally used 'only with regard to the principal functions of the reasonable man'.[5]

---

[1] Émile Boisacq, *Dictionnaire étymologique de la langue Grecque* (4th ed.; Heidelberg, 1950), *s.v.*
[2] Franz Passow, *Handwörterbuch der griechischen Sprache*, s. λόγος.
[3] *Ibid.*   [4] ἔπος from the same root as εἶπον, Boisacq, *op. cit.*, *s.v.*
[5] Passow, *loc. cit.*; cf. Anathon Aall, *Der Logos, I. Geschichte seiner Entwicklung.*

Essential for the proper understanding of *logos* is the fact that the various meanings could, for the Greeks, converge into *one* concept and thus into one comprehensive unity;[1] accordingly *logos* expresses the mental function that is highest according to Greek understanding. As we have seen, *dabhar* performs the same service for the Israelites; therefore, these two words teach us what the two peoples considered primary and essential in mental life: on the one side the dynamic, masterful, energetic —on the other side the ordered, moderate, thought out, calculated, meaningful, rational. It is the concept of ordering which develops ever more broadly and deeply until it attains the highest stage: the lawful and reasonable, seen from the human as well as from the divine standpoint. In the Classical Period the religious viewpoint still remained quite in the background; what in this epoch corresponds to the divine *dabhar* as the manifestation of Jahveh is, therefore, not yet the divine *logos* but the personal and visible appearance of the gods, the theophany. Only in the Hellenistic Age, in Neo-Platonism and Stoicism, does the development of the concept of *logos* achieve its highest religious stage; it is at the same time adulterated with oriental elements,[2] and is therefore no longer typically Greek. A comparison between *dabhar* and *logos* is yet thoroughly possible, and if one would expose the deepest roots of the *logos* concept in the New Testament, it is also necessary.

We have to render *dabhar* as well as *logos* by 'word', but our concept 'word' renders only one part of the content of *dabhar* and of *logos*; the most important part is not touched by this rendering, and at the same time the great distinction between *dabhar* and *logos* is hidden within the very term 'word'. 'Word' is, so to speak, the point of intersection between two entirely different ways of conceiving of the highest mental life, a fact that can be pointed up by means of the following diagram:

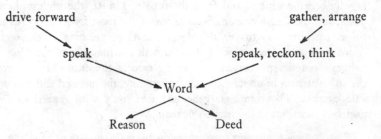

drive forward   gather, arrange

speak   speak, reckon, think

Word

Reason   Deed

<hr />

[1] As H. Kleinknecht correctly emphasizes (*Theologisches Wörterbuch zum Neuen Testament*, ed. G. Kittel, IV, 76 ff.).

[2] *Tiele-Söderblom Kompendium*, pp. 398 ff. M. Pohlenz, 'Stoa und Semitismus', *Neue Jahrbücher für Wissenschaft*, II (1926), 257.

When, therefore, the Fourth Evangelist pronounces the word *logos* at the beginning of his Gospel, the many different profound meanings of *dabhar* as well as of *logos* harmonize into a beautiful and mysterious unity for him as well as for his Greek-speaking readers familiar with the Old Testament in the same way as the sound of several church bells rung simultaneously. Dürr and the many New Testament exegetes of the same opinion may be right in their view that the Old Testament tone is strongest; yet when the Evangelist speaks three times of the eternal being of the *logos* (v. 1 f.), undoubtedly it is the Greek spirit which is breathing upon us, for it is characteristic of the Hebrews that their words *effect* and of the Greeks that the word *is*:

> It is a self-evident presupposition to the Greek that in the things in the world and primarily in its very progression a *logos*, a perceptible, knowable law, governs, which first makes possible knowing and understanding in the human *logos*. This *logos* constitutes the essence and the being of the cosmos and of man. Socrates and Plato carry consistently to a conclusion the genuine Greek conception of the *logos* idea. The *logos* as the basic fact of all life in community is the decisive point of Socratic as well as Platonic politics. The *logos* says 'how a being is' (Plato *Cratylus* 385b).[1]

dabhar is a power-laden word and, as such, belongs to the ancient oriental type of 'word', but this word of God is not like that in the rest of the ancient Orient, for it is neither principally a divine emanation nor essentially a material hypostasis in a nature religion or fertility religion. *dabhar* is always the act of *one mind* and, therefore, is of an entirely different sort in principle from the ancient oriental word. Attempts at this idea do exist in the rest of the Orient too, but they have never been able to impress their stamp upon the concept 'word'. As an act of mind *dabhar* is very much akin to the Greek *logos* idea; we recall Passow's observation that *logos* is used only with regard to the principal functions of the reasonable man. We have here a classic example of how a far-reaching formal similarity can be combined with a material difference in kind, and a quite contrary formal distinction with a radical and material affinity.

E. COLLECTIVE CONCEPTS AND IDEAS

1. *The Hebrew Collective Concept*

We can approach our problem from another side. Plato's doctrine of Ideas, which sees as 'realities with true being' what to our modern way of

---

[1] Kleinknecht, *op. cit.*, pp. 78 ff.

thinking are considered to be mere concepts, has its material counterpart in Hebrew thought. The concepts of the Israelites are not abstractions drawn from concrete individual things or individual appearances, but they are real totalities which include within them the individual things. The universal concept rules the Israelite's thinking. When, for example, he thinks of a Moabite, he is not thinking of an individual person who has among other qualities that of stemming from Moab, as Johannes Pedersen argues. The characteristic Moabite qualities trained up a peculiar type, the sum of Moabite traits. The type is called *mo'ab*, and the individual Moabite, *mo'abhi*, is the embodiment of it. We are so accustomed to begin with the individual that, involuntarily, we call this manner of conceiving the universal a personification, wherein lies something artificial, a figure of speech. This is not so; the granted point of departure for thinking is the universal, the type which contains the common traits and imparts to the group the stamp of its will. Therefore, the type deals and acts as a unity and is dealt with as a unity. Moab and Edom speak and act when their kings have dealings with Israel, because the Moabite and the Edomite are revealed by and large in their words and actions. *mo'ab* is thus related to a Platonic Idea of the Moabite.

The Hebrew language is full of what we call 'collectives', because the Hebrew always see the general; in the designation 'collective', we give evidence of our own individualism for by that term we refer to a sum of individuals. We should perhaps do better to say 'generalized terms', or 'terms of totality', or 'class terms'. Wheeler Robinson uses the expression 'corporate personality' and means by it, on the one hand, that the individual is identified with the group (family, tribe, or nation), and on the other hand, that the group including its past and future is interpreted as one personality.[1] The decisive matter is not the number, whether several examples or only a single one is intended, but whether the peculiarity or the essence is embodied in the individual or individuals in question.

Thus, for example, *'ets* designates not the concept 'wood', but rather as the Platonic Idea of wood, everything real which has the properties of wood. *We* start from individual wooden things and form from them the concept wood as something common to all wooden things; the concept wood has, for this reason, much less reality than wooden things. For the Hebrew, however, *'ets* is the given and the real, and wooden things are concretizations of it. The Hebrew *concept* designates, consequently, the

[1] H. Wheeler Robinson, 'Hebrew Psychology', *The People and the Book*, ed. A. S. Peake, pp. 353–82; *idem*, 'The Hebrew Conception of Corporate Personality', *Werden und Wesen des Alten Testaments*, ed. J. Hempel ('Beihefte zur ZAW', 66), pp. 49–62.

concrete at the same time as the 'abstract', the particular as well as the collective. Hence, *'adham* is 'man' and 'humanity' in one; *'ish* is both 'man' and 'men'; *rekhebh* is 'a chariot' or 'several chariots'. The particular individual is only a manifestation of the regnant type; in certain class terms the individual can be designated by a denominative termination *î* (*mo'abh—mo'abhî*), and this shows again that it is the individual that is derived. The many cases, however, in which the same form is used equally for one and for many show that the relation of the individual to the class is not that of being an isolated excerpt, but it is that of what we might call an exemplar in which the class appears. So, too, is the relation between individual and race; the individual Moabite is no excerpt from a mass of Moabite individuals, but he is a revelation or manifestation of 'Moabite-ness', in the same way as the particular cow is a completely valid manifestation of 'cowhood' (i.e. the Idea of the cow). Whether one speaks of *a* lion or *the* lion is therefore of no great moment; in either case it is the class *lion* which is revealed. Nor is the abstract separated from the concrete; *ṭôbh* is at the same time 'goodness', 'to be good', and 'a good (person)', and hence, it is goodness in its manifestations. For this reason, there is no sharp distinction between word-classes; this is one of the basic characteristics of Semitic languages. In the root *mlk* is involved the meaning 'kingship', and according to the modification of the word, it can mean 'king', 'kingdom', and 'act as a king'.

2. *Platonic Parallels*

It is not difficult here to see the similarity to the Platonic Idea. If it is true that Hebrew roots express the concept or the idea, this means that that to which Plato is driven in arduous intellectual exertion is vouchsafed to the Semites in their language; the kind of thinking associated with Platonism is natural to the Semites. Johannes Pedersen, to whose work we referred above,[1] gives the relationship with the doctrine of Ideas:

> Hebrew, like other Semitic languages, has preserved its primitive character and gives an immediate expression of the processes of thought. The words that make the language call forth images, but the Israelite sees more in them than something that is different from the actual matter. The matter lives in the word. The Hebrew language is principally composed of two kinds of words, nouns and verbs, the nouns designating the souls, the things, the *ideas, that which is and acts,* the verbs designating the action, the activity, the movement issuing from the souls and acting upon them.[2]

[1] Pedersen, *Israel I–II*, pp. 109 f.   [2] *Ibid.*, pp. 112 f. (Italics my own.)

Here Pedersen also uses the word 'idea' and defines it very neatly as 'that which is and acts'. The difference from Platonic thinking here is principally in the kind of acting; the action of the Hebrew noun is active, dynamic, visible, and palpable like the action of the Orientals, while the action of the Ideas is like the effect of a magnet or of the sun, passive and impalpable but still real enough. A magnet draws iron to itself and in that action remains immobile; the sun raises water into the air by evaporation and gives to all life strength for growing, but in all that it remains at rest and still. With the object of the action the situation is reversed; the stronger and more active is the subject, the more passive the object. If my hand lifts a piece of iron from the ground into the air, the entire activity is undertaken by me and the thing is completely passive. On the contrary, if I lift the piece of iron with a magnet, the iron itself leaps into the air and it appears as though the magnet is doing nothing and the iron everything, when actually the iron is just as passive as in the former case; or perhaps better, while the magnet is just as active as I was and accomplishes just as much as I did with my hand.

So long as we are dealing with mechanical objects, the state of affairs is clear and the conclusiveness of the image sufficiently great; less clear is the dominant rôle that the sun plays in the life of plants, trees, and animals. All living and growing, all movements seem to come from themselves, and they do in a certain sense; yet the sun bestows strength upon everything, directly or indirectly. Now Plato consciously compares the operation of the Ideas in mental life with the operation of the sun on the physical realm. There is no justification for underestimating the enormous activity which he ascribes to the Ideas, especially the highest Idea, the Idea of the Good, i.e. God, nor for misrepresenting the corresponding activity which it requires of man. The activity takes the form of a striving upward, but the desire and strength for this striving stem from the Ideas themselves, just as the need and striving of plants for the sun are aroused and sustained by the sun itself. It is therefore misleading, indeed false, to say that in Socratic-Platonic religion man ascends to God on his own strength and redeems himself. The rôles played by God in Jahvism and in Platonism are, in the formal sense, quite different, but in the material sense they are similar in so far as both are the origin and abiding foundation of all religious life and also require of man moral dealing. In Jahvism the religious moral activity of man ordinarily takes the form of obedience to the passionate zeal of God, but it can be urged that Jahveh must be sought with all the heart (Jer. 29.13).

In order not to be misunderstood, we add by way of conclusion that the Platonic doctrine of Ideas cannot be reduced to a formula; it comprises everything mental from the idea of a chair or some other thing to the Idea of the Good, i.e. God himself. An equitable comparison, therefore, between Platonism and Jahvism must take precautions that similar things be compared with one another: the idea of a thing with the root of the Hebrew verb for the thing, the highest Idea of the Good with the highest name for the God of Israel.

2

Impression and Appearance

A. THE IMPRESSION OF BUILDINGS

WHEN WE observe and study a thing, we involuntarily make for ourselves an image of it somewhat analogous to a photograph. When we mean to speak about the thing and describe it, we try to develop by means of words the same image in our hearers. The Greeks did the same thing. The Israelites, on the other hand, had no interest in the 'photographic' appearance of things or persons. In the entire Old Testament we do not find a single description of an objective 'photographic' appearance.[1] The Israelites give us their impressions of the thing that is perceived. We shall further elucidate this first of all by some examples of buildings.

Noah's ark is discussed in detail in Gen. 6.14 ff. (P): 'Make an ark of gopher wood; you shall make it with large rooms and caulk it inside and out with pitch. And you shall make it this way: the length shall be three hundred cubits, the width fifty cubits, and the height thirty cubits. Make a roof above for the ark . . . and set the door of the ark in its side; build it in three levels with large rooms.' It is striking in this description that it is not the appearance of the ark that is described but its construction.

---

[1] R. Bultmann maintains that the appearance of a statue is described in Dan. 2.31–35 (*Gnomon*, XXVII[1955], 551 ff.). It is first of all necessary to make clear what in the Greek sense as well as in ours the description of an appearance is; for this purpose, Bultmann himself can be cited. He speaks of the specifically Greek view of what is or of reality as fashioned material: 'Those things are real which one can grasp, whose shape can be experienced tactually, whose dimensions and outlines can be measured. . . . Seeing is, at the same time, a tactual experience of the forms which constitute the object in its being' (R. Bultmann, 'Zur Geschichte der Lichtsymbolik im Altertum', *Philologus*, XCVII [1948], 17). This is the same thing as we have called 'photographic appearance' in distinction from appearance in the Song of Solomon. In this sense, there is certainly no description of an appearance in the Old Testament, especially not in Dan. 2.31–35. It is definitely not said here whether the statue represents a man or a fabulous being. Only the material interests the narrator (cf. Song of Sol. 5.11, 14 f.). Moreover the statue is not an image of something spatial or perceptual but of a world historical occurrence, which will appear successively in the course of several centuries. A Greek would not have been able to contrive so curious a symbol; the image is pertinent, however, for the Hebrew narrator, since world history is for him a unity, and when God destroys the last Kingdom (v. 34), he simultaneously destroys all the earlier ones (v. 35).

What interests the Israelite, therefore, is how the ark was built and made. He talks of this the whole time, and the appearance is not directly alluded to by a single word; it is impossible for us to form an intelligible image of the ark. Yet as building specifications, the description is natural and consistent: first a rough sketch of the whole construction—build out of gopher wood an ark with many rooms in it using pitch as caulking material; then the details follow in order—bottom, sides, roof, door, and interior.

The description of the wilderness sanctuary also belongs to the P stratum (Exodus 25-28). At the beginning it is recounted that Jahveh showed Moses a model of the whole thing, but what the model looked like is nowhere reported. From beginning to end the account deals minutely and systematically with the making of all the objects, but in spite of all its quite pedantic accuracy it is not possible for us to form a clear image of the sanctuary:

> . . . you shall make the tabernacle with ten curtains of fine twisted linen, and blue and purple and scarlet stuff; with cherubim skilfully worked shall you make them. The length of each curtain shall be twenty-eight cubits, the breadth of each curtain four cubits; all the curtains shall have one measure. Five curtains shall be coupled to one another; . . . and you shall make loops of blue on the edge of the outmost curtain in the first set; and likewise you shall make loops on the edge of the outmost curtain in the second set. . . . (26.1 ff.)

This tone continues throughout the narrative. Even the sacred furniture standing in the sanctuary is similarly described:

> . . . they shall make an ark of acacia wood; two cubits and a half shall be its length, a cubit and a half its breadth, and a cubit and a half its height. And you shall overlay it with pure gold, within and without shall you overlay it, and you shall make upon it a moulding of gold round about. And you shall cast four rings of gold for it and put them on its four feet; etc. . . . (25.10 ff.)

Further it describes how the table for the bread of the Presence, the golden lampstand, the altar for burnt sacrifice, and the screen for the door of the tabernacle are to be made. Nothing is said even of the appearance of the sacred garments for Aaron and his sons, only how they are to be made (28.1 ff.; cf. the repetitions: 36.8-39.43).

This manner of describing objects, however, is not something peculiar to the Priestly document; the other sources do likewise. It is accurately described how Solomon had the Temple and the palace in Jerusalem built (I Kings 6.7); the narrative of the building is repeated in summary fashion later on (II Chron. 1.18 ff.). The novelty in the latter account is that Solomon makes the Temple (I Chron. 28.11) according to David's model or plan (the word *tabhnîth*, employed also at Ex. 25.9, can mean either), without our hearing anything about the appearance of the model or plan. This is apparently of no interest to the Israelite.

The silence of the sources with regard to the appearance of famous edifices and furniture can be explained in the following way: when an Israelite sees an edifice, his consciousness is at once concerned with the idea of how it was erected, somewhat like a housewife who cannot be satisfied with the taste of a cake but is particularly interested in what its ingredients are and how it was made. The edifice is thus not a restful harmonious unity in the beauty of whose lines the eyes find joy, but it is something dynamic and living, a human accomplishment; to be affected by it and to admire it, this is his joy and desire. In certain cases we, too, can feel the same way as the Israelite. When a European approaches the pyramid of Cheops, he likewise considers first how the ancient Egyptians accomplished the construction of such a colossus. The Israelite also, when he confronts other objects such as buildings, is interested in them not for their appearance but first for their use; they are for him tools or implements of human or divine actions, as is to be shown below in greater detail. We turn next to the Old Testament descriptions of man's exterior appearance.

B. THE IMPRESSION OF MEN

1. *The beauty of renowned persons*

When considering man, the Israelite first seeks his qualities. He recounts to us his impression of him; ordinarily the man's appearance holds no interest for him. This issues from two observations. In the historical and presumptively historical writings it is never reported how a person looked. Here and there it is briefly said that a person is handsome, like Joseph (Gen. 39.6), Saul (I Sam. 9.3; 10.23), David (I Sam. 16.12), and Absalom (II Sam. 14.25). First of all, the beauty is not expatiated so that we are unable to guess the Israelite ideal of beauty; secondly it is clear in the foregoing cases that beauty characterizes the persons in question. Joseph's handsomeness works alluringly upon Potiphar's wife, Saul's handsomeness betrays his regal class, David's blossoming handsomeness shows us that we have before us an extraordinary youth, Absalom's handsomeness is the ground partly for his self-consciousness as well as for his being favoured and for his popularity.

2. *The descriptive lyrics in the Song of Solomon*

Not only through the silence of sources but also through what they say are we enabled to establish the lack of interest in the appearance of things. In one Old Testament book, the Song of Solomon, we apparently have extensive descriptions of human appearance; these descriptions, which we designate by the Arabic word *wasf*, show immediately with their grotesque images, however, that here are no descriptions in our sense of the word. If we proceed from the knowledge we have attained that the Israelite considers persons in order to discover their qualities, it is not very difficult to understand the peculiar images in these descriptive images. In the form of a simple riddle, easy to solve, the *wasf* describes the dominant and admirable qualities of two principal persons, particularly the bride or fiancée.

Let us take first of all the image of the tower which is used of three parts of the maiden's body, of the nose (7.4), of the neck (4.4; 7.4), and of the breast (8.10):

> Your neck is like the tower of David,
>   built for a fortress,
> Whereon hang a thousand bucklers
>   all of them warriors' shields (4.4 Kautzsch).

The word *talpiyyôth* (v. 4a) is used here alone in the Old Testament and what it means is uncertain, whether 'fortification, entrenchment' or 'lookout', '(far) view'. In either case, it is clear that it is a tower built for war, not for the sake of a beautiful sight. We translate it, therefore, by 'fortress' in order not to awaken in a modern reader false associations. The custom of hanging up shields, of which we read in Ezek. 27.11, had the purpose of giving to the onlookers, particularly any sort of aggressor, a conception of the size of the tower's garrison. Hence this verse doubtlessly says that the maiden's neck resembles an exceedingly strong battle tower. The next time the tower image is used of the maiden's neck as well as of her nose:

> Your neck is like an ivory tower,
>   your head like Carmel.
> Your nose is like a tower of Lebanon
>   a watcher toward Damascus (7.4–5a Kautzsch).

The literal sense is clearest at this point. The proposal on rhythmic grounds of putting verse 5a after 4a is a very happy one and is generally accepted. The breasts are likened to towers, again the battle tower (8.10), for in the first half of this verse the maiden likens herself to a wall, i.e. to a city wall which also serves as protection in warfare. These towers and

this wall, which had withstood all assaults until now, she has handed
over of her own free will to the great conqueror, the bridegroom:

> I was a wall,
>   and my breasts were like towers;
> Then I became to him
>   like a surrendered city (8.10).[1]

The meaning of the tower image is clear from this verse, and it is illuminated by a modern marriage custom reported by Consul Wetzstein in
Damascus: On the morning after the wedding night, the king, i.e. the
young bridegroom, is asked in solemn assembly how went the campaign
which he undertook against a fortress previously unconquered; he is to
give an answer to that question to his people.[2] The tower images therefore signify insurmountability, inaccessibility, pride, purity, and virginity.
Staerk remarks on this verse that the comparison of the virgin breast
with a fortress is also found in German folk lyric.[3] The meaning of the
image is the same also in the other instances; it is remarkable that no
exegete has arrived at this possibility of interpretation.

The tower image is really exquisitely apt for expressing the proud
inaccessibility of a pure maiden; we express the same maidenly bearing
verbally. When we think of a young lady who wants to resist a young man,
she does today precisely what the tower images describe; she holds her
nose high (thy nose is a tower), her neck is straightened, and she holds
her head high (thy neck is a tower), and she holds herself proudly aloof
(Ger. 'sie brüstet sich') (my breasts are towers). Obviously, the Song of
Solomon aims to express by means of the tower image the same three
feminine reactions and motions; this means therefore that for the
Israelite, as for the Semites generally, the tower is something dynamic,
a fact which we can also feel, and in part, even repeat verbally: the tower
rises or towers.[4] The synonymous image of Carmel (7.5) which, as everyone knows, rises steeply from the Mediterranean Sea is well translated
by the expression, 'she holds her head high'. In the tower image there is
also something more, something threatening, something inspiring terror.
This subordinate idea is expressed also in other images.

With the solution of the riddle of the tower image, we now have a key

---

[1] In v. 10a, ka can be deleted in agreement with the ancient versions, but this is not
necessary; the translation of 10b follows M.M.M. [translator's rendering].
[2] J. G. Wetzstein, 'Die syrische Dreschtafel', Zeitschrift für Ethnologie, V (1873),
270 ff.
[3] W. Staerk, Lyrik (Psalmen, Hoheslied, und Verwandtes) (Die Schriften des Alten
Testaments, ed. Hugo Gressmann et al., Vol. III, 1), p. 299.
[4] In Norwegian, 'kneiser', which is used of a tower as well as of a proud maiden.

for the understanding of a series of other images. The maiden's brothers
by their protection will make their sister even more inaccessible:

> If she is a wall,
>> we will build upon her a battlement (of silver);
> But if she is a door,
>> we will enclose her with boards (of cedar) (8.9).

We omit *kaseph* (9a) and *'arez* (9b) for metric and material reasons;
they have been inserted out of misunderstood and exaggerated politeness.
Battlements are built of stone and not silver; a good bar for a door is
made of sturdy oak and not fine cedar. The idea that lies in the images
of the tower and the wall can be deepened even more; the maiden is like
a fortified, unconquerable royal city, such as Jerusalem or Tirzah (I Kings
14.17; 15.21, 33; 16.6; etc.):

> You are beautiful as Tirzah, my love,
>> comely as Jerusalem,
>> terrible as an army with banners.
> Turn away your eyes from me,
>> for they frighten me—(6.4 f. Kautzsch).

In v. 4 a line ought perhaps to be deleted on *metrical* grounds, and that is
apparently the last one unless a member parallel to the 'terrible army
with banners' has been omitted. On material grounds nothing is to be
omitted. For us the connexion of beauty with formidableness is unusual,
but the wrath of a young woman who triumphantly protects her honour
unites them. Tirzah, Jerusalem, terrible army with banners, and flashing
eyes express the same laudable quality clearly and potently. Seen from
another side, the unapproachability of the maiden consists of purity and
virginity. For that, too, this book has a richness of striking images:

> Who is this that looks forth like the dawn,
>> fair as the moon, bright as the sun,
>> terrible as an army with banners (6.10).

The correctness of this rendering is assured by the fourth member of
this double verse, the sense of which, according to recognized canons of
Hebrew style, should be the same as in the parallel members. The word
for 'bright, pure', *barah* (10b), which also designates moral purity (6.9;
Pss. 19.8; 24.4; 73.1; Job 11.4), points in the same direction.

The dove is also an image of innocence, moral purity, and blameless-
ness; it says expressly, 'my sister, my love, my dove, my perfect one'
(*tammathî* from *tam*—'complete', 'perfect') (5.2). Little embellishments

of the image can underscore still more the principal idea: the wild and
timid dove lives hidden high up in the mountains:.

> O my dove, in the clefts of the rock,
>   in the covert of the cliff,
>   let me see your face,
>   let me hear your voice
> for your voice is sweet
>   and your face is comely (2.14).

Innocence shines from the eyes of the bride:

> Behold, you are beautiful, my love;
>   your eyes are doves (1.15; 4.1).

Purity and innocence are the highest form of feminine beauty.

The maiden who stands there as a bride is something not yet in existence. The bridegroom, as the poem says, has sixty wives and eighty
concubines (the occurrence of the countless handmaidens is surely to be
omitted on metric grounds, 6.8); so many must there be that he is king
for a moment, even King Solomon. His bride is first among them all;
she is also first in the eyes of her mother and all the other wives and para-
mours, who are particularly expert in this very field. The number one
gains thus a content, becomes the expression of a quality as occasionally
even in our own language; but in this case the uniqueness is innocence
and purity, the *conditio sine qua non*:

> Sixty queens (have I) and eighty concubines,
> The first, however, is my *dove*,
>   (the first) my *perfect one*,
> The first to her mother,
>   the flawless to her that bore her.
> The maidens saw her and praised her,
>   queens and concubines, and extolled her (6.8 f. Kautzsch).

A distinct image of purity is water:

> Your eyes are pools in Heshbon,
>   by the gate of Bathrabbin (7.4).

In the context the images speak of minatory unapproachableness; as
mentioned above (8.9b), virginity is expressed also by detachment from
the outside world:

> A garden locked is my sister,
>   a garden with a fountain sealed (4.12 Kautzsch).

The Massoretic Text emphasizes still more the detachment:

> A locked garden is
> my sister, my bride,
> A sealed fount,
> a locked spring.

Here and in v. 15, 'spring' is considered not as an expression of purity but as a dispenser of refreshing water (cf. Prov. 5.15 ff.), a meaning which elucidates the context. Cool spring water is in southern lands even more than among us a means of highest and purest delight. The images that speak of the purity, innocence, and proud unapproachableness of the beloved are so numerous and so dominant that they give their stamp to the entire collection of lyrics. On this ground alone, not to mention others equally important, it is impossible that the Song of Solomon sings the praises of free love.[1] The old interpretation that the Song of Solomon contains marriage songs is consequently confirmed splendidly by a proper understanding of the images.[2] The rest

---

[1] Sexual morality among the Bedouin is still exceedingly strict; marital infidelity or moral transgressions on the wife's part before marriage can be punished by death. 'Free love' is thus no harmless matter as it is in modern metropolitan life, nor was it so in ancient Israel as the prescriptions in the Pentateuch show. From this background it is hard to see how G. Jacob (*Das Hohelied auf Grund arabischer und anderer Parallelen von neuem untersucht*, p. 27) with Staerk's assent (*op. cit.*, p. 293) can write: 'It would have certainly produced an inconceivably philistine effect if the nuptial chorus had filled the royal week exclusively with the praise of legitimate love. On such occasions, love in general forms the theme, and what is more, chiefly free love to which joyful voices are appropriate.' How could anyone glorify an action which for the wife was subject to passionate indignation or the death penalty, and that at her own wedding! That would be an unprecedented insult.

The collections of G. H. Dalman (*Palästinischer Diwan*) and Enno Littmann (*Neuarabische Volkspoesie*) show that today there are obscene songs in Palestine and vicinity; they also stand poetically on a very much lower plane and show generally a modern urban corruption of the ancient love poetry. The love-lyrics collected among the Bedouin by Alois Musil (*Arabia petraea, III. Ethnologische Reisebericht*) are on an entirely different level artistically as well as morally; obscene allusions are not to be found here.

[2] For the ancient period a third type of love-lyric must be reckoned with, the songs which were sung at the more or less savage festivals of the Canaanite fertility religion. Here, eroticism had been elevated to religion. The sexualizing of religion is not difficult to explain psychologically, but in Israel it was forbidden and was passionately contested by the prophets. The prophets did draw from the fertility cult some powerful images for the relation between Jahveh and Israel (Hosea 1–3; Jeremiah 2) and thus chastised the enemy with his own weapons since they branded the people's flirtation with the fertility gods as fornication. How, precisely, the relation between the cultic love-lyrics and the customary nuptial lyrics was formed is a difficult question into which we cannot enter here. Concerning the use of love-lyrics (Isa. 5.1 ff.) we have seen in any case that already in ancient times it was possible to use the love-lyric as a parable of the relation between Jahveh and Israel, to be sure *in malam partem*. After the Exile when the roots of fertility religion had been severed, it became possible for Judaism to apply the love-lyric *in bonam partem* to the relation between Jahveh and his people. When we consider how tenacious an adopted religion is, it seems not inappropriate to assume that certain motifs in the fertility religion lived on in Judaism and

of the images in the book must obviously be explained in conformity
therewith.[1]

We have already referred to the second principal group of the bride's
qualities which are candidly praised in the Song of Solomon, the womanly
power of attraction, her charm. The images used for it are flowers, palm
trees, colours, jewels, and artistic objects, the pleasantly scented and the
pleasant-tasting. This has been known for some time, and we need therefore detain ourselves on this but briefly. At the transition from the first
to the second group stand the flowers. The bride sings and the bridegroom replies:

> I am a crocus (RSV mg.) of Sharon,
>   a lily of the valleys,
> As a lily among brambles,
>   so is my love among maidens (2.1 f.).

Sharon, the fruitful plain south of Carmel, is proverbial for its richness
of flowers especially in the Spring. The lily is not the white lily but the
dark, aromatic sword-flag which also blooms among the richly luxuriant
brambles. The beauty here described is not the fragile beauty of Heine's
lyric, 'Ah, sweet as any flower',[2] but in any case it is more delicate than

---

particularly the longing to experience the relation between Jahveh and his people as an
intimate one, a longing which must have increased in Judaism proportionately as Jahveh
became more and more transcendent. Thus it can be explained psychologically that in
late Judaism the love-lyrics of the Song of Solomon, which especially glorify the
absolute fidelity of the bride, could find application as religious parables (certainly not
allegories!) in the cult of the feast of unleavened bread. In any event we cannot accuse
the Jews, who will have sung similar lyrics at their own weddings, of any ignorance of
the nuptial character of the lyrics. The famous utterance of Rabbi Akiba in *Tosephta
Sanhedrin*, xii, 'Whoever sings from the Song of Solomon in the wine shops and [thus]
turns it into a [profane] lyric, has no share in the world to come', thus proves not that
the true meaning of the Song of Solomon as a love-lyric had found a final refuge in the
public house, but that this particular love-lyric was borrowed at the time from profane
use and dedicated to religious cultic use.

[1] The Song of Solomon, like the rest of the Old Testament, mentions everything
sexual with robust candour, even the sexual members; but these could not be shown
(Gen. 9.21 ff.; I Macc. 1.14). Thus the candour was auditive. The Greeks observed
sexual life as uninhibitedly as the Hebrews, but their candour in this regard was otherwise oriented; they could display their nude bodies without shame—cf. their gymnastics
and their sculpture—but they would have taken umbrage at the robust expressions
of the Hebrews. Their candour was thus visual.

[2] 'Du bist wie eine Blume', set to music by Robert Schumann (Opus 25, no. 24) and
translated by Theodore Baker as follows:

> Ah, sweet as any flower and fair and pure thou art,
> Yet as I gaze, foreboding mournfully fills my heart.
> I fain would on thy tresses my hands in silent prayer,
> Praying that God would ever keep thee so pure and sweet and fair.

Schumann Vocal Album, trans. Theodore Baker ('Schirmer's Library of Musical
Classics', no. 120 [New York: G. Schirmer, Inc., 1896, 1930]), pp. 28 f.

the powerful and virile beauty of the bridegroom (v. 3a). Beauty is not form but charm:

> How sweet is your love, my sister, my bride!
> how much better is your love than wine,
> and the fragrance of your oils than any spice!
> Your lips distil nectar, my bride;
> honey and milk are under your tongue;
> the scent of your garments is like the scent of
> Lebanon (4.10 f.).

The beloved is a garden with a spring of fresh water; in the garden grow exquisite fruits:

> nard and saffron, calamus and cinnamon,
> with all trees of frankincense,
> myrrh and aloes,
> with all chief spices—(4.14).

The bride commands her beloved to go into his garden and eat its fruits, and the bridegroom answers, 'I come' (4.16c–5.1).

A third group of images praises the maiden's feminine voluptuousness and her bodily vigour that promises fruitfulness; this group includes edible animals and grains. It is natural that this group is less freely represented than the other two:

> Your hair is like a flock of goats,
> moving down the slopes of Gilead.
> Your teeth are like a flock of ewes,
> that have come up from the washing,
> all of them bear twins,
> and not one among them is bereaved (4.1b f.; 6.5b f.).
> Your belly is a heap of wheat,
> encircled with lilies.
> Your two breasts are like two fawns,
> twins of a gazelle (7.3 f.).

In the descriptive songs the images are of a mixed shade because of alternation among all three groups. As one image, e.g. the tower, can be applied to various parts of the body, so the same part of the body can be represented by two or three groups of images; hence the breasts are called towers (8.10), fawns (7.4), and date-clusters (7.8).

The prevalent quality in the description of the young man is his power and size, especially his strength and endowment. During his marriage he is a king (1.4, 12), indeed the most famous of all kings, Solomon (3.7 ff; 8.11 f.); he has a guard of gallant warriors armed with swords (3.7 f), and he has a sedan chair made of the wood of Lebanon, fashioned of silver and gold, and upholstered in purple (3.9 f). What is of particular interest from our viewpoint is the description of his person:

> My beloved is all radiant and ruddy, distinguished among ten
>> thousand.
> His head is of the finest gold;
>> his locks are wavy,
>> black as a raven.
> His eyes are like doves beside springs of water,
>> bathed in milk, fitly set.
> His cheeks are like beds of spices, yielding fragrance.
> His lips are lilies, distilling liquid myrrh.
> His arms are rounded gold, set with jewels.
> His body is ivory work, encrusted with sapphires.
> His legs are alabaster columns, set upon bases of gold.
> His appearance is like Lebanon, choice as the cedars.
> His speech is most sweet, and he is altogether desirable.
> This is my beloved and this is my friend,
>> O daughters of Jerusalem (5.10–16).

The text is partially corrupt, but is clear enough for us to recognize the three principal groups of masculine qualities. The colours (vv. 10 f.), flowers, and sweet-scented, pleasant-tasting things (v. 13) describe his power of attraction, beauty in the narrow sense; the doves, the water, the milk, the pool (?), and the bath (v. 12) speak of his purity and faithfulness; the images that are to us insipid, which say that the parts of the body are made of gold, alabaster, ivory, and jewels, tell of superior physical endowment (vv. 11, 14 f.), while Lebanon and the imposing cedars tell of imposing power and size (v. 15). That the description implies that the body becomes stiff and immobile from an external viewpoint is simply not in the images. Other images tell us directly that the bridegroom is fleet and nimble (2.17; 8.14).

A comparison between the images of masculine and feminine beauty is instructive. The bride is graceful; her beauty comes fully into its own in the dance (7.1). The bridegroom is nimble; his beauty comes into its own in the rapid course in earthly nature (2.17), i.e. the hunt. She is slender like the stately palm tree with its slender supple branches (7.7 f.); he is tall, strong, and steadfast like the cedar of Lebanon (5.15). In the antiphonal songs he calls her a lily among brambles, and she calls him an apple tree among wild trees (2.2 f.).

3. *The ideal of beauty*

In accordance with his fundamental conception Kant defines beauty as something formal. According to him neither the colours in painting nor the tonalities in music can be reckoned as beauty; they can only reinforce the beauty of the drawing in painting or of the composition in music. Here the Greek-European conception of art has been pushed to the extreme—hardened, and exaggerated. Aesthetics becomes thus a kind of space-consciousness. Now the Kantian aesthetic can be made something more acceptable if, with Hans Ording, the form or the idea as the life-giving principle in itself be permitted inclusion.[1] Then beauty is closely related to the spiritual (mental) which is included in the form. This might safely meet Plato's conception as well. As an extreme example of this we can cite the beauty of a geometric figure which presents a successful and elegant solution of a geometric problem. Here the beauty is found not in the lines as such, for those who do not grasp the meaning of the figure do not experience the beauty; the beauty is found in the clarity, facility, and elegance with which the figure reveals the range of mathematical ideas. According to this standard, *beauty is spirituality revealed in material objects.* This definition suits not only human beauty, but also divine beauty, and not only the Greek conception of beauty but the Israelite as well. The sensuous may be more or less underlined, but it must always contain *something* spiritualized in order to be valued as beautiful; gross sensuousness is always ugly.

In antiquity the humanly beautiful is always intimately related to what is good and acceptable to men; good and beautiful are thus synonyms for the Greeks as well as for the Israelites. What is living and what is conducive to life are beautiful to the highest degree. Savage nature, the sea particularly during a storm, the desert, and the mountains are ugly, even sinister. The passing away of the sea is a part of blessedness (Rev. 21.1). Not until men begin to weary of the cultivated field do a feeling and a taste for savage nature develop. It was not accidental that it was the great critic of civilization, Jean-Jacques Rousseau, who discovered the beauty of the Alps (afterwards everyone could see it), while an artistic soul like Martin Luther twice crossed the Alps without, so far as we know, finding anything at all beautiful in them.

If the intellectual motive in the experience of beauty is common to both Greeks and Israelites, the kind of sensuous motive is characteristically different. For the Greeks beauty lies in the plastic and consequently in the tranquil, moderate, and harmonious expression of the intellectual motive. Music and rhythm are given to men to order and bring into harmony the unharmonic movements that arise in their souls.[2] The

[1] Hans Ording, *Estetikk og kristendom*, p. 146.
[2] Plato *Timaeus*, p. 48.

Greeks especially are unsurpassed as sculptors and architects. Marble suited them to reproduce even the divinity; hence the statue of Zeus by Pheidias awakes in the viewers a feeling of devotion and mental affection.[1] The Greek artists were naturalists and realists who reproduced impressions of nature faithfully. Plato saw in art an imitation or copy of the sensuousness which was thus inferior to the model in both value and meaning. It is possible that the materialism which came to light in Sophism also seized the artists of that time and bred a conception of art contrary to the spirit of Plato. It is certain that Plato's conception of *beauty* corresponds to the one developed above. A good example of this is his description of the beautiful and ever more beautiful in the *Symposium*. Beauty is first discovered in a beautiful figure; then one learns to understand that the beauty of one body is the sister of the beauty of any other body. It would be unreasonable not to observe the beautiful as a beauty always remaining the same. When he has understood this, he loves every beautiful figure and refuses to love one only. Then he begins to treasure more highly the beauty of the soul than the beauty of the body so that he also loves the one who has a beautiful soul but a less beautiful body. In this way his eyes are opened to the greater beauty that lies in laws and human organizations. From here it is but a step to the beauty of knowledge and human thinking; now he has the whole 'vast sea of beauty' before his eyes. When he is strengthened and perfected in this beauty, the highest and most wonderful beauty is revealed to him. The beautiful is eternal, without birth or death, and it neither waxes nor wanes. This beauty is never relative but is absolute; therefore, it is not beautiful in one regard and ugly in another, nor is it beautiful for one and ugly for another, etc. The beautiful is not a body, nor a part of a body, nor anything corporeal; it is the beautiful in itself which in distinction from all else neither is born nor passes away nor alters. It is the divine beauty itself in immutable and unadulterated form.

It is worth noting how Plato exerts himself to make clear that the intuition of the higher and particularly of the highest form of beauty depends upon whether the man is willing to pay the price of toil, sacrifice, and renunciation which is required; the Israelite must pay a similar price to get God's blessing (Pss. 15; 24.3 ff.). The soul of the beholder must therefore gradually be changed so that it is likened to the constantly ascending forms of beauty. The consequence of the intuition is also sublime. When anyone sees the divinely beautiful, he gives birth to true virtue and educates it: he becomes the darling of the gods and immortal.

[1] T. R. Glover (*The Ancient World: A Beginning*) assembles several testimonies of this.

It is seen how the beautiful, the true, and the good are inseparably related. Aesthetics has here been raised to the religious sphere. The highest beauty, the divine, is also the most spiritual (mental), and yet it is clear that this beauty is somehow or other conceived plastically as well as naturalistically: it is a still, broad, immutable, vast sea (*Symposium* p. 210). Spirituality is a necessary precondition of perfect rest, for movement and alteration belong to the sensuous; when the sensuous is more and more put off, a kind of spiritual or ethereal corporeity remains as a substratum for the eternal, immutable, and immobile. This beauty in itself is at the same time the true and the real.

For the Israelites also, beauty begins in the sensuous. That is beautiful, first of all, which accomplishes its definition and fulfils its purpose; when a thing is as it should be, it is beautiful. Accordingly 'beautiful' and 'good' are synonyms. The most regular word for beautiful is *ṭôbh*, which we ordinarily translate 'good'. The distinction between what the Israelite finds beautiful and what the Greek finds so is characteristic. The Israelite finds the beautiful in that which lives and plays in excitement and rhythm, in charm and grace, but also and particularly in power and authority. It is not form and configuration which mediate the experience of beauty, as for the Greeks, but the sensations of light, colour, voice, sound, tone, smell, and taste, as we saw above in the Song of Solomon. When we call these sense-impressions secondary, there is obviously in that judgment a disparagement which is connected with the fact that for us they *do* stand on the second level. For the Israelites, however, the secondary sense-impressions are basic and decisive, and for this reason they should properly be called primary. When we have become familiar with this idea, it does not strike us as offensive that, for example, the divinity smells with pleasure the smoke of sacrifice (Gen. 8.21). The degree to which such a conception is susceptible of spiritualization we can see from Rev. 5.8 (cf. 8.3 f.): the prayers of the saints rise like incense to the presence of God, i.e. God who smells the prayers with pleasure, just as men can taste and see that Jahveh is good (Ps. 34.8).

The Song of Solomon teaches us that a man's beauty is found in his pre-eminent qualities which are expressed by means of the body in a dynamic way. The Israelite poets are impressionists; they repeat only their impressions. Saul was fairer than all the other Israelites; of his beauty only one trait is recounted: he was a head taller than everyone else in the nation, i.e. he was an impressive, regal figure (I Sam. 9.2). David also was fair, but apparently he was not taller than others for his size is never mentioned; here it is still clearer that his beauty lay in his vitality, leadership, and extraordinary skill which even his appearance had to betray. Thus one source recounts that he had a ruddy complexion and beautiful, that is expressive, eyes (I Sam. 16.12); another source says that he could play and speak well, that he was valorous and skilled in warfare (v. 18).

For the beauty of nature as such, the Israelite has little feeling; beautiful and powerful nature praises its creator. It is the work of God who also has complete power over it (Pss. 8; 19.1–7; 104; Job 38–41; Isa. 40.26, 28; 42.5; 45.12). The colours of nature play a less important rôle for the Israelites than for the Greeks. The rainbow is mentioned in only two places, and remarkably neither in the Psalms nor in the book of Job. In Genesis (9.13) the rainbow is a sign given by God; in Ezekiel the beauty of the rainbow is praised to be sure, but, as it appears, only because of its brilliance and splendour. On the same grounds it is admired at Ecclus. 43.11 ff., and apparently also at 50.7. The preferred colours are white and red.[1] 'Bright and gay colours were preferred, but only lighter or darker tones were generally distinguished.'[2] This is related to the fact that it was not colours but light and what illuminates which were for the Israelites the ideal of beauty: Light is sweet, and it is pleasant (*tôbh*) for the eyes to behold the sun (Eccles. 11.7). If white and red were most preferred, this is connected with the fact that they come closest to light and fire and therefore illuminate most. In sunlight and firelight, white, golden, and red pass over one another and appear thus as colours that stand very close to one another. In this way we can better understand that 'white' and 'red' are synonyms:

[1] Hugo Gressmann ('Farben', RGG[1], II, 827–29) is hardly right when he bases the Hebrew preference for red on the fact that it is the colour of blood, since blood defiles and pollutes (Isa. 59.3; Lam. 4.14). Perhaps on this ground the colour of blood is hardly mentioned in the Old Testament for it does not have much in common with the beloved colour of red. On one occasion blood is designated as red because stylistic grounds required it:

> Why is thy apparel red,
>   and thy garments like his that treads in the winepress?
> I have trodden the winepress alone,
>   and from the people no one was with me;
> I trod them in my anger
>   and trampled them in my wrath;
> their lifeblood is sprinkled upon my garments,
>   and I have stained all my raiment (Isa. 63.2 f.).

Here, first of all, is mentioned the clothing dotted with red flecks and then comes the explanation that the flecks come from the blood; even in this poem, however, shed blood is dirty and not pretty. To be sure, the blood of the sin-offering purifies, but in this case the appearance is put aside altogether and attention is directed only to the life in the pulsating blood.

[2] H. Guthe, *Kurzes Bibelwörterbuch*, p. 174.

Her princes were purer than snow, whiter than milk;
their bodies were more ruddy than coral . . . (Lam. 4.7).

My beloved is white and red,
distinguished among ten thousand (Song of Sol. 5.10 Kautzsch).

The bride is red as the dawn, bright as the sun and the full moon
(6.10).

If we consider white and red as colours on a colour-chart, they are mutually exclusive; moreover, the complexion of the Israelites was not exactly white. Both verbs used in Lamentations (4.7) demonstrate what is meant: *zakhakh* means 'be pure, glistening' with the secondary meaning 'be innocent', and *tsaḥaḥ* means 'glisten, be dazzling white'. The adjective *tsaḥ* (Song of Sol. 5.10) is formed from the latter verb, 'dazzling white'; as a substantive it means 'glow'. In both cases, therefore, the idea is approximately the same as in Song of Solomon 6.10: illuminating and irradiant beauty in combination with purity.

Various forms of *tsahabh* mean in the Old Testament 'golden bright' and in modern Hebrew 'brilliant red'. Generally the Hebrews do not distinguish sharply between red, brown, and golden; they were bright and shiny colours for them. Even in later times the bright colours were most valued (Luke 23.11; Acts 10.30; James 2.2; Rev. 15.6; 19.8). God did not surround himself with colours but shrouded himself in light as in a mantle (Ps. 104.2); for the Israelites, Jahveh's glory (*kabhodh*) appeared on the top of the mountain like a devouring fire (Ex. 24.17). To Jerusalem the prophet says: Thy light is come and the glory (*kabhodh*) of Jahveh has shined upon you (Isa. 60.1 Kautzsch). 'In every case *kabhodh* is a cosmic predicate of the divinity which is morally indifferent.'[1] *kabhodh* as the beaming manifestation of Jahveh belongs to the religious sphere. If it is really hard for us to translate Jahveh's *kabhodh* as beauty, this is connected with the fact that we, like the Greeks, have to conceive the beautiful in a sensuous-harmonious way. The Israelites experienced it in quite another way; the beautiful needed to have no graceful, harmonious form.[2] They found the highest beauty in the formless, dreadful fire and in the life-giving light.[3] That *kabhodh* is really a kind of beauty results from the fact that even the beauty of nature is so designated: the glory of Lebanon shall be given to the desert (Isa. 35.2).

---

[1] W. Eichrodt, *Theologie des Alten Testaments*, I, 143.

[2] It is not difficult to see the interrelationship between Hebrew-biblical mentality and modern non-figurative art: negatively expressed, they are both non-figurative; positively, they are dynamic.

[3] European painters, *e.g.* Rembrandt, have often used light to express holiness and divine glory.

C. THE IMPRESSION OF THINGS

When we look back at the images employed in the descriptive lyrics and the interpretation of them until the present time, we find that the images which translate an odour, a taste, or a beautiful colour were readily understandable to Western minds and have also been correctly interpreted; the apparently static images belonging to the field of visual perception appeared incomprehensible and unsavoury, although it has been known, surely, that similar images have been employed in the contemporary Orient and experienced as fully intelligible. Once we recognize that such images also represent qualities, they are easily understood. This recognition leads us to a deeper understanding of a definite side of the Israelite conception of things generally, which would otherwise have been hidden from us. Material things, i.e. visible things, have a meaning for the Israelites, a comprehensible content; this meaning and content is the dominant quality. Hence the meaning of the tower is 'indomitability', and the meaning of gold is 'opulence', as we saw in the Song of Solomon.

1. *Images of weakness, of transitoriness and of reliability*

The meaning of 'flesh' is 'weakness'; the Egyptians are men and not God, and their horses are flesh not spirit (Isa. 31.3). The meaning of 'grass' and 'flower' is transitoriness:

> All flesh (i.e. all men) is grass,
>   and all its beauty is like the flower of the field.
> The grass withers, the flower fades,
>   when the breath of the Lord blows upon it;
> . . . . .
> The grass withers, the flower fades;
>   but the word of our God will stand for ever (Isa. 40.6 ff.).

Rock as an image for God is a universal human image and was used previously by the Sumerians; the meaning is not the same everywhere. Thus we think, for example, of the firmness and imperturbability of the rock: it never budges. The qualities are, according to the Israelites, not absolutely characteristic of mountains, as we saw above (pp. 49 ff.). The Israelite thinks more of the security which the mountain furnishes because it is high and inaccessible; it is therefore a suitable place of refuge for the wild dove (Song of Sol. 2.14). Whoever finds himself upon a rock is out of danger (Ps. 27.5). When God is called a rock, he is thought of as a refuge:

my God, my rock (*tsûr*), in whom I take refuge,
my shield, and the horn of my salvation, my stronghold (Ps. 18.2).
O Lord, my rock and my redeemer (Ps. 19.14).
He only (i.e. God) is my rock and my salvation (Ps. 62.2, 6).

2. The image-bearing quality of things in the J narrative of Creation

Because things have a meaning, they are symbols given in nature, which are quite immediately comprehensible to every Israelite without explanation. They have something to say; even the stones can speak (Luke 19.40). So natural was it for the Hebrews to think and speak in metaphors and similes that exegetes forget it occasionally and substitute the direct meaning for the image. As an example we can cite the Jahvist's creation narrative. As has been known for a long time, the meaning of the dust and ashes is inferiority; so Abraham presumed to speak even though he was dust and ashes (Gen. 18.27). Job thus describes his deep misery:

God has cast me into the mire,
    and I have become like dust and ashes (Job. 30.19).

The Psalmist in despair complains:

. . . thou dost lay me in the dust of death (Ps. 22.15).

So when it says, 'then the Lord God formed man of dust from the ground' (Gen. 2.7), *wayyitser yhwh 'elohim 'eth-ha'adham 'aphar min-ha'adhamah*, there can be no doubt about the fact that man's littleness is thereby designated. One cannot, therefore, with Gunkel, strike out '*aphar*, for earth ('*adhamah*) by itself does not have the meaning of littleness; on the other hand, '*adhamah* must be there to designate the phonetic and actual connexion between man and earth. Therefore the author must use the double expression, dust from the earth, i.e. earth-dust; both words recur later in a profoundly significant way:

In the sweat of thy face shalt thou eat bread,
    till thou return unto the ground;
for out of it wast thou taken:
for dust thou art, and unto dust shalt thou return (3.19 AV).

Thus the meaning of man's creation out of the dust is given: man is little. The account therefore tells the hearer what man is in himself, man is dust; he was not only once made out of it, but that is his abiding nature. Not only the first man, but every man is formed out of dust:

For he knows our frame,
He remembers that we are dust (Ps. 103.14).

Not only to Adam but to every man God says:

Turn back (i.e. to dust), O children of men! (Ps. 90.3)

The idea that man is made out of dust is universal and in itself very natural.

Our question is, however, whether the author of Gen. 2.7 conceived of God as a potter; an Egyptian image shows the god Chnum forming human beings on a potter's wheel.[1] It is quite possible that the Jahvist knew of this conception, but it is not to be concluded from this that he thought of Jahveh as a potter. Appeal cannot be made to Jer. 18.2–6, for at that point the image depicts Jahveh's power to destroy men. It is doubtful whether the Egyptian himself thought of creation as crudely as the image of the potter Chnum permits us to suppose; he could also say of Chnum: 'He has formed the four-footed beasts by the breath of his mouth, he has breathed bloom and (. . .) on the field.'[2] According to Egyptian thinking, creation through the word does not stand in opposition to creation or formation by hand. This is directly attested in a hymn to Ptah Tenen of Memphis, where it says of the sun god Re, whom the Memphitic system subordinated to Ptah, 'To him, whom thy mouth has begotten, whom thy hands made'.[3] The unreconciled juxtaposition of creation through the word and by the hand shows that they are two expressions for one and the same thing. This psychological mystery is perhaps explained thus: for the ancients the word was more substantial and matter more spiritual (meaningful) than for us. All the more must we expect that for the reader of Genesis as already for the redactor, the account in chapter two did not exclude creation through the word (ch. 1). Moreover, pictorial representation of God and man was forbidden in Jahvism, and it is certainly not likely that the God of Israel would have set his people so poor an example. These considerations cannot, however, be decisive; we must interrogate the text. According to Gesenius-Kautzsch (117 hh), in expressions 'which mean *to make, to form, to build something out of* something . . . besides the accusative of the object proper, another accusative is used for the material of which the thing is made'; in addition to Gen. 2.7, Ex. 38.3 is mentioned as an example: all the vessels thereof he made of bronze. The following paragraph (117 ii) says that the second object of such verbs can be thought of as accusative of the product. The decisive matter for the grammarian seems to be which word has before it the *nota accusativi*—'eth. Materially and linguistically, however, the distinction between the two groups can be insignificant: he builds the stones into an altar = he builds an altar from the stones, 'eth ha'abhanîm mizbeah (I Kings 18.32). You shall build an altar of

---

[1] Cf. J. Skinner, *Genesis* ('International Critical Commentary', 2nd ed.), p. 56.
[2] Dürr, *op. cit.*, pp. 27, 151.   [3] *Ibid.*, p. 25.

unhewn stones, *'abhanîm shelemoth tibhneh 'eth mizbeaḥ* (Deut. 27.6). Our distinction between an accusative of the material and an accusative of the product is not thought of in an Israelite way; Driver calls attention to the fact that the more distant accusative in both cases, strictly speaking, forms an appositive to the nearer.[1] This means that both accusatives taken together form a unity. The material here is not raw material, nor is the thing made the product of the work in this sort of construction; the concept is a unity—the material thing that we can see has been made.[2]

We can illustrate this difference between Israelite and European thinking by means of an imaginary debate: European: 'Here we have three kettles, one iron, one copper, and one silver kettle. The material is different, and the thing they all have in common is the form of a kettle. A thing is therefore a form with a content.' Israelite: 'I do not understand. Take away the material from your kettle and nothing remains. Form without content is pure unreality; for the thing is identical with its material.[3] That which is common among these vessels is their use. They are made in order to serve as kettles or to be able to serve as kettles. An implement is therefore material fashioned and used for a definite purpose.'

Gesenius-Kautzsch (177 kk) illustrates the appositional meaning of the second accusative by a good example from Ex. 20.25: You shall not build it (the stone of the altar) *gazith*—(as) hewn. We are now able to interpret correctly the meaning of Gen. 2.7: Jahveh Elohim formed man (as) earthdust; or—if we may allow ourselves to invent for this purpose an adjective 'dusten' for 'out of dust', on the analogy of golden, wooden, etc., Jahveh Elohim formed man dusten. Man and dust form an inseparable unity. Man is dust because God made him (as) dust. Thus, for example, Gunkel's *eisegesis* that Jahveh—with his own hand—formed man out of moist earth as a potter forms his image out of damp clay, is simply not in the text.[4] There is no mention here of Jahveh's hand nor of a raw material, only of God's powerful deed and man's smallness. God's act or deed is of the same order as that in 1.26. The text of 2.19 would have agreed more with Gunkel's conception: Jahveh Elohim formed *min ha'adhamah*—out of the earth—all the beasts of the field and the birds

[1] Ges.-K. § 117 ii.
[2] This line of thought can be rendered fairly well in German. *Alle seine Geräte machte er kupfern* (Ex. 38.3). If we say, '*Geräte aus Kupfer*', copper is the material, the raw material out of which the implements are made; if we say, '*kupferne Geräte*', copper is the material of the finished implements.
[3] Ges.-K. § 141 b.
[4] H. Gunkel, *Genesis*, p. 6. In other places it is expressly said that Jahveh's hands have formed man, but the context demonstrates that it is not meant literally; e.g. we are the clay, and thou art our potter, we are all the work of thy hand (Isa. 64.8), or, thy hands have made and fashioned me (Ps. 119.73).

of the heaven. But even here the conception is to be rejected on linguistic grounds, for according to Gesenius-Kautzsch (117 hh), the expressions for *make something out of something*, *build*, *shape*, *form*, among them the verb *yatsar*, are construed with two accusatives; moreover, a construction with *min* before the material is not even mentioned, and in addition, *ha'adhamah* would have had to have the meaning 'earth as a material' (v. 19) and the meaning 'land' (v. 7). Presupposing that there is no grammatical or linguistic exception, the most obvious thing is to attempt a translation like this: Jahveh Elohim formed all the beasts of the field stemming from the land; or, Jahveh Elohim formed the animals as something which is of the land. The meaning of this verse is then not very much different from that of 1.24; the earth is not the material out of which the beasts are made but is the place from which they originate. This is quite clear in Ecclesiastes: all have come out of the dust and all return to the dust again (3.20 Kautzsch). We have the same idea also in Gen. 3.19. The difficulty of the expression in Gen. 2.7, 19 is closely related to the fact that different ideas can be expressed with one sentence: man (beast) is created by Jahveh, he is earth, and he comes from the earth.

The constructions and images found in the account of the so-called creation of woman are entirely different; here there is express mention of the material with which Jahveh worked. He took out one of the ribs and filled up the place with flesh (2.21); of the 'making' of the woman there is decided expression: Jahveh Elohim made the rib which he had taken from the man into a woman (v. 22). In order correctly to assess the account of the 'making' of woman, it must be asked whether the woman is created not like the man out of dust, but perhaps as something more delicate; obviously, however, the woman is also dust and is created as dust. The account (2.7) goes for her too, she is included in it. So on the other hand, the making of woman has great consequence for the 'man'; he became a husband, *'ish*. Husband, *'ish*, originates at the same time as wife, *'ishshah* (v. 23). The account (2.21 ff.) reports, therefore, not the creation of woman, but the *differentiation* of humanity into man and woman. This obviously does not mean that, in the opinion of the narrator, man was originally androgynous; his standard is doubtless the development of man from childhood to maturity. The narrator's purpose is to disclose the essence of man,[1] and to that belongs also the essence of sexual differentiation. From the viewpoint of a male narrator it is very easy to

---

[1] Rudolf Bultmann (*Primitive Christianity in its Contemporary Setting*, p. 18) is right when he says, 'In the last analysis, the Old Testament doctrine of creation' speaks of 'the present situation' of human existence through 'the incomprehensible power of Almighty God'.

explain the sexual distinction, for a human being first becomes conscious of himself as a man when he sees a wife in another human being. Thus the natural succession of origin is first the human being, then man and wife.

It is quite clear that, if it is a matter of the differentiation of humanity, this must be accomplished in a *bodily* way. This is true also because when the body is especially emphasized, as we have seen above, it is the bearer of the psychical qualities of humanity, with the result that bodily separation is an expression of complete psychosomatic separation of humanity into man and wife, male and female. Therefore, a part of the man's body must be laid as the foundation in the origin of woman; why that part has to be a rib is not altogether clear. On account of v. 23, it had to be a bone; then it would be hard to find something better than a rib which encloses and protects breast and heart. In any case, the choice must have fallen upon the rib because it had a deeper meaning for the author. As an analogy we can cite that among the Greenlanders the woman is said to have originated from man's thumb;[1] the thumb is the strongest, most valuable, and most practical member of the entire body. Among the Arabs 'rib' is an affectionate name for a bosom companion; if we may assume the same use of the word among the Israelites, the account preserves a beautiful as well as a profound meaning, and the succeeding 'shout of the bridegroom' (v. 23) becomes quite comprehensible.

If Gunkel is right in his assertion that we have here a paradigm of the aetiological myth,[2] it should surely be assumed that the story would explain also why the man is lacking a rib. Yet the man does have all his ribs intact *after* the creation of woman, and this supports the suggestion that the rib is mentioned not because of its material but because of its meaning. The account goes on (2.18 ff.) to describe man's longing for companionship, at first quite indefinitely and indirectly in God's words that it is not good for man to be alone; he will make a support, a helper fit for him. The companionship that the man needs is thus in the first place a companionship in work, as v. 20 underlines again. For man's sake God first created the beasts and the birds and led them to man; then man gave them names, and by this act he was reckoned to be their master. Allowing for all the formal distinctions, the lordship described here is the same as that in the P account (1.26, 28); he upon whom God bestows the authority to name the beasts has by that act achieved lordship over them. In this he found no fit helper. Then God makes woman, and man discovers that in distinction from the beasts she is completely like him (2.23a) and belongs to him; he then gives her name to her (v. 23b). When a man realizes that

---

[1] Gunkel, *op. cit.*, p. 13; Skinner, *op. cit.*, p. 68. [2] *See* preceding note.

a woman belongs to him, he is obliged thereby to forsake his parents' house in order to be with his wife in faith and love (v. 24a; that the young woman was also obliged to do so was so obvious to the narrator that he does not even consider it necessary to say so). *dabhaq*—'cleave, cling' is never used of cohabitation when speaking of people, but it is frequently used of strong love (Gen. 34.3; I Kings 11.2) and unbreakable trust, even in greatest need, of a king (II Sam. 20.2) or of a mother-in-law (Ruth 1.14). When man and wife remain joined in faithful love, the separate duality becomes once again a unity, one flesh, one human being (v. 24a). *dabhaq* thus speaks of the faithful and active love of a man for his wife (that she loves her husband is either obvious or of no concern for the Israelite). Sexual intercourse is naturally included, but it is not mentioned because, for the narrator, it is only one consideration of love and not, as in our oversexed age, the most important matter; this is the way in which we must understand the last half of v. 24, *wehayu lebhasar 'ehadh.* Nearly all the ancient versions add *shonehem*—'their twoness, the two of them'; it is omitted as unnecessary. Here *basar*, as it does frequently elsewhere (cf. v. 23), has the meaning 'man in his psychosomatic unity' (Ezek. 21.4, 10; Isa. 40.5; Ps. 63.1); the sense of the passage then is something like this: the husband cleaves to his wife in all faithful love, so the two become once again *one* human being, the sundered body becomes one body. Humanity in its wholeness is first and last in this creation narrative as it is in the other one; man and wife are a fuller definition of humanity or man (cf. 1.26 ff.).

Even if v. 24b should not be original, the ancient versions still offer a noteworthy commentary on our verse; in ancient times the readers did not find the meaning of the passage in the fact that the unity should be fleshly, but they found it in the fact that the separated flesh should again form a unity. Thus the emphasis is not upon *basar*, but upon *'ehadh.* The commentary that we have in I Cor. 6.15 f. also points in the same direction; the unity between man and wife is not something momentary that is achieved in sexual intercourse, but it is an enduring companionship and unity which is exhibited *through* sexual intercourse. The most beautiful expression of this unity is the child in whom both have literally become one flesh.[1]

3. *Comparison with Plato's* Symposium

As Gunkel also noticed, the same matter is dealt with in Plato's *Symposium* by Aristophanes (192 f.). Although neither Plato nor Aristophanes

[1] M.M.M., *in loc.*

can be accused of prudishness, it is here asserted with particular emphasis that the desire of each for the other is not of a sentient sort; it is an indefinite passion for completion, companionship, and unity as in Gen. 2.18–20. What they want, they do not themselves know and cannot say; they only sense it and can only vaguely intimate it. What they desire is to be together always and never to be separated. They want to be fused and united in order to become one again.

According to Aristophanes' myth, men were originally round creatures double their present girth, having four arms and legs, two faces, four eyes and ears, two privy members, etc. Zeus commanded Apollo to divide men because of their insolence. This dividing is accurately and graphically described; it is the author's purpose that a clear picture of the dividing be given. The form of the myth is quite different from that in Genesis 2, but the meaning is exactly the same. In the different *forms* of the myths is revealed the difference in the kinds of ideas and thinking between the two peoples; in the *material* similarity is expressed the same high mental quality of the two peoples.

4. *Personification in the Old Testament*

By personification we do not mean without further clarification what is known in German theology as *Hypostasierung*[1] and in English theology as Personification,[2] but the attempt to 'understand' nature (trees, plants, animals, mountains, etc.) by analogy with human psychic life and to represent the inner connexion between the two. Just as concepts of God and of the divine realm can be formed only through images and analogies taken from the sphere of human experience, so contact and living relation with nature can be achieved only when nature is elevated to the psychic level. We shall elucidate the matter first by several examples. When the nation of Israel returns from exile, all nature will participate in the joy:

> the mountains and the hills before you
>   shall break forth into singing,
> and all the trees of the field shall clap their hands (Isa. 55.12).

Against this background the next verse also must be understood:

> Instead of the thorn shall come up the cypress;
>   instead of the brier shall come up the myrtle (v. 13).

When the desert is changed into a garden, it is hardly for the purpose of making the journey more pleasant, but it is to be interpreted as a sign of

---

[1] S. Mowinckel, 'Hypostasen', RGG², II, 2065–68.
[2] G. Foucart *et al.*, 'Personification', ERE, IX, 781–803.

nature's participation in the miraculous return of the People of God. The great herald of the notion of creation experiences the unity of the whole world and expects that what was created by Jahveh will act also in his spirit:

> Sing, O heavens, for the Lord has done it;
>> shout, O depths of the earth;
> break forth into singing, O mountains,
>> O forest, and every tree in it!
> For the Lord has redeemed Jacob,
>> and will be glorified in Israel (Isa. 44.23).

> Break forth together into singing,
>> you waste places of Jerusalem (Isa. 52.9).

Even the wild beasts rejoice over Israel's good fortune, and they thank God:

> The wild beasts will honour me,
>> the jackals and the ostriches;
> for I give water in the wilderness,
>> rivers in the desert,
> to give drink to my chosen people (Isa. 43.20).

Likewise also the isles and the desert shout for joy (Isa. 42.10 f.).

Obviously this viewpoint does not detract from the divine sovereignty and absolute authority which stands squarely in the foreground, particularly in Deutero-Isaiah. How well the two viewpoints could be united in pious thinking is shown in the sixty-fifth Psalm. Just as nature rejoices in the Deutero-Isaiah:

> The pastures of the wilderness drip,
>> the hills gird themselves with joy,
> the meadows clothe themselves with flocks,
>> the valleys deck themselves with grain,
> they shout and sing together for joy (Ps. 65.12 f.),

so the joy of the earth stems from God:

> Thou makest the lands toward the east and
>> toward the west to shout for joy (v. 8).[1]

Nature shouts for joy also in Pss. 96.11 f.; 98.4, 7 f. In the nineteenth Psalm it says impressively:

> The heavens are telling the glory of God,
>> and the firmament proclaims his handiwork.

---

[1] Kautzsch (*Die Heilige Schrift des Alten Testaments*, II, 169) renders in German as follows, '*die Länder gegen Morgen und gegen Abend*'. His footnote: '*wörtlich: die Aufgänge (d.i. die Gegenden im Aufgange) des Morgens und des Abends*' [Tr.].

Day to day pours forth speech,
and night to night declares knowledge (vv. 1 f.);

of the sun its says:

(he) rejoiceth as a strong man to run a race (v. 5b, AV).

The morning stars sang with joy when God created the earth (Job 38.7).

The Book of Job says that he who fears God is in covenant not only with God but with nature as well, and that for him there is help from nature:

At destruction and famine you shall laugh,
and shall not fear the beasts of the earth.
For you shall be in league with the stones of the field,
and the beasts of the field shall be at peace with you (5.22 f.).

From this viewpoint it is easier to understand nature fighting for Israel against Sisera:

Lord, when thou didst go forth from Seir,
when thou didst march from the region of Edom,
the earth trembled, and the heavens dropped,
yea, the clouds dropped water.
The mountains quaked before the Lord,
yon Sinai before the Lord, the God of Israel
. . . . .
From the heavens fought the stars,
from their courses they fought against Sisera.
The torrent Kishon swept them away,
the onrushing torrent, the torrent Kishon.
. . . . .
So perish all thine enemies, O Lord!
But thy friends be like the sun
As he rises in his might (Judg. 5.4 f., 20 f., 31).

There is no reason to suspect divinities in the warring stars even though star gods were worshipped earlier as well as later. The stars can be construed in the poem as active heavenly bodies; Jahveh does battle with hail (Job 38.22 f.). The powers of nature, even, are mobilized for war. At the Red Sea the Israelites undoubtedly saw that nature contributed materially to their miraculous deliverance; in the late poem (Exodus 15) everything is attributed directly to Jahveh; in the Song of Deborah, in the book of Job, and in Deutero-Isaiah nature, too, is active.

In order to make these personifications of nature and her powers somewhat more comprehensible to modern man, we shall cite some analogies from a modern poem. We find several of them in Björnstjerne Björnson's little book *Århundredernes legende*,[1] but in the German translation[2] the majority of the personifications, including the pithiest of them, were simply omitted because they are just intolerable to rationalistic minds. In the account of little Paul it says: 'The old house where they dwelt was delighted to hear a child's voice again, the trees too; they spoke of him among themselves.[3] The birds had become so melancholy, the flowers too.'[4] In the account of the frog, a poor drudge of an ass by exertion of his utmost effort rescued a frog which had been chased by four schoolboys before being run over by a cart; one of the boys who had picked up a stone to kill the frog cast the stone far away, 'for from the heavens above, which had now become dark, he heard clearly, "Let it alone!" '[5] The young fisherman's wife Jeannie, who went to visit the poor, hopelessly ill widow, knocks at the door, and when no answer is forthcoming, she knocks again; she was going to force the door 'when the door sprang open by itself. It is sometimes as though things can feel as we do.'[6] Trees and flowers that talk, a merciful donkey, clouds that speak, and a door that springs open, all of these come from something more than poetic licence; they are expressions of a deep conviction: 'In everything that lives there is a reflexion of the eternal.'[7] This means that the universe as God's creation possesses an inner unity and is tuned to a definite pitch, and this pitch is goodness.

Corresponding to man as the image of God is nature as the image of man (Rom. 8.20–22). It is difficult if not shocking to conceive of both; yet it cannot be said that it is more absurd to understand nature from the viewpoint of human psychic life than—as is often the case in modern times—to understand human psychic life as a marginal instance of biology. When the attempt is once made to understand 'the wholly other', one is forced either to raise the lower and less significant to the higher level or to permit the higher to descend to the lower level. In the former case too great an honour is rendered to the lower; in the latter case a decided injustice is done to the higher. From the Jewish-Christian stand-point it has to be said that the universe as God's *creation* possesses an inner homogeneity, and as *God's* creation the homogeneity is a reflexion of the divine nature. The decisive events, even the evil ones, have cosmic consequences or cosmic correspondence (Gen. 3.17 f.; Isa. 24.5 ff.).

---

[1] Björnsterne Björnson, *Århundredernes legende*.   [2] Bj. Björnson, *Legenden*.
[3] Bj. Björnson, *Århundrederndes legende*, p. 95.   [4] *Ibid.*, p. 98.
[5] *Ibid.*, p. 19.   [6] *Ibid.*, p. 119.
[7] *Ibid.*, p. 16. This little book is a prose rendering of Victor Hugo, *La légende des siècles*, where personification of nature also appears frequently; e.g. from 'Booz endormie': '*Une immense bonté tombait du firmament*', and from 'Eviradnus': '*Je ne sais si la roche ou l'arbre l'entendit.*'

Adam's blameworthy fall as well as Christ's righteous act has cosmic meaning (Rom. 5.12 ff.; I Cor. 15.20–28; cf. Rom. 8.20 f.).

We can perceive, here and there, the inner unity between human acts and cosmic realities. Driving storms on England's coasts in 1588, and an unprecedented cold in Russia in the winter of 1812, in each case contributed decisively to freeing the world of tyranny.[1] The thoughtful Christian has customarily seen expressions in both instances of God's universal rule, and this is naturally permitted; but the question arises whether in our age with its accurate meteorological prediction this explanation is easier for our faith to tolerate than something on the lines of an assumption of a uniform cosmic sequence, a prestabilized harmony in which even material powers co-operate to effect God's will.

D. THE IMPRESSION OF GOD

1. *The Israelite Image of God*

When we pose the question: How did the Israelites conceive of their God? the sources give us two quite different answers. When the Israelites represented God pictorially they made him a bullock, derisively called in the Old Testament a calf (Ex. 32.4; I Kings 12.28 ff.; Hos. 8.5; 10.5); it is seriously questioned whether in any period Israel conceived of Jahveh theriomorphically.[2] On the other hand, all the theophanies and expressions about Jahveh in the Old Testament are anthropomorphic. He was called a man of war (Ex. 15.3), Lord, king, father, etc.

Is there an unbridgeable chasm between the theriomorphic and anthropomorphic expressions of Jahveh's essence? If we are thinking in a Greek way, yes, for a person cannot be simultaneously theriomorphic and anthropomorphic. If we are thinking Hebraically, no, for neither theriomorphic nor anthropomorphic expresses God's appearance but only his being and his properties. This is a necessary consequence of our interpretation of the images in the Song of Solomon. What the representation of Jahveh as a bull should mean in the Israelite cultus is not difficult to divine. In the Song of Solomon, the edible beasts are symbols of fruitfulness. Jeroboam's bulls in Dan and Bethel (I Kings 12.25 ff.) must be

---

[1] To illuminate the matter from the other side, and in part also to confirm it, a word of Napoleon's in 1812 may be quoted: 'I feel myself driven toward a purpose which I do not know. As soon as I have reached it, as soon as I shall no longer be necessary, an atom will suffice to shatter me. Until then all human powers will be capable of nothing against me' (Karl Heim, *Glaube und Leben*, p. 368).

[2] Johannes Hempel, 'Gott, Mensch, und Tier im Alten Testament', *Zeitschrift für systematische Theologie*, IX (1932), 217 ff.

understood against the background of the Canaanite fertility cult as expressions of Jahveh's life-giving power. This is indicated also by the pejorative name which Hosea and other pious Israelites applied to the bulls: they are calves, they possess no procreative power; they are impotent! It is quite as wrong to take literally the anthropomorphic expressions about Jahveh.

No one has mentioned as many parts of Jahveh's body as the author of Psalm 18, but if we put together all the expressions that he uses, they do not give a uniform picture. A fire burned within him, a cloud of smoke arose from his nostrils, and bright flames poured forth from his mouth (v. 8); through his nostrils breathed an angry breath which swept the earth like a destructive tempest (v. 15); the darkness which encircles Jahveh (v. 9) fits ill with the fire (v. 8). In the same verse the poet uses simultaneously two images which, if they are visually conceived, are mutually exclusive:

> He rode on a cherub and flew;
> he came swiftly upon the wings of the wind (v. 10).

We exert ourselves in vain trying to bring these two images into visual agreement, e.g. by attempting to make the cherub a personification of the wind, or by making the wind into an aerial divinity. From a 'motor' standpoint they agree completely; Jahveh comes fast as the wind and lifted high because the powers of nature and the angels are his servants (Ps. 104.4).[1]

If the mention of bodily members were to be understood as a description of appearance, we should have expected that in the most ancient and primitive times the descriptions of Jahveh would have abounded only to decrease more and more as time advanced; yet, just the opposite is the case. What is perhaps the oldest poem in the Old Testament, the Song of Deborah (Judges 5), describes at the beginning Jahveh's wrath and dominion over the powers of nature as does Psalm 18, without mentioning any bodily members at all. The prophets Amos and Hosea, too, are much soberer and more restrained in their description of Jahveh than Deutero-Isaiah. In the oracles of Amos no bodily members are mentioned, and Jahveh's form, described in the prose passages (7.1 ff.; 8.1 ff.; 9.1 ff.), which the prophet saw in his visions can hardly be regarded as an actual

---

[1] The man's bodily members are also cited in the Old Testament to designate the physical qualities of the man, a fact noted especially by Aubrey Johnson (*op. cit.*, p. 88): 'In Israelite thought man is conceived . . . as a unit of vital power . . . that is to say, the various members and secretions of the body, such as bones, the heart, the bowels and the kidneys, as well as the flesh and blood, can all be thought of as revealing physical properties.'

picture of the divinity; we must assume, however, that even in the visionary state Amos was clear about the fact that the patterns shown were *only* a portent of the judgment. These visions are to be classified among the so-called imagistic visions, in which experiences the character of sensory preception is lacking.[1] In the book of Hosea we find no suggestion of Jahveh's appearance, a fact which ought not to be given too much significance since whole oracles are formed as direct speeches of Jahveh. Isaiah's well-known Temple vision mentions Jahveh's throne and his train, but no single bodily parts (Isaiah 6).[2] In the prophet of the Exile, on the contrary, corporeal images of Jahveh are frequent:

> Behold, the Lord God comes with might,
>   and his arm rules for him;
> behold, his reward is with him
>   and his recompense before him.
> He will feed his flock like a shepherd,
>   he will gather the lambs in his arms,
> he will carry them in his bosom,
>   and gently lead those that are with young (Isa. 40.10 f.).

> The Lord goes forth like a mighty man,
>   like a man of war he stirs up his fury;
> he cries out, he shouts aloud,
>   he shows himself mighty against his foes.
>
> . . . . .
>
> Now I will cry out like a woman in travail,
>   I will gasp and pant (42.13 f.).

The best explanation is surely that the references to bodily members are not to be construed as actual descriptions but as figurative expressions which describe his qualities with poetic licence. The meaning of the images is everywhere pellucid and is confirmed by the use of images customary in the Old Testament. This is particularly clear in the case of that part of God's body the mention of which jars us most, the nostrils. The Hebrew word for nostril, *'aph*, also means 'wrath'. Breathing heavily and snorting with the nostrils are for the Hebrews bodily expressions of anger, just as a frown or a raising of the eyebrows is for us. The images:

> the foundations of the world were laid bare,
>   at thy rebuke, O Lord,
>   at the blast of the breath of thy nostrils (Ps. 18.15),

and

> At the blast of thy nostrils the waters piled up (Ex. 15.8)

[1] Ivar P. Seierstad, *Die Offenbarungserlebnisse der Propheten Amos, Jesaja, und Jeremia*, p. 57.
[2] *Ibid.*, p. 92.

are therefore highly intelligible for the Israelite because when God's nostrils are mentioned, he must at the same time think of divine wrath. An expression very commonly used of God as well as of men is *harah 'appô*, 'his wrath was kindled'; *haron 'aph* means 'the divine fire of wrath'. The fire inside God which issues as smoke and flames from his nostrils and his mouth (Ps. 18.8) is therefore also a deeply meaningful image of wrath. The two functions of God's nostrils, breathing and burning, which cancel one another out when we think of them as actual bodily descriptions, agree completely when we construe them as images of wrath which have their proper psychological basis in human psychic life: a man becomes hot and breathes heavily when he becomes angry.

It is also quite clear that the *arm* means might, strength, or energetic assistance upon which one can rely:

> Cursed is the man who trusts in man
> and makes flesh his arm,
> whose heart turns away from the Lord (Jer. 17.5).

The arm here simply means 'helping power'; thus there is also no reference to any part of Jahveh's body in the following:

> The Lord has bared his holy arm
> before the eyes of all nations;
> and all the ends of the earth shall see
> the salvation of our God (Isa. 52.10).

The *hand* also signifies might or power; the Israelites say as we do, 'To be in the hands of a man', i.e. in his power (Josh. 9.25; I Sam. 17.47). Jahveh's hands, particularly his right hand, are images of his power:

> Thy right hand, O Lord, glorious in power,
> thy right hand, O Lord, shatters the enemy (Ex. 15.6).
> The sea is his, for he made it;
> for his hands formed the dry land (Ps. 95.5).
> Thy hands have made and fashioned me (Ps. 119.73).

The hand (hands) is on the whole for the Israelites as for us a part of the body through which a great deal can be given expression: spread out his hands = invite (Isa. 65.2), clap the hands = be joyful. How little the Israelites needed to make a visual image in such an instance is shown by a stylist of the rank of Deutero-Isaiah:

> All the trees of the field shall clap their hands (Isa. 55.12).

The meaning of the metaphor *eye* is clear in itself: in our eyes (Ps. 118.23), in the sight (eyes) of the Lord (Ps. 116.15) = to our way of thinking or God's respectively. The eyes were opened (Gen. 3.7), Jahveh opened the servant's eyes (II Kings 6.17) = they saw and recognized what earlier they had not been able to. The Hebrews could express things more boldly than we can: 'I was eyes to the blind', says Job (29.15); the eyes of all Israel were directed toward the king (I Kings 1.20), i.e. the people waited tensely for the king's decision.

To incline the *ear* to someone (Ps. 17.5) is the same as hearing or listening (Ps. 78.1). How little the Israelite conceived of the ear visually is demonstrated by an expression of Jeremiah:

> Behold their ear is uncircumcised
>   and they cannot hearken (6.10 AV);

therefore,

> circumcise yourselves to the Lord,
> remove the foreskin of your hearts (4.4.).

In both cases, the impurity is there and must go.

Of particular interest is the description of Jahveh's theophany in the poem Isa. 30.27–30, which Mowinckel thinks stems from a pre-Exilic disciple of Isaiah. The text is corrupt, but these verses which describe Jahveh and his wrath are well attested. Therefore, we limit the quotation to vv. 27, 28a, 30 f.

> There comes Jahveh's 'appearance' from afar,
>   his nostrils burn, thick clouds arise,
> his lips are boiling over with rage,
>   his tongue is like a devouring fire,
> and his breath is like an overflowing stream
>   reaching up to the neck. . . .
> Jahveh makes his majestic voice heard
>   and the descending blow of his arm seen
> in furious anger and a flame of devouring fire,
>   with a cloudburst and tempest and hailstones;
> for at the voice of Jahveh Assyria will be terror-stricken.[1]

In v. 27, we have translated '*aph* by 'nostrils' rather than 'wrath'; in that way the rising clouds of smoke in the following are well founded. With the fiery tongue we bear in mind a similar description of God such as in Ps. 18.8 and can limit ourselves to a reference to what was observed there. Here too, the visual images do not agree; in v. 28, God's breath is an overflowing stream, but in v. 27, his tongue is like fire. What makes this passage especially valuable is the introduction: Behold there comes Jahveh's *shem* from far. With Guthe[2] we have translated *shem*, which

[1] English rendering of M.M.M.   [2] Guthe, *Kurzes Bibelwörterbuch, s.v.*

properly means 'name', as Jahveh's 'appearance'. In reality the difference is not great; Jahveh's appearance is his lips, his mouth, his nostrils, his voice, and his breath. Since these bodily parts and bodily phenomena are images of qualities, the description of Jahveh's appearance is, really, a description of his essence, of his spiritual personality as it is accessible to men, thus a description of his 'name'. Since the poet calls the theophany Jahveh's *shem*, he has given us the key to the correct understanding of the anthropomorphisms; Jahveh's *shem* is the sum total of his qualities and activity. When men see God's acts, they see in them God so far as he is knowable to men, his essence and his qualities.[1] The name is thus a manifestation of divinity; it can even dwell in a house (Jer. 7.12), inhabit a place (Deut. 12.11; 14.23; 16.2; 26.2; Neh. 1.9). In the name of the covenant-God his person is met face to face and his action is experienced.[2]

On this basis the theophany in Exodus (33.18–23) is not hard to understand; sight and hearing pass imperceptibly into one another (cf. Isa. 2.1; 13.1; Hab. 1.1). Moses asks: 'Show me thy glory!' Jahveh answers, 'I will make all my goodness pass before you, and will proclaim before you my name *Jahveh*; and I will be gracious to whom I will be gracious and will show mercy on whom I will show mercy' (vv. 18 f.).

Jahveh's glory is revealed in resplendence, but this resplendence is not of a natural sort such as of the sun; rather it is precisely divine resplendence, explicitly an expression of his essence. Yet Jahveh's essence is free goodness, grace, and mercy; all this is contained in his name. The meaning of the account seems to be that Moses could see Jahveh's goodness and hear his grace and mercy, if it is at all possible here to distinguish seeing from hearing. Jahveh spoke further, 'You cannot see my face; for man shall not see me and live' (v. 20). *Face* cannot here, as the following verse shows, designate that part of the body where eyes, nose, and mouth are to be found; it must mean Jahveh personally without mediation through visible and audible manifestations. Just as little is Jahveh's hand (22 f.) which covers Moses to be conceived visually, as though Jahveh had a huge hand; that would give just as grotesque an image as a visual conception of the tower image in the Song of Solomon. Jahveh's hand appears here as his gracious means of protecting Moses from danger. Hebrew has two words for *face*: *'appayim* and *panim*. The former is the dual form of *'aph*, nose, and therefore means, strictly speaking, 'nostrils' (Gen. 2.7); it is thus the most prominent part of the face which gives its name to the whole. This part governs the concept generally; so *'appayim* is used particularly in the expression 'to fall with the face against the

[1] Eichrodt, *Theologie des A.T.*, I, 102. (Cf. Rom. 1.19 f.)   [2] *Ibid.*, I, 103.

ground'. Consequently, this word cannot be used of God's face. *panîm* means God's face, properly the side turned toward one, then the face of a man or of God; once in a great while it is used also of the face of an animal; further: front side and especially surface, e.g. of the earth or of water. The inner connexion between face and surface shows that the original conception is dynamic; it is in every case a question of the side that is turned toward one. The Greeks also used a part of the body as a designation of 'surface', and what is more it was 'back': ὁ νῶτος, τὸ νῶτον; here the *tertium comparationis* is a plane. Since the face is the uncovered part of the body, it reveals the personality: embarrassed children involuntarily hide their faces in order to hide themselves. It is characteristic that the Greeks (and we) think in the concept *face* of the person who is *seen*: πρόσωπον—face, what is looked at; but the Hebrews by using *panîm* think of the acting subject: I turn toward someone. Since one does not see himself, the concept is not visual but motor-dynamic. We have presupposed that *panîm* is formed from *panah*—'turn'. Even if Haupt's idea that *panîm* is the plural of *peh*—'mouth'[1] is right, the concept is not visual but motor-dynamic, for when the mouth defines the conception of the whole face, indeed of the person, it is observed only as an organ of speech. The many meanings and uses which *panîm* has in the Old Testament are derived without difficulty from 'the side turned toward one'; to see the *panîm* is to see and meet the person himself (Gen. 32.20); so also the Apostle Paul uses it (Col. 2.1; I Thess. 2.17; 3.10); *panîm* is used also of a personal meeting with God;[2] to hide the *panîm* = hide oneself in grief (II Sam. 19.4) or—especially of God—in anger (Pss. 13.1; 27.9; etc.).

It is said of Jahveh that he knew Moses face to face (Deut. 34.10), that he spoke with him mouth to mouth (Num. 12.8), that he spoke to Moses face to face like a man to his friend (Ex. 33.11). In all three cases the subject is Jahveh who bestows his grace upon Moses to come near to him and to give him clearer revelations than to any other man. These sentences cannot be reversed, so that Moses ascends to Jahveh and speaks with him mouth to mouth, face to face, and converses with him as a friend.[3] For modern man the problem of the possibility of God's revelation is scientific and epistemological; for the Israelites it was moral and religious. The questions that we pose are thus not posed in the accounts and sayings in

[1] Buhl, *Gesenius' Handwörterbuch über das A.T.*, s. *paneh.*
[2] Cf. Eichrodt, *Theologie des A.T.*, II, 12, and the monographs there mentioned of Baudissin, Böhmer, and Nötscher.
[3] On the change in the divine name in Exodus 24, *see* Thorleif Boman, 'Jahve og Elohim i Jonaboken', NTT, XXXVII (1936), 159 ff.

question; therefore we do not find direct answers to our questions here.

We must understand the anthropomorphic actions in the accounts of the Jahvist against this background of the Old Testament conception of God. Nowhere in this account are Jahveh's bodily parts mentioned. Western minds naturally infer that if Jahveh carries out definite actions analogously to man, he must also possess the members and bodily parts necessary for the action. Thus he must have a hand to be able to form man and woman or to make clothes (Gen. 3.21); he must have lungs and mouth to be able to breathe (Gen. 2.7), feet to go about (Gen. 3.8), or a hand to be able to close a door (Gen. 7.8). Our conclusion is not demanded according to Israelite thinking, for it is possible for the Israelite to say that the trees clapped their hands and the mountains shouted for joy (Isa. 55.12) without having to account for where the hands of the trees and the mouths of the mountains are.

We should not, in the *first* place, conceive of the anthropomorphic actions of God more grotesquely than the text plainly states. This we have already shown in the case of the creation of the man and his wife. *Secondly*, we may permit ourselves to question the author: with what bodily parts did Jahveh make heaven and earth, make it rain, and cause trees to grow out of the earth? If the accomplishment of such actions requires a being who breaks all human boundaries, then it must be justifiable to think that it is the same being who accomplishes also the apparently very human actions and that a narrator of the rank of the Jahvist did not, in the course of so short an account as Gen. 2.4–25, work with two entirely different conceptions of divinity. Jahveh can execute the unprecedented, and he can also do the smallest things; in both he always remains the same in power, goodness, care, wisdom, and moral earnestness. These characteristics add up to Jahveh's being, and when we observe his actions in the J narrative more rigorously, we shall find that just those very qualities are what is common to all of them. In spite of all their external dissimilarities, therefore, the divine actions are essentially alike since their uniformity lies not in the forms of their appearance but in their meaning. The anthropomorphic divine *actions* in J thus serve the same purpose as later the visible, i.e. anthropomorphic, *manifestations* of Jahveh serve in the Psalms and Deutero-Isaiah, etc.: they reveal his qualities and his invisible being.

Jahvism's absence of portraiture extended not only to sculpture and painting but also to the religious consciousness: the leading minds made very definite images of their God, it is true, but never *visual* ones; their images of God were motor, dynamic, and auditive. For this reason there is an internal and real relation between the ancient, formally naïve accounts of Jahveh's actions and the later appearances of Jahveh in over-powering theophanies or in his energetic, creative word which is also a divine manifestation.[1] Thus it says at Isa. 22.14: Jahveh Sabaoth has revealed himself in my ears.

2. *Imago dei*

The Old Testament did coin a theological expression for the appearance or manifestation of God. In the P creation narrative it says: Let us make man in our image, after our own likeness (*betsalmenû kidhmuthenû*) . . . so God created man in his own image (*betsalmô*), in the image (*betselem*) of God he created him; male and female he created them (Gen. 1.26 f.).

The first question is what *tselem* and *demuth* mean. Paul Humbert, who has made a very thorough linguistic and religio-historical analysis of the two concepts, maintains that both *tselem* and *demuth* have every-where a completely concrete meaning.[2] The distinction is that *tselem* designates the complete likeness of a picture or a statue to the original, while *demuth* designates only the approximative likeness, i.e. similarity. Thus in Genesis 1, it is a theologian and great religious thinker conscious of the appearance and likewise of the form of God who is speaking. Neither in the Old Testament nor in the related words of ancient oriental languages is found any spiritual or moral meaning for *tselem* or *demuth*.[3] On the other hand, asserts Humbert, it is not possible to underline enough in Genesis 1 the pronounced character of theological reflection, priestly deliberation, and monotheistic austerity.[4] Beyond a doubt, Humbert is right in this. Gunkel also stresses that P above all others avoids anthropo-morphisms as much as possible.[5] How is it to be explained, then, that P is the one who speaks of God's *tselem* and thus gathers into one aggregate all anthropomorphisms and consequently underlines them? Gunkel be-lieves that he can solve this difficulty with his usual assumption that P took over the concept of God's image from his older model. According to him the ancient idea is already reinterpreted in the Psalms (8.6 ff.), where similarity to God is combined with man's dominion over the beasts (cf. Ecclus. 17.2–4). But, according to Gunkel, the identification of similarity to God with dominion over nature contradicts the text of Genesis 1, according to which dominion over the beasts is adjudged to

[1] *See* p. 67, above.
[2] Paul Humbert, *Études sur le récit du Paradis et de la chute dans la Genèse* ('Memoires de l'Université de Neuchâtel', 14), pp. 155 ff.
[3] *Ibid.*, p. 162.   [4] *Ibid.*, p. 166.   [5] Gunkel, *op. cit.*, p. 112.

man by another special blessing, especially that of 5.3, where it is quite clearly a matter of form.[1] Against Gunkel it must be objected that it is not possible to imagine how a theologian working scientifically, and that is what we are dealing with in Gunkel's notion,[2] who is otherwise capable of masterfully reworking the pagan elements of the ancient model, would allow the worst kind of anthropomorphism to stand and would stress it with particular emphasis. Humbert attaches importance to the distinction between *tselem* and *demuth*: according to him, P intended thereby to stress that man is not substantially identical with God but only similar to him. In this Humbert is unquestionably right, but this does not prevent God from having a bodily form (v. 27).

It is quite right to note, with many scholars, the wording of Gen. 1.26 ff. One has a feeling of how the theologian is struggling with the expressions in order, on the one hand, not to trespass upon God's sovereignty and sublimity and, on the other hand, to protect the worth of man. Man is a creature like the beasts, the birds, and the fish, and so he belongs to another category than that of the creator; yet man is created in accordance with a special divine decree and is set as master over the beasts; consequently man belongs to another category than that of the beasts. Man is hence neither God nor beast; what is he, then? Our writer tries to express this by means of the concept of image, and right there one notices the struggle. Man is to be formed after the analogy of an Elohim-being (note the plural in v. 26); the creation of man is therefore something great, but still it is nothing unprecedented, nothing that impairs God's sovereignty. Still, man is not as perfect as an Elohim-being; he is formed only similarly thereto and not after its model. If this misunderstanding is averted, it can be said that man is created in the image of the highest God, i.e. in accordance with the type (v. 27). Because of the ambiguity of the word *Elohim*, it is impossible to say whether the other Elohim (v. 27) means God or Elohim-being; there is little choice for both meanings are protected in the passage (vv. 26 ff.). We need not unduly underestimate the capability of Israelite theologians, thinkers, and philosophers to see religious problems and penetrate them; more extensive proof of this will be given later on.[3] Even though the notion of the image of God occurs but seldom in the Old Testament (outside of Gen. 1.26 f.; 5.13; 9.6, it is to be found only at Ps. 8.6), the New Testament as well as Christian dogmatics has with sure instinct singled out this very notion as particularly valuable.

In the term 'image of God', P has expressed what appears to us at first

[1] *Ibid.*   [2] *Ibid.*, p. 117.   [3] On pp. 197 ff.

glance to be a contradiction; if, however, we recall what the proper meaning of the descriptive lyrics in the Song of Solomon has taught us, the idea of a divine form is sensible and is not only compatible with a well-thought-out monotheism but is even necessarily related to it. For the Hebrews and for their Semite relatives, as we have shown above, the members of the body are expressions of qualities. The form as a unity is thus the concentrated expression of the entire personality and its essence. Formally *tselem 'elohîm* is something concrete and physical; actually it is something spiritual. We have shown how single members of God's body are expressions of divine qualities; here we have the theological term for the totality of divine qualities and hence for his whole being. This construction of the image of God is confirmed by Hehn who calls attention to the rôle played by image (*tsalmu*) in the Assyro-Babylonian Orient; the image was a manifestation and something like a living incarnation of divinity and in this capacity was able to accomplish mighty acts.[1] The *tselem 'elohîm* thus does not simply say how God looks in himself but only how he appears before men and is known by them. The corporeity of God is mentioned (Gen. 1.26 f.) only as a form of revelation vis-à-vis humanity.

The comparison between Judges 5 and, for example, Deutero-Isaiah taught us that the so-called anthropomorphisms do not belong to the oldest stratum of religious language; at the earliest stages of Old Testament religion, Jahveh worshippers did not reflect on the possibility and kind of God's revelation, but spoke of it only as a fact. The 'anthropomorphisms', i.e. the mention of the parts of God's body as expressions of his qualities, belong to a later stage of development; they arise spontaneously in Israel when the pious become aware of their smallness in the face of God's sublimity and when they begin to reflect upon the mode and manner of God's revelation to mortal man. Later generations, having failed to grasp the profound meaning of the 'anthropomorphisms', have taken umbrage at their mere humanness, and have preferred more neutral means of revelation like word, spirit, and wisdom. The 'anthropomorphisms', because of their profound descriptive power, continue to stand as peerless expressions of the divine being; there is indeed, as P clearly understood, nothing in the sensible (not divine) world which comes so near to divinity as man himself. Yet it was not, as Humbert says,[2] P's idea of the *imago dei* which prevented the theriomorphism of Egyptian religion from influencing Israel. The Jahvist had already brought this accomplishment to fruition; at one time the Egyptian influence was considerable, but in P's time the Israelite Wise Men had come to terms with the spiri-

[1] Cited by P. Humbert, *op. cit.*, p. 164.   [2] *Ibid.*, p. 170.

tual currents from the east, as Genesis 1 itself sufficiently demonstrates. It can be said rather that there is a straight line from the naïve anthropomorphism of the Jahvist to P's sharply delineated theological concept. If God is to reveal himself to man, it must therefore occur in human manifestations, and if man is to speak about his God in the clearest and most perfect way, he must have recourse to some kind of 'anthropomorphism'.

We must agree with Humbert that in the Priestly document's reflective, systematic range of ideas the theme of *imago dei* really plays a leading rôle, for it permits him to distinguish clearly between theology, anthropology, and zoölogy. As the entire account of Genesis 1 tends to come to a climax in the appearance of man as the end and crown of creation, the creation of man culminates in this highest destiny as God's image, which places him in proximity to God and creates a cleavage between man and the animal world. It is a matter here of a conception, carefully worked out through theological reflection, to which P later adheres (Gen. 5.1; 9.6) and which, moreover, gives a basis to man's enduring mastery over the beasts. Far from being something subordinate in P's range of ideas, the concept of the image of God forms one of the high points in the doctrine of creation which he perfected with consummate architectonic skill. With the aid of *imago dei* God gives man his stamp and thereby puts his seal upon his creation.

Humbert is also right in his observation that in itself it is not surprising that the concept of the *imago* appears only in the P document, for since the redaction of this document was undertaken not earlier than in the fifth century, the concept is therefore a late achievement of Israelite thought.[1] That the concept of the *imago*, when it was first coined, immediately exerted its influence is shown by Ps. 8.6, where it achieved lyric expression also in the cultus;[2] in Humbert's opinion, Genesis 1 also belongs to the liturgy, and what is more, to the ritual of the New Year festival. There are, of course, the Wise Men who knew the meaning of the *imago* concept and used it (Ecclus. 17.3, 4; Wisd. 2.23), and we must mention Philo as well (*de Opificio Mundi* 25, 69, 72). The *imago dei* idea is, consequently, no secondary and peripheral detail, but it is a zenith in Old Testament theology and anthropology.

Excursus: Jewish Pictorial Art in the Diaspora

As was stated in the Foreword, it lies beyond the scope of this monograph to examine the mixture of Israelite-Semitic and Greek-European

---

[1] *Ibid.*, p. 174.   [2] Mowinckel considers Ps. 8 older than Gen. 1.

cultures. Yet we should like to show briefly at this point how in the growth of such a mixed culture both roots can easily be maintained.

Israelite faith permitted no bodily representation of God either in sculpture or in painting; the Decalogue's ban on images corresponds to Jewish character and Jewish thinking. In the homeland, in later times at least, it was construed as a prohibition against religious pictorial art of any sort. In the Diaspora under Greek influence the Jews took a less rigid stand without thereby relinquishing their Jewish uniqueness. The excavations at Dura on the Euphrates in Syria show with the discovery of a synagogue that a biblical historical art of a high order was developed in the synagogues of the Diaspora. The following motifs are represented there: the sacrifice of Isaac, Enoch or Abraham, Moses at the burning bush, the Exodus, the death of the Egyptians in the Red Sea, Aaron with sanctuary and Torah shrine, the water miracle in the desert, the return of the Ark from the temple of Dagon, and in the form of a Torah shrine Ezekiel, Ezra with the scrolls, and many others. They come from the year AD 245, thus shortly before the ruin of the city.

The pictures are different in form and content from the pagan pictures (probably Palmyrene), for which reason R. Wischnitzer conjectures that the pious rabbi and leader of the synagogue inspired the artist and directed him step by step. A comparison with the pagan temple-painting in Dura is instructive. Where the pagan paints his god or forms him out of stone, the Jew paints the symbol of God's word: the Torah shrine and lamp or else the *action* of his God and so the sacred history. He does not employ God's image, face, and form, but at most employs a hand of God to indicate his *action*. The great men of Old Testament religion are depicted not because of their piety or their heroism but because God has acted in them or has spoken to them by acting, or like Ezra because he is reading God's word. Thus this art is truly Jewish in kind; the invisible being of his God is made visible in his *acts* through which he also *speaks*.[1]

E. APPEARANCE IN GREEK THINKING

As we have occasionally mentioned above, the Greeks experienced reality differently from the Israelites and more analogously with us. They consider reality as an objective, given quantity with which our senses, particularly our sight, bring us into contact. They recount and describe what they see, and in so doing they show no inclination to tell stories, they do

[1] Rachel Wischnitzer, *The Messianic Theme in the Paintings of the Dura Synagogue*; cf. G. Kittel, *Theologisches Wörterbuch z.N.T.*, II, 380–84.

not narrate things verbosely, and in their speech they are not prolix. Philosophers and poets had not yet discovered the art of writing thick volumes of slender content. To the extent that they recount only what is important, what has made or is to make an impression, the Greeks resemble the Israelites more than us; however, they speak not of their impressions but of what they actually saw or what really could have been seen. Only from the choice of subjects described can we imply what made an impression upon them.

In the *Critias* (pp. 116 f.), Plato describes the citadel on the Island of Atlantis with its walls, ramparts, and its canal leading to the sea; inside the city were to be found a royal palace and temples with statues and sculptures. Although the building of the city is described, we still have a graphic picture; some of the stones were black and some were red, some of the buildings were monochrome and some were polychrome because stones of different colours were combined for optic pleasure. In the temple of Poseidon was placed a golden sculpture of the god driving a chariot to which were hitched six winged horses, and it was so high that his head touched the ceiling; round about it stood a hundred Nereids riding on dolphins, etc. The reader can see and imagine the whole thing in his mind. The very complicated picture of the cave in the seventh book of the *Republic* (p. 515 E) is also accurately and graphically drawn.

Ever since Homer in both poetry and prose the Greek landscape has been vividly in mind, as Gunnar Rudberg in particular has observed;[1] according to him it is the largest and best-preserved source of knowledge about Greek culture for it participates in and defines many images in art and in philosophy. When, for example, in the *Symposium* Plato is moved deeply and eulogizes in elevated style the broad sea of beauty, he selects an image from Greek nature in order to express the ineffable.[2] The mountains are numerous, yet not high and rugged but regular and harmonious, having gentle contours; nature forms a plastic, architectural whole, mathematically and harmoniously constructed. Light plays on this landscape and varies according to place or time of day. Greek architecture is intimately related to the landscape; it grows out of the landscape, so to speak, and fits into it. In the *Phaedrus* (p. 230) Plato describes a summer day by the shore of the Ilissus under a blossoming plane tree with a mighty crown, behind a high, shady, and fragrant hedge; close by flows a lively brook with cool water; the breeze blows soft and mild; it

---

[1] G. Rudberg, 'Theoria', *Ur Hellas' liv*, p. 98.
[2] Plato *Symposium*, p. 210; Pindar and Aeschylus before him used this image, and he himself used it in the *Protagoras*.

floats like music in the air as an answer to the cicadas; most delightful is the high, soft grass which is like a soft pillow for the head. Even if Plato had not expressly said so, we should still have sensed from his description that this was a holy place. Thus even the Greek nature images frequently have a deeper meaning which, however, is never expressed but only experienced by participation; consequently, the objective and coherent perception is never abandoned.

Sun and sunlight are frequently eulogized, not however as in the Old Testament where the sun is a source of light and heat but because it is so beautiful and enhances the beauty of man and nature with its brilliant rays. Likewise the most brilliant colours, white and red, are not the most beautiful, but it is blue that is the beautiful colour, for heaven is blue, the broad sea and the far mountains are blue, and even the eyes of Pallas Athene are blue.[1] The Old Testament has no word for 'blue'; there is mention only of the dye obtained from the murex, *tekheleth*, which is the colour of silk, wool, threads, and the like, and it becomes the designation for a bluish colour. The origin of this term is not something seen, therefore, but it is in an action.

Plato gives us visual images even of the universe; earth and stars are spherical.[2] Perception is of decisive significance for philosophy, for all our concepts, including that of time, are given through sight.[3] According to this kind of thinking Plato is, therefore, absolutely right when he calls time a moving image of immutable eternity.[4] Principles and symbols in the earliest Greek philosophy were visually construed and are not concepts in the later European meaning; the same is true of the *elements* of pre-Socratic thought and of the Ideas of Plato. Aristotle carried on what had been begun by Plato. Observation produces a theoretic and religious side; the life of the philosopher is a βίος θεωρητικός, a *vita contemplativa*. For Aristotle, the word θεωρία means, in part, observation and the inquiry connected with it, and in part, the doctrine which is thereby set forth, our notion of 'theory'. In the *Protrepticus* it is said that pure idea is *theoria* and deserves to be esteemed most highly as sight among the senses is esteemed;[5] in the *Metaphysics* (xi, 7), *theoria* is called 'the most

---

[1] Homer *Iliad* ii. 166, 172, 279 [Liddell-Scott, *s.v.*, calls it 'light blue or grey', Tr.].
[2] Plato *Timaeus*, esp. p. 48, and the myth in the *Republic* x, pp. 616 f. The astronomer Aristarchus, a contemporary of Euclid, taught that the planets revolved about the sun as the moon does about the earth.
[3] Plato *Timaeus*, p. 47.   [4] *Ibid.*, p. 38.
[5] W. Jaeger (*Aristotle: Fundamentals of the History of His Development*, trans. R. Robinson [2nd ed.; Oxford: Clarendon Press, 1948], pp. 54–101) develops the hypothesis that the no longer extant *Protrepticus* of Aristotle underlies chs. 6–12 of Iamblichus' *Protrepticus*.

pleasant and most excellent', and in the *Nichomachean Ethics* (x, 8), perfect happiness, too, becomes a contemplative activity (*theôrêtikê*).[1] In Aristotle, much more than in the lofty Plato, perception is directed toward earthly things. The *theoria* of Greek philosophy is cognate with the Greek's artistic images and his poetry. The association of the Platonic Idea, in particular, with the dominant form-tendency of Greek art since ancient times has been expressed often enough; however, the observation is no less valid for the rhetorical arts and for the essence of Greek thought-form in general. The most ancient natural philosophy's notion of the cosmos was already such a view in contrast to the computative, experimental natural science of our day.[2]

Descriptions of *persons* in Greek literature[3] are formally similar to the descriptions of nature; they are for the most part indirect. Persons reveal themselves through words and deeds, mostly through involuntary actions. Seldom are external portraits drawn, and when they are, it is for the purpose of outlining the character of the person in question. Homer describes Thersites as an insolent and cowardly figure who can, however, speak well and wittily in a loud voice. He would be well suited to speak for his people, but his hateful appearance discloses his true character; he is bandy-legged and limps, his back is crooked, his shoulders bend forward, his head is pointed, and his hair is thin and unkempt.[4] Plato describes Socrates' accuser, Meletus, as young and unknown with long hair, a thin growth of beard, and a pointed nose;[5] consequently he is represented as unimportant and unsympathetic. Obviously the Greeks knew that external and internal beauty or ugliness did not always correspond to one another; external beauty could be seductive like the faces and songs of the Sirens, and external unattractiveness could be misleading as in the case of Socrates or Theaetetus, both of whom had turned-up noses and protruding cow eyes.[6] In different ways the beautiful soul became apparent in such cases; thus the remarkable power of attraction of Socrates, chiefly for the youth, is known and presupposed in all of Plato's dialogues, and here and there it is even praised, as in the speech of Alcibiades in the *Symposium*. Thus there is no irony in the profound prayer of Socrates with which the *Phaedrus* ends, '. . . give me beauty in the inward soul; and may the inward and outward man be at one'. All descriptions of persons in Greek literature would therefore—as in the Old Testament (Song of Solomon)—only characterize the persons; the

---

[1] G. Rudberg, *Ur Hellas' liv*, pp. 115 ff.
[2] W. Jaeger, *Padeia: The Ideals of Greek Culture*, I, xxi f.
[3] G. Rudberg, *Platon*, pp. 179 ff.　　　　[4] Homer *Iliad* ii. 221–24.
[5] Plato *Euthyphro*, p. 2b.　　　　[6] Plato *Theaetetus*, p. 114.

particular interest in appearance which is so predominant in modern literature and which was surely present then in individual men was prohibited in higher literature.

The Greek *gods* from Homer and Hesiod on were conceived visibly and clearly together with their epithets; they appeared to human eyes as glorious and exalted supermen. It was therefore a pious activity worthily to represent their figures in statues; obviously it was known that the image was not identical with the god concerned, but on principle the image was able to give an idea of the god and to inspire sacred veneration and awe in the observer. The excavations at Mycenae have turned up numerous representations on gold rings of divine epiphanies in human form but no representations of divine presence at cultic activities.[1] Too extensive conclusions need not be drawn from this discovery, but at all events the images confirm the impression obtained from Homer, that in the heroic age the leaders of the upper class associated with the gods freely and without distress in everyday life and that the representation of the gods in beautiful human forms was also usual in the period when 'Homeric' religion was in full bloom.

Kerényi speaks of the atmosphere dominant in Homeric poetry; it is a quite distinct phenomenon of Greek existence. It shows us immediately how spectacle and solemnity are related essentially for the Greeks and represent in *one* the highest religious and mental revelation.[2] There is another view of the gods which is perfectly clear but which is not granted to all; Kerényi calls it the solemn view, which in a characteristic Greek way means a complete pellucidity.[3] The gods came in order to observe and be observed. Zeus rules the world and is even so only spectator; the standpoint of the spectator is for the Greek already divine in itself. The participant in a cultic act or mystery drama is called θεωρός 'spectator', which was soon connected by folk etymology to θεός, 'god'.[4]

We must also define briefly and schematically the peculiarity of Homeric religion in relation to the religion of the subjugated original inhabitants of Greece (who lived on in the popular faith) and also in relation to foreign, frequently oriental, influences (which are to be traced in the world-escaping, ecstatic doctrine of salvation founded in Orphism and continued in Dionysiac religion and the Mysteries).[5] Popular piety felt the influence

[1] M. P. Nilsson, *Geschichte der griechischen Religion*, I, 290 ff.
[2] Kerényi, *Die Antike Religion*, p. 101.   [3] *Ibid.*, pp. 103 ff.
[4] Kerényi (*ibid.*, pp. 116 ff.) cites W. F. Otto (*Die Götter Griechenlands* [Bonn: Cohen, 1929]) who speaks of a higher knowledge in which apprehending and perceiving are one and the same. This unity of perceiving and knowing and experiencing is well known and familiar from the Johannine literature in the New Testament, and from that viewpoint we can understand better and participate in the Greek standpoint.
[5] 'Die Religion bei den Griechen', *Tiele-Söderblom Kompendium*, pp. 342 ff.

of the powers of the netherworld, the chthonic powers; sacrifice to the netherworld deities and to the dead bears a more sombre character and came to light for the most part artistically. The people paid to the old rough and coarse wooden images inside the temple a superstitious veneration; they sacrificed also to trees and stones, springs, wood-spirits, and nymphs. In historical times a cult of animals was dedicated only to the snake. The animals that appear as attributes of the Olympian gods, the eagle of Zeus, the owl of Athena, the cow of Hera, the bull or the ram of Dionysus, and the snake of Asclepius, are surely remnants of an animal cult which was spiritually vanquished by Homeric religion. The originally Thracian cult of Dionysus was celebrated by the Bacchantes on the mountains with nocturnal orgies and wild dances. When the frenzy had reached its height, the 'maenads' tore asunder every living thing that crossed their path and consumed the bloody flesh raw; it was the god himself or the beasts sacred to him which were consumed. In the tragedy, *Bacchae*, Euripides describes how the frenzy of the barbarian Thracian god has suddenly appeared all over Greece like a powerful epidemic of inspiration, contagious ecstasy, and unheard-of deeds of strength. Even after the Greek mind had subdued the savage powers, the original barbarian kind of Dionysiac cult appeared now and then in the release of religious passion and savage power.

Against this background the Olympian religion of the ancient heroic age stands out as a unique achievement of the Greek mind. With veneration and yet worthily the Greeks associated with their gods in broad daylight; practically nothing of magic and other superstitions is found. Fear of sinister, mysterious, demonic powers yielded to the luminous, more cheerful faith in the Olympian gods who appear in clear and beautiful human forms and whose will, attitude, and appearance aroused nothing sinister or terror-inspiring. It is quite right that the history of religions knows no other circle of gods so anthropomorphic,[1] and that here and there Homer described them in a manner altogether too human; yet the sharp boundary between god and man was never overstepped as in the Mysteries. If an individual did so, it was considered the greatest sin, indeed *the* sin. This demonstrates that we are dealing with a genuine religion which in this regard may be compared with that of the Old Testament; even in the Jahvist *hybris* is the original sin (Gen. 3.1 ff.; 11.4). We must also recall that the concept 'anthropomorphic' can mean three things:

   a. In a purely formal way it can designate the concrete as distinguished

[1] *Ibid.*

from the abstract and philosophical. If we want to conceive God not simply as a divine impersonal neuter but as mind and person, we are compelled to draw necessary concepts and images from the human realm. The difficulties we face in this process, especially if we conceive God visibly, we shall touch upon below.

b. Materially, used in connexion with religious concepts, it means 'human' as distinct from 'animal', 'vegetable', 'physical (i.e. inanimate)', or 'demonic'.

c. It can also signify 'human' as distinct from 'divine'.

The Olympian gods are anthropomorphic in each of these senses. Certain features are altogether too human and unworthy of gods, yet we ought never to forget that the first meaning is predominant and characteristic; the fear of *hybris* stood in the centre of the religion and prevented a confusion of human and divine. On the other hand, we ought never to forget what a spiritual achievement Olympian religion represented when belief in the anthropomorphic (in the good sense) gods burst forth, a belief which afforded ample room for the unfolding and blossoming of the noblest spiritual and mental life.[1] The uniqueness and strength of Greek piety is shown not only in temple worship, prayer, and personal devotion within Olympian religion, but also in its astonishing capacity to temper, ennoble, and hellenize the 'un-Greek' religions of Dionysus and the Mysteries, and to remain true to itself until the last centuries of Greek culture.[2]

Plato already experienced and tried to solve the problem of Greek piety mentioned above: how are god and the divine to be conceived? In any case, they can be seen. Plato tried above all to see the eternal and invisible, and see it he did. We need not go into his ideas about the relation between the visible and the invisible, the body and the soul, time and eternity; in that way we avoid also a discussion of his so-called mysticism and dependence upon the Mysteries. Yet he conceived the divine personally as well as impersonally; the gods are named by their usual names, and if anything improper is told of them, the guilt is the poets'. In the *Timaeus* he also speaks of the δημιουργός, the good creator and father who formed the world; under him stand the inferior gods. Elsewhere, e.g. in the *Republic*, however, the highest is the idea of the good, the symbol of which is the sun. Tiele and Söderblom are of the opinion that Plato's religion is not in his doctrine of Ideas but is

[1] Even in this regard, despite contrary formal distinctions, Greek religion is related to the religion of the Old Testament; Jahveh is not despotic and capricious like the oriental gods, but he has revealed himself in law and his deeds and commandments are therefore clear in regard to ethics.

[2] *Tiele-Söderblom Kompendium*, p. 350.

expressed in what he says about the personal god;[1] Rudberg, on the contrary, maintains decisively that the idea of the good is the highest in Plato's thought and bases his assertion, among other things, upon the fact that the creator god in the *Timaeus*, designated by the purposely pejorative name δημιουργός, 'workman, craftsman', is a half-mythical figure who is the object only of opinion, δόξα, and not of knowledge.[2]

It is doubtful whether the question is correctly put if the personal and the impersonal in Plato's religious thought are opposed one to another; Plato's god is personal as well as impersonal. When a man prays, and there is prayer in Plato's dialogues, god must necessarily be conceived personally for one does not speak with something impersonal. Since Plato undoubtedly understood prayer to be the highest religious function, those places where he speaks of a personal god or gods need not be considered too insignificant. If, however, an attempt is made to conceive a person visibly, and this is a Greek presupposition, two difficulties arise. First, it is impossible to gather all divine qualities and functions into one single image; they must be distributed among several persons, and then they can be conceived. This leads necessarily to polytheism; the peculiar features or primary concerns in this are not the many gods but the need to visualize, which demands a divine plurality. The more one is able to leave external visibility out of the question, the more it is understood that the old traditional concepts of the gods, indeed every image of every god, are really just one 'image' of one invisible personal reality, and the concept of god or gods is faced freely, as is precisely the case with Plato. Secondly, it is clear that the concept 'person' must have at least three forms in order to express its full content. We can designate the three forms by the three personal pronouns, he, you, and I; as modern philosophy and theology have recognized,[3] they are indissolubly connected with one another and condition one another reciprocally. Christian theology tried in a later period of its history to express the fuller concept of 'person' by means of the essentially good but unlikely and logically censurable notion of the Trinity. If Plato does not mention the *person* of god in conveying to us his final ideas about the divinity, the cause for this need not be that he has not reflected sufficiently upon the concepts 'person' or 'personality'.[4] It is possible that he had become clear about the fact, or understood intuitively, that the psychological concept 'person' is incapable of representation logically or graphically. When Plato the

[1] *Ibid.*, p. 395.   [2] Rudberg, *Platon*, p. 179.
[3] Martin Buber, *I and Thou*; Friedrich Gogarten, *Ich glaube an den dreieinigen Gott.*
[4] Rudberg, *Platon*, p. 179.

logician thinks and talks about religion, the concept of person disappears, and the divine appears as the highest idea of the good, the true, and the beautiful. In the encounter between logic and phantasy, in any event, Plato became conscious of the Ideas.[1] When, however, the religious man Plato is engaged personally, he speaks of god or prays to him, as, for example, in the *Timaeus*.

Thus the appearance as well as the perception of both god and the divinity of the Olympian gods, who could solve all difficulties by merely appearing is of decisive significance all the way from Homer to Plato's most profound thoughts on the highest Ideas. The idiosyncrasy of this thinking is coherent, in general, with the distinctive ancient concept of the world. For the ancients 'image' is not only a copy of a visible object, but it can also mean 'a radiating, a becoming visible and manifest of the essence in such a way as to have a share (μετοχή) in the very substance of the thing itself'.[2] Thus, εἰκών means, in plain words, the coming into appearance of the kernel, the essence, of a thing; it participates in reality. When Christ is designated as the εἰκὼν τοῦ θεοῦ τοῦ ἀοράτου (Col. 1.15), the expression is best to be explained in a Hebraic way and means that Christ is the aggregate of the qualities of the invisible God. However, it can also be interpreted in a Greek way and then means that Christ is the becoming visible on earth of the invisible God. The sense remains the same although, as regards form, the interpretations are opposites.

The distinction between Greek religiousness and Semitic-Israelite religiousness is superficially striking; seen from the psychological viewpoint, they show an odd similarity: they are both faithful to reality. W. F. Otto delineates the distinction: 'The worldliness and naturalness with which the religion of the Greeks is reproached is encountered in their plastic art also. Here too the difference from the oriental is immeasurable. Organic structure takes the place of monstrosity; instead of symbolism and denotation we have what we have learned—through the Greeks—to understand as forms of nature. . . . Before our eyes a miracle takes place: the natural has become one with the spiritual and eternal (pp. 5 f.). . . . The ancient Greek religion comprehended the things of this world with the most powerful sense of reality possible, and nevertheless—nay, for that very reason—recognized in them the marvellous delineations of the divine.'[3] Stanley A. Cook writes about the Semites: 'The Semite, unlike the Egyptian, was interested only in this world, and

[1] *Ibid.*, p. 215.
[2] H. Kleinknecht, 'Der griechische Sprachgebrauch von *eikon*', *Theologisches Wörterbuch zum N.T.*, ed. G. Kittel, II, 386 f.
[3] Walter F. Otto, *The Homeric Gods*, pp. 5 f., 10.

this difference between them reappears throughout their culture (p. 202).
. . . The poetry is intensely realistic. . . . Things to be of any interest
must be of deep personal interest, and passion then generates a feeling
of human relationship even with the inanimate (p. 196). . . . It has been
said that the Arabs of the classical period and their descendants, the
bedouins of the present day, are perhaps one of the races most untouched
by the solemnities of religious awe that have ever existed (Sir Charles
Lyall). Certainly, their poems will breathe a "pagan" passionate love of
life (cf. also David's Lament in II Samuel ch. 1); and it is, in any case,
one of the paradoxes of the Semites that they have given the world its
greatest religious geniuses (p. 197).'[1]

Worldliness, naturalness, and a sense of reality are therefore just as
characteristic of the Semites as the Greeks; they merely express these
qualities differently.

[1] Stanley A. Cook, 'The Semites', *The Cambridge Ancient History*, Vol. 1 (1923),
pp. 196 f., 202; cf. 530 f.

3
Time and Space

A. THE GREEK-EUROPEAN CONCEPTION OF TIME

IN A short but significant essay, 'Zeit und Raum im Denken des Ur-christentums', Ernst von Dobschütz deals with the contrast between Greek and Hebrew thinking.[1] He shows how the Hebrews' thinking moves in time, while it is just as characteristic of the Greeks to employ space as their thought-form. As an example he mentions how the biblical idea of the increasing depravity of mankind from Adam until the present was retold by a Greek author as something that took place spatially. The author describes his sojourn in Eden, the land of the blessed, and his journey thence to Gaul; the lands became progressively worse the farther he got from Eden. Von Dobschütz even thinks that the intrusion of the space scheme into early Christian thought can be applied as a scale for measuring its hellenization. Von Dobschütz is mistaken in details; it is quite incorrect to say that the Greek philosophers erected no extensive theories about the time notion. Precisely the opposite is the case, as G. Delling has indicated.[2] Aristotle, for example, and even Plato before him, reflected as profoundly upon the time notion as Kant did; of course, Plato expressed himself less exhaustively than Aristotle. It is wholly natural that the Greeks devoted much thought to the time notion, since, if spatial thinking was easy for them, the time problem must have presented particular difficulty and provoked them to reflection.

It could be urged further against von Dobschütz that Greeks and Romans also knew of a blessed primeval age; Hesiod already in the seventh century BC put into poetry the myth of the five races of men. The first, the golden race, lived in the first blessed age when the earth of itself produced rich harvests and men were as gods. Then followed the silver race, the copper race, the race of Heroes, and the iron race.[3] To

---

[1] *Journal of Biblical Literature*, XLI (1922), 212 ff.
[2] *Das Zeitverständnis des Neuen Testaments.*
[3] Paulus Svendsen, *Gullalderdröm og utviklingstro*, pp. 13 ff.

all appearances the similarity with the Old Testament accounts of the primeval age is great; it must also be supposed, when the method of ancient poets is taken into consideration, that Hesiod employed ancient sources. Since Hesiod's father had emigrated from Asia Minor, an oriental influence is very possible. Thus, in P as well as in Hesiod, men were originally vegetarians (Gen. 1.29); only after the Flood were they permitted to eat meat (9.3). Seen more accurately, however, the difference between the two conceptions of mankind's primeval history is very great. Hesiod speaks of no history and no development; Cronus created the entire golden race from which after its earthly life protecting spirits arose for later races. Subsequently an entirely new race, the silver race, was created by Zeus, which lived its life and then died out. The reason for the silver race's not being of the same quality as its predecessor is to be found not in human guilt but in divine will. The next generations were also created anew by the gods. The descriptions of the five generations are five independent pictures devoid of internal relation; nor does Hesiod speak of an uninterrupted descent of mankind, for between the copper and iron races Zeus created the glorious race of the Heroes.

The belief in far away places where prosperity ruled for a long time after the golden race and, to some extent, still rules is typically Greek: Elysium, the Isles of the Blest, Atlantis, the gardens of Alcinous, etc.[1] The concept of the mount of the gods, Olympus, is also Greek in its plastic visible mode, but it does not properly belong in this context. In the main, therefore, von Dobschütz is correct in his thesis.

We must begin with our notion of time which agrees with the Greek, since it is so obvious to us that most men, even philosophers, accept it uncritically as the only possible one. Our notion of time has achieved plastic expression in the words we use for time. Western minds represent time as a straight line upon which we stand with our gaze directed forward; before us we have the future and behind us the past. On this line we can unequivocally define all tenses by means of points. The present is the point on which we are standing, the future is found at some point in front of us, and in between lies the exact future; behind us lies the perfect, still farther back the imperfect, and farther yet the pluperfect. At first one does not think about whether this straight line is finite or infinite, for all our attention is concentrated upon the present and upon the times that are grouped about it; however, the line is obviously without limit, and that is as true for the forward direction as it is for the backward.

[1] *Ibid.*, pp. 20 f.

The Greek language also has corresponding verb-forms which can be delineated in quite similar manner on a straight time-line; therefore the popular time conception of the Greeks is as rectilinear as our own. Referring to Delling, Cullmann cites a sentence from Aristotle as proof that Aristotle believed time to be cyclical: ὁ χρόνος αὐτὸς εἶναι δοκεῖ κύκλος τις.[1] The citation is not conclusive because it is lifted out of its context. In the next chapter where Aristotle analyses the essence of time —time, that is, which is almost exclusively physical, which is manifest in motion from place to place[2]—he achieves such depth and subtlety that a modern commentator, filled with admiration, can say that his analysis of the essence of time opens a direct path to the four-dimensional algebra to which so much attention is given in connexion with the theory of relativity.[3] The word κύκλος referring to time is adapted to colloquial speech and is to be understood figuratively (N.B. δοκεῖ); it is chosen at that point because there chronometry is under discussion.[4] If, however, time is to be measured on a *line*, everyone is compelled to make use of the apparently circular movement of the sun about the earth as a standard, either directly or indirectly with aid of a clock (sun-dial, mechanical watch) which copies the movement of the sun. The annual movement of the sun defines the year for Indo-Germanic peoples; both changes in the sun's movements, Christmas and Midsummer's Day, are ancient Indo-Germanic festivals, but they are not attested in the Old Testament. This is not accidental, for the Hebrews' perception of time is otherwise oriented, as we shall see later.

The possibility of chronometry by means of clocks rests, of course, upon the uniformity of all circles. The circle has another peculiarity which makes it especially fitted for chronometry; it is at the same time limited and unbounded. Chronometry is a practical requirement; much more decisive for Aristotle's philosophical conception of time is the definition he gives a few pages prior to the one mentioned above: ὁ χρόνος ἀριθμός ἐστι κινήσεως κατὰ τὸ πρότερον καὶ ὕρτερον,[5] which can be translated freely as: time is the continuous dimension of successive movement, or in more modern terms: time is the dimension of succession. According to Aristotle, therefore, we must represent time by the image of a line (more accurately: by the image of movement along a line), either a circular line to indicate objective, physical, astronomical, and

---

[1] Aristotle *Physics* iv. 14 (223b. 28 f.).   [2] *Ibid.*, iv. 10–14 (217b. 29–224a. 18).
[3] P. H. Wicksteed and F. M. Cornford, *Aristotle. The Physics* ('Loeb Classical Library'), I, 382.
[4] Cf. Aristotle's reasoning, *Physics* iv. 14 (223a. 18–224a. 18).
[5] *Ibid.*, iv. 11 (220a. 25 f.).

measurable time, or a straight line as demanded by the grammatical time of past, present, and future in which are laid those actions that we express in temporal terms. It is an illusion to believe that these two ways of looking at time are so different that they cancel each other out; they do have in common the principal feature, conception of time by the metaphor of a line, and what form the line takes is epistemologically of no importance or, in any case, only incidental.

As Henri Bergson has already developed extensively, the concept of space governs all our thinking to such an extent that we even conceive of time spatially.[1] We speak of a space of time, a point of time, a time span, a segment of time; the past lies behind us and the future before us. As we saw above, the conception of time contained in our verbs can be illustrated accurately by means of points on a straight line. Kant has given scientific expression to this popular conception,[2] with certain reservations to be sure. He calls time the internal sense and knows that time cannot be perceived externally, because it is possible only by analogy to understand the time sequence by means of a line continuing to infinity. Over against these reservations stand other expressions: first, time itself is a notion (indeed an internal one); secondly, the image of the time-line permits all the properties of time to be included save one, that the units of time follow one after another; and thirdly, he employs spatial expressions occasionally without reservation, for example, time has a dimension—it can be divided into different time—each definite quantity of time is possible only by limitations of a single time, and he says, 'For in order that we may afterwards make inner alterations likewise thinkable, we must represent time (the form of inner sense) figuratively as a line, and the inner alteration through the drawing of this line.'[3] If we omit the spatial images and other expressions of Kant and concentrate upon his abstract thinking about time, it is noteworthy that he is forced to recognize that time, as opposed to space, does not pertain to the external world. It is not necessarily united with movement from place to place but only with consciousness; therefore it follows that time is primarily the category of inner life, of events, and of history. Even after all this, time remains a form, a scheme of thought, a point of view like space, and therefore it is ultimately thought of spatially or in a spatial analogy. The ambiguity of Kant's conception of time is surely related to his attempt to construe scientific time and psychological time as a unity.

Wundt has subjected the conceptions of time to a psychological-

[1] *Essai sur les données immédiates de la conscience*, chap. II.
[2] *Critique of Pure Reason*, pp. 67 f., 74 f., 77.   [3] *Ibid.*, p. 255.

physiological analysis;[1] however, since he starts, as a matter of course, from what we understand as the natural time concept and examines only this one (Bergson's interpretation of time is not even mentioned), his arguments are of no interest for our analysis of Hebrew thinking. For the same reason his extensive psychology of language can be of no profit to us;[2] here he asserts that our notion of tense is founded in an immediately empirical way,[3] but this is simply not the case. In the same volume he does mention the Hebrew language once, but then only the psychologically indifferent phenomenon of the verb's standing first in the sentence.[4] Of the peculiar conception of time inherent in the Hebrew language he appears to know nothing. Bergson's criticism of the interpretation of time by all civilized European peoples remains unrefuted.

Plato's interpretation of time deserves particularly to be observed by a theologian; while the sober Aristotle analyses the time of natural science, Plato occupies himself with the time of religion.[5] Therefore, the problem of the relation of time and eternity arises for him; eternity for him is not endless astronomical time, but the life-form of the divine world to which God also belongs. Time designates for him the life-form of the world of nature, the world produced by God. By way of analogy with the origin of the world, which he defines as a reflection of divinity, Plato calls time a moving image of eternity (*Timaeus* 38). When God, the Demiurge, made the world, simultaneously he made an image of eternity progressing in number (i.e. an image which moves forward measurably), eternity itself being immovable and at rest. This image we call time. This time can be divided into days, nights, months, and years; all these are *parts* of time. The past and the future are merely *forms* of time. We can see here how Plato already distinguishes between physical time and psychological time: divisible time is physical time, but present, past, and future are psychological categories. Yet both physical and psychological time belong to the sensible and transitory world in the same way as time, divine time, the archetype of time, is called eternity. There is, thus, a formal similarity between eternity and time as between the original and a reflection, and there is a qualitative dissimilarity as between a perfect

---

[1] W. Wundt, *Grundzüge der physiologischen Psychologie*, III, 1–98.
[2] W. Wundt, *Völkerpsychologie*, Bd. I, Teil. i–ii.
[3] *Ibid.*, p. 193. Lévy-Bruhl's inquiries (*op. cit.*) into the time-conception of primitive peoples have refuted this notion once and for all.
[4] *Ibid.*, p. 379.
[5] Karl Barth (*Church Dogmatics*, ed. G. W. Bromiley and T. F. Torrance, Vol. I, *The Doctrine of the Word of God*, 2nd half-volume [1956], pp. 45–121) also presupposes that time can be a category not only of natural science and psychology but also of religion.

type and a pale imitation. We see here also how the spatial governs Plato's line of thought; time is only a pictorial, moving imitation of immovable and unalterable eternity which represents perfection. Although the main bearing of Plato's analysis of time is a thrust toward eternity, the stature of his mind is demonstrated by the fact that he analyses time much better than most subsequent thinkers for two reasons: first, he distinguishes between parts of time and forms of time; second, he is clear about the fact that if time is illustrated in the form of an image, it must be conceived of as moving. According to Plato, time is as unbounded as the world, and just as finite; the characteristic feature of eternity, however, is not its possible boundless temporal extension but the divine content with which it is filled. It follows, therefore, that eternity, too, is something spatial, identical with the boundless sea of sublime beauty which he so exquisitely describes in the *Symposium* (210c). When we employ the term 'spatial' here, we must beware of a misunderstanding. In Plato's thinking eternity is spatial not in the sense that it is three-dimensional, and still less four-dimensional, but only in the sense that it is without alteration, hence without unrest, disturbance, privation, decay, and destruction. The 'tooth of time' does not gnaw upon it.

The Greek conception of time is put into words not least adequately by the fact that time is *assessed* by Plato as well as by Aristotle as something vastly inferior to space, partly as an evil. Aristotle is in agreement with the maxim that time destroys (κατατήκει ὁ χρόνος): everything grows old under the pressure of time and is forgotten in the course of time, but nothing grows new or beautiful through time. Hence we regard time in itself more as destructive than constructive. That which exists eternally, e.g. a geometrical proposition, does not belong to time.[1] This contempt for time by so clear and sober a mind as Aristotle's tells us more about the difference between Greek and Hebrew conceptions of time than all attempts to understand the Greek concept of time philosophically. For this reason, too, everything pertaining only to space, e.g. geometry, was so highly regarded, and the Greek gods and the divine world had to be conceived as exempt from all time, transitoriness, and change because time, change, and transitoriness are synonymous terms.

---

[1] Aristotle *Physics* iv. 12 (220a. 30 ff.).

B. THE ISRAELITE CONCEPTION OF TIME

1. *The time of the heavenly luminaries*

a. *The uselessness of the Western concept of time.* In order properly to explain the Hebrew consciousness of time, it would be most natural following our treatment up to this point to analyse the Hebrew synonyms and expressions for time and to quote copious examples and passages from the Old Testament. In his monograph of 1871,[1] still unsurpassed in its thoroughness, C. von Orelli employs this method. This method really presupposes that what is meant by 'time' is self-evident; 'time' must be established as a scheme of thought or a categorical form in order to have a standard by which the Israelite conception of time can be measured and evaluated. Practically all Western people now consider—the majority naïvely and uncritically, others consciously and on philosophical grounds —our conception of time as the only one possible epistemologically. An isolated radical critic like Henri Bergson, who denies the entire European conception of time, has scarcely been heard seriously; his conception of time has been considered an interesting and ingenious curiosity. Thus von Orelli takes as a basis the Aristotelian concept of time since he depends philosophically upon the studies in logic of the Aristotelian Trendelenburg.[2] The Jewish linguist Sal. Pappenheim penetratingly criticizes the time concept and its word-forms and attempts to classify them from the viewpoint of more modern, especially Kantian, philosophy which, even in von Orelli's opinion, has formerly prejudiced linguistic understanding.[3]

From a European standpoint von Orelli can assert correctly: 'However differently the concept of time has been regarded or evaluated in individual philosophical systems, it can hardly be defined without bringing it into closest relation with *motion.*'[4] Von Orelli thinks man possessed the idea of motion in space before he made time an object of his interpretation. Spatial conceptions are gained immediately from sense perceptions; temporal conceptions are formed indirectly with the help of spatial conceptions. The dependence of temporal conceptions upon spatial conceptions applies not only to individual words, but whole complexes of conceptions are transferred from the spatial to the temporal. The series originally in juxtaposition spatially serves as a means for representing the series in succession temporally; by means of spatial precedence

---

[1] C. von Orelli, *Die hebräischen Synonyma der Zeit und Ewigkeit genetisch und sprach-vergleichend dargestellt.*
[2] *Ibid.*, p. 11.   [3] *Ibid.*, p. 9.   [4] *Ibid.*

temporal priority is expressed, and by means of spatial gaps temporal interval is expressed.[1]

As we shall see later these specifications do not fit the Hebrew consciousness of time, and von Orelli almost discovers it himself. He observes that in Indo-European languages as well as in Semitic languages the use of spatial expressions to designate temporal notions is remarkably inconsistent. To be sure, he mentions only the notions 'before' and 'behind' which can designate the future as well as the past, but he supplies illustrations of the ambiguity from Arabic as well as from German, Latin, and Greek. His explanation of this remarkable linguistic phenomenon, to which we shall return later, is somewhat striking; he is not clear, however, on the fact that behind the double temporal meaning of the same words are two different notions of time. He would then have found that in the Indo-European languages the future is quite preponderantly thought to lie before us, while in Hebrew future events are always expressed as coming after us, and that this conception stands in a necessary relation to the Hebrew conception of time as a whole. The inconsistency discovered by von Orelli in Arabic does not occur in Hebrew so far as it has been possible for me to examine the examples occurring in the Old Testament. In this instance, reference to a parallel Arabic usage has only clouded our understanding of the peculiarity of Hebrew.

b. *Sun and moon as time-determinants; perception of time.* Before we analyse the Hebrew designations for time, we must attempt in some way to grasp the Hebrew notion of time. We pose the problem in the simplest possible way when we ask how the Israelites became conscious of physical or astronomical time. How were they able to answer these questions: What time is it now, i.e. what is the hour? What season of the year are we in right now? As the Greeks did and as we do, the Israelites determined these times with the aid of the sun, moon, and the stars (Gen. 1.14), but in a totally different way. The distinction is expressed even in the different designations for sun, moon, and stars; the Greeks called them heavenly *bodies*, and Plato knows that they are spherical.[2] The Greeks, therefore, first consider the form of the heavenly bodies; they observe where they are in the heavens and in that way they (and the other Indo-Europeans) determine time. The most important time determinant is the sun; Christmas (25th December) and St John's day (Midsummer Day, 24th June), which are defined by means of the sun's position in the sky, are ancient Indo-Germanic festivals. These were unknown in Israel; there the holy seasons were defined with the aid of the quite variable and

[1] *Ibid.*, pp. 13 f.   [2] *See* p. 115, n. 2.

movable moon. The Hebrews call the heavenly bodies *lamps, me'oroth* (Gen. 1.14 ff.), or *lights, 'ôrîm* (Ps. 136.7); both names refer to their *function*. Lamps and lights help us to see; they illuminate and warm.

The heavenly luminaries emit differing intensities of light and warmth, and in that way they define time. The time when the sun is the dominant light- and warmth-giver is the day, but the time when the moon is the dominant light and together with the stars gives illumination is night (Gen. 1.16). The Hebrews did not express themselves that way, to be sure; for them, time is determined by its content, and since light is authoritative and decisive, the light was called day and the darkness night even before the creation of the heavenly luminaries (Gen. 1.5). After their creation it was their chief task to separate light and darkness from one another and thus to separate day and night (v. 18). The transition from day to night is abruptly recognizable in the south, not slow and almost unnoticeable as in the far north. The separation of light from darkness effects not only the distinction between day and night but also between good and not good, for God saw that the light was good and separated the light from the darkness. The qualitative distinction between light and darkness is so sharp in the Old Testament that light can be used identically with good fortune and blessing, darkness with ruination and curse. When Jahveh's salvation comes, 'then shall thy light rise in darkness' (Isa. 58.10).

> When I looked for good, evil came;
> and when I waited for light, darkness came (Job 30.26).
> The Lord is my light and my salvation (Ps. 27.1).

The heavenly luminaries are, therefore, signs of Jahveh's kindness, as it says in Psalm 136, in almost verbal agreement with Gen. 1.14–16:

> O give thanks to the Lord, for he is good,
> for his steadfast love endures for ever. . .
> to him who made the great lights . . .
> the sun to rule over the day . . .
> the moon and stars to rule over the night . . .:

they are signs of his glory and power:

> O Lord, our Lord, how majestic is thy name in all the earth!
> . . . whose glory above the heavens is chanted . . .
> When I look at the heavens, the work of thy fingers,
> the moon and the stars which thou hast established;
> what is man that thou art mindful of him,
> and the son of man that thou dost care for him? (Ps. 8.1–4).

The revelatory activity of the heavenly luminaries is clear and easy to understand, for:

> The heavens are telling the glory of God;
>   and the firmament proclaims his handiwork.
> Day to day pours forth speech,
>   and night to night declares knowledge . . .
> their words (go) to the end of the world (Ps. 19.1–4).

It is not difficult, therefore, to understand what *'othoth* (Gen. 1.14) is to mean. Gunkel cannot be right, that sun and moon in their appearance and disappearance become signs (Jer. 10.2), for, as we have said, day and night are determined by illumination and not by the movement of the heavenly bodies. Moreover, the signs mentioned in Jer. 10.2 are astrological omens of disaster, and it is expressly said that the heavenly luminaries are not to have that task for the Israelites. The joyful tone of the creation narrative and the designation of the light as good rule out Gunkel's interpretation. Skinner finds the proposed attempt at solution unsatisfactory but does not offer one of his own. Keller thinks that the term *'othoth* lies along the same line as *mo'adhím* and asserts that for this reason the stars have a cultic function.[1] It is illuminating that *'oth* has here the same meaning as in Gen. 9.12 ff., where P designates another heavenly light, the rainbow, as *'oth*.[2] The meaning of Gen. 1.14, then, is: As the rainbow, when it appears occasionally, is the sign and guarantee of the covenant of grace with Noah, so are sun, moon, and stars the daily signs and guarantees of his mercy shown forth in the whole of creation. P's mentioning the heavenly luminaries as signs thus becomes quite ingenious: sun, moon, and stars speak of God day and night everywhere, as the Psalms express more fully, but the rainbow does so only now and then and also from a particular viewpoint, namely that the waters are never again to rise to become a flood (Gen. 9.15).

mo'adhím (Gen. 1.14) is never used for the natural seasons of the year (*vide* Skinner, *in loc.*) but always for a time understood or defined by circumstances, in general for designating the holy seasons of the Priestly year which are defined in terms of the moon (Ps. 104.19). This meaning seems to be the only one possible here since the seasons of the natural year are specifically mentioned: P's preference for cult affairs makes this explanation probable. Thus the enumeration of the functions of the heavenly luminaries in Gen. 1.14 is artful and ingenious; first, they are to tell God's kindness, power, and glory, then to mark out the sacred

---

[1] Carl Keller, *Das Wort OTH als 'Offerbarungszeichen Gottes'*, p. 129.
[2] The combination of sun, moon, stars, and rainbow also in Ecclus. 43.1 ff.

seasons, and finally to date the secular times, the daily as well as the less frequent ones.

Not only day and night but also definite times during the day were designated by the kind and intensity of the sun's light and warmth. Nehemiah gives as the time for opening the city gates, 'Let not the gates of Jerusalem be opened until the sun is hot' (7.3); this is the Hebrew equivalent of our expression, 'when the sun stands high in the heavens'. The same expression *ḥom hashshemesh* is also used as a time-designation in I Sam. 11.9. A synonymous expression *ḥom hayyôm*—the heat of the day, is used in I Sam. 11.11 and in Gen. 18.1: Abraham sat in the door of the tent 'in the heat of the day' (cf. II Sam. 4.5). Joshua's prayer expresses the subjective, perceiving time experience:

> Sun, stand thou still at Gibeon,
> and thou Moon in the valley of Aijalon (Josh. 10.12).

The poet is thus not speaking of the objective, external, and visible position of the sun in the firmament but of the sunlight in Palestine. The corresponding instance in Homer's *Iliad* (ii, 412) is described in a characteristically Greek way; Agamemnon prays Zeus not to let the sun *sink into the sea* before he has won the victory. Although the motion of the sun is admittedly mentioned in the Old Testament, it is not mentioned as an indication of time in the Indo-Germanic manner, as von Orelli incorrectly asserts,[1] but as an expression of its power and glory:

> So perish all thine enemies, O Lord!
> But thy friends be like the sun as he rises in his might (Judg. 5.31).

> (The sun) comes forth like a bridegroom leaving his chamber,
> and like a strong man runs its course with joy.
> Its rising is from the end of the heavens,
>   and its circuit to the end of them;
>   and there is nothing hid from its heat (Ps. 19.5 f.).

c. *Time-rhythms rather than time-cycles or time-lines.* The heavenly luminaries as determinants of time thus excite various sensations in men through which they define time objectively; to this corresponds man's subjective perception of time. Even the beasts who may not be capable of observing sun and moon have a keen sensation of time which is connected with bodily rhythms. As subjective time-determinants for man we may cite sleep and wakefulness, work and rest, meal-times; we also have shorter rhythms, such as heart-beat, pulse-beat, and respiration. It is common to all of these that they can determine a point in time or an

[1] Von Orelli, *op. cit.*, pp. 32 ff.

interval of time without using any sort of spatial movement. The same can also be said of the heavenly luminaries as time-determinants; the difference between light and darkness, their regular alternation, the phases of the moon, the weaker and stronger heat of the sun in the course of a day are time-rhythms and not time-movements. So for the Hebrews the seasons of the year, too, are eternal rhythms:

> seedtime and harvest,
> cold and heat,
> summer and winter (Gen. 8.22).

We Europeans with our customarily spatial mode of thinking frequently think of temporal rhythms by means of the obvious image of a circle or cycle; the reason for this is the circular movement of the sun which from time immemorial has been used for temporal orientation, since the image of the circular movement of the sun was transferred to the corresponding time.[1] The Hebrews, however, orient themselves temporally not toward the circular movement of the sun, but toward the regular change of the moon's phases, toward the rhythmic alternation of light and darkness, warmth and cold, as already indicated. The use of such images as circles and cycles must be explained correspondingly. Human life runs its course as an eternal rhythm: earth—man—earth. If we depart a bit from our customary way of thinking and reflect quite dispassionately, we shall find in this alternation no trace of a circular line but purely and simply a rhythmic alternation. In Hebrew this is dôr; it is quite possible that von Orelli is right in his contention that dôr is derived from the same root as dûr—circular course, circle. This does not establish, however, that the Hebrews thought of a generation as a circle; it is every bit as possible and probable that, on the contrary, they thought of the circular course as an eternal rhythm of beginning, continuation, and return to the beginning. Lines and forms, as we shall see later, play no rôle for them, hence not even the circular line. For them the great reality is rhythm, and the circular course is a rhythm of which they learned primarily not from the movement of the sun (and not even fundamentally from this of whose movement only a half-circle is visible), but from the round dances and their rotating themselves in the dance. The characteristic of this rhythm is what von Orelli also emphasizes, that 'regularly taking place it rounds itself off into a thing complete in itself'.[2] The participants in a dance also form an unbroken unity since they give one another their hands.[3]

---

[1] *Ibid.*, p. 32.   [2] *Ibid.*

[3] Cf. the illustrations in Guthe, *Kurzes Bibelwörterbuch*, p. 542.

For us the turn of the year is the time when the annual cycle is at an end; for the Israelites it is the time when the beginning of the year returns. It is therefore called *teshûbhah*—return (II Sam. 11.1; I Kings 20.22, 26; I Chron. 20.1; II Chron. 36.10); they can also use *teqûphah*—rotation or turning (Ex. 34.22; II Chron. 24.23), even for the coming round of the day (I Sam. 1.20), the same notion, of course. No basis exists for assuming any other idea in Ps. 19.7: during the night the sun is hidden (in its tabernacle, v. 5), then appears at one end of the heavens out of hiddenness, and returns in the evening at the other side of the heavens into hiddenness (into its tabernacle). The use of the preposition *'al* in place of *'adh* confirms this explanation.

An isolated unit of time, therefore, has a rhythm which for the sake of comparison with rhythmic speech can be given the form: unaccented—accented—unaccented, or to compare it with the pulse-beat: weak—strong—weak. Thus in Hebrew the period of day and night is a rhythm of dull—bright—dull; evening—morning—evening (Gen. 1.5, 8, 13, 19, 23, 31). For the seventh day nothing is said about evening and morning, for the seventh day is in itself a day of rest and, as such, is the end (and beginning) of the greater rhythm of the week: rest day—week day—rest day. The monthly rhythm begins with the new moon; the dullest phase of the moon is the fixed point in reckoning the month.[1] Accordingly, the rhythm of the month is: new moon—full moon (or moon phases)—new moon. A year is: beginning—the months—return to the beginning; the turn of the year in ancient times fell in the autumn after the completion of the harvest,[2] therefore in a time when the strength of the year was at its lowest. A human life is origin from the earth—life—return to the earth; this rhythm is expressed in Job:

> Naked I came from my mother's womb,
> and naked shall I return (1.21).

The 'thither' (AV), *shammah*, need not be pressed; it is demanded by the rhythm. The sense can be rendered somewhat as follows: Naked I came out of hiddenness (my mother's womb), naked I returned to hiddenness (the grave). Generally the time-rhythm has the form ⌣ — ⌣.

d. *Duration and Instant*. A longer period of time is thought of as a continued rhythm passing over into a higher time-rhythm, etc. The shortest rhythm, the day, passes into the week-rhythm, then into the month-rhythm, and this into the rhythm of the year, since the learned P writer considers the year as originally a lunar year. The seven-beat rhythm of

---

[1] *Ibid.*, p. 178.   [2] *Ibid.*, p. 282.

the week is continued in the sabbath year and the jubilee year.[1] Whether the Hebrews thought of the time-rhythm or -rhythms as circles or as straight lines is as pointless a question as whether the successive beats of the pulse form a straight line or a circle. In any case it is a question of a series of perceptions which could be conceived as lines only with the greatest difficulty.

If, for his own purposes, a European insists on making an image of the time-rhythm, the image of the endless straight line says precisely the same thing as the circle, or rather the image of *motion* along the lines in question says the same thing; one can be convinced of this easily by an example. In a continuous number, the periodic recurrence can be shown in either way equally clearly: for example, the decimal number, $1:7$ $=0.142857\ 142857\ \dots\ 142857$, appears in a straight line, but the six numbers can be placed serially on the circumference of a circle at equal intervals; by movement along either line, the same group of numbers is encountered repeatedly. Thus if it is true that calculable time forms a rhythm with the ceaseless return of the same time-content, it is understood why in Semitic languages the notion of recurrence coincides with that of duration. Thus *'ôdh* means first the return of something, then its recurrence, and this idea passes over into duration.[2]

The shortest span of time, or, Hebraically expressed, the shortest perception of time, is *regha'*—a beat, or as von Orelli so suitably suggests, the pulse-beat of time.[3] The word is not used with *'ayin* (eye) either as a verb or as a noun, as is German *Augenblick* (twinkling of an eye). If, as von Orelli assumes,[4] the movement of the eye formed the middle term of the conception, then certainly the conception is different from that in our notion, 'twinkling of an eye'. 'In *regha'* there is originally something violent.' The difference can be so explained that in the former instance the winking is observed with the eye, and in the latter case it is experienced as a twitching of the eyelid. An external observation decidedly lies behind the expression 'without an eye twitching' (Ger. *mit keiner Wimper zucken*), for the movement of the lash can very well be seen, but cannot very well be sensed. Certainly, then, a visual perception is beneath the time expression 'twinkling of an eye', while the Hebrew *regha'* refers to some sort of bodily sensation such as pulse-beat, heart-beat, or twitching of the eyelid. In any case, the shortest time in Hebrew is not a point, nor a distance, nor a duration, but a beat. Synonymous with *regha'* is *petha'* from the verb *patha'* = *pathah* 'open'. As adverbial accusative and with

---

[1] *Ibid.*, pp. 282, 250 ff.   [2] Von Orelli, *op. cit.*, p. 30.
[3] *Ibid.*, p. 28.   [4] *Ibid.*, p. 27.

prepositions, *petha'* and the adverb derived from it, *pith'om* (for *pith'om*), are used like *regha'* to designate abruptness. In many places these words are completely synonymous, yet between these notions appears a fine line of difference based on their origin. *regha'* is more the rapacious, violent, stormy suddenness with which something takes place; *petha'* signifies that something arrives imperceptibly, surprisingly, and unnoticed, and when the eyes are raised unexpectedly, it is suddenly there. This notion of an unexpectedly occurring surprise appears at Eccles. 9.12 (*et al.*), in the comparison with the fish and birds who notice nothing until they find themselves 'suddenly' ensnared; likewise at Prov. 7.22 in the case of the young man hearkening to temptation who pursues the harlot 'straightway', i.e. suddenly he has no more self-control. The unforeseen occurrence in suddenness is found also at Isa. 47.11; Num. 6.9; 35.22, where *pith'om* means 'absolutely unintentional'.[1] I do not believe, however, that these last-named words allude to the mere opening of the eye; they portray how in sheer surprise the mouth as well as the eyes opens involuntarily when something unexpected is suddenly seen.

We have examined the ideas underlying the expression of *calculable* time and more than once have found that the Israelites understood time as something qualitative, because for them time is determined by its content. We shall now look into this side of the Israelite understanding of time.

2. *Psychic Time*

a. *The identity of consciousness.* For us space is like a great container that stores, arranges, and holds everything together; space is also the place where we live, breathe, and can expand freely. Time played a similar rôle for the Hebrews. Their consciousness is like a container in which their whole life from childhood on and the realities which they experienced or of which they had heard are stored. Because every person is and remains identical with himself, a consolidating unity adheres to each person's psychical content which could be expressed thus: all this is my world, my existence. A man who lives from the psychical impressions that the external world makes upon him has a world in his consciousness; he lives in time, but even while he actually lives in time, moments and intervals of time play a very subordinate rôle. It is the same I that once played as a child, went to school as a youth, and entered competitive life; body and appearance have changed, life's experiences have come, but the man himself, i.e. his consciousness, has remained the same self.

[1] *Ibid.*, p. 29.

Seen from the inside his personal experiences form a unity, a world; in that world he moves freely and with ease. Thus even while the Hebrew lives in time, time-distinctions play a very trifling rôle for him. Even in the divine consciousness all time measurement disappears (Ps. 90.4), because Jahveh remains identical with himself (Ex. 3.14; Isa. 41.4; 44.6; 48.12).

Consciousness comprises an entire life as a unity and cannot be divided like space; even an event is a coherent whole. It is essentially inadmissible to break up or analyse this unity into a series of segments or rapidly consecutive points of time. Let us reflect upon an event that is unrelated to space and that belongs, therefore, only to time, e.g. a melody. When a song is being sung, its beginning, in our spatial manner of thinking, already belongs to the past and its end still to the future; but essentially the song is a living unity which, even after it has been sung to the end and logically belongs to the past, is something present and in the highest sense real. The possibility of conceiving as a unity a melody that has been sung demonstrates that for us, too, the now, the earlier, and the later are a unity, and so too are past, present, and future. We would not follow Bergson when he tries to explain melody as the harmonious working together and fusion of sounds, but we would regard melody, word, speech, meaningful acts, and above all our own individual psychical existence as originally temporal data which are comprehensible without explanation for every man who has any conscious psychical life.

Moreover, we Europeans must learn to regard events as facts that are and abide. The sound waves that mediate the melody to us disperse (as indeed all light waves, too, vanish or are somehow turned into heat), but the melody itself lingers and never perishes for us, as psychology teaches us. In a similar way significant historical events remain indestructible facts in the life of a people. The consequences of the events can be altered in a positive or negative direction by new deeds or failures, but the events themselves can never be altered; they belong to the permanent stock of the people's life. If this is the actual state of affairs regarding what has happened, we understand that the difference between past and present is less important than the qualitative distinction between events; a decisive event of antiquity can balance many current events in the evaluation of the present. In the light of inevitable disaster, today's feasts could appear as dreadful unrealities so long as threatening misfortune must be reckoned with as an accomplished fact. Thus a general can say, 'We have lost the war', even when the war is in full course and ordinary folk suspect nothing.

The life of a people endures for centuries, even millennia, yet it is a *life* just because the people remains identical with itself throughout its entire history. The people's consciousness of itself as a unity, as an individual, is expressed in the notion of a patriarch. In Jacob's blessing (Genesis 49), the sons of Jacob are now persons, now tribes; the poet passes from one viewpoint to the other without the slightest difficulty. The patriarch and the tribe are one life even though centuries separate them. The prophets rediscover the bad as well as the good characteristics of the patriarch in the people (Hos. 12.4; Isa. 41.8). It is an entirely Israelite idea when St Paul asserts that if the Jews were to repent once, all Israel would be saved. In a similar way the story of Adam and Eve embodies the history of mankind.

It is clear what meaning God's consciousness must have had for the Hebrews; the life of a man encompasses a small part of the history of existence, the life of a people a greater part, the life of humanity a still greater part, but the life of God encompasses everything. God's consciousness is a world consciousness in which everything that takes place is treasured and held fast in the eternal and is therefore as indestructible as 'matter'. Without a world consciousness, all the history of humanity and of the universe would end in nothing; for a people, however, for whom life and history is everything, the concept of a divine world consciousness is as necessary as the concept of eternal being was for the Greeks. For the Israelites, the world was transitory, but Jahveh and his words (and deeds) were eternal (Isa. 40.8).

b. *The content of time.* For the Hebrews who have their existence in the temporal, the content of time plays the same rôle as the content of space plays for the Greeks. As the Greeks gave attention to the peculiarity of things, so the Hebrews minded the peculiarity of events. It is quite interesting that although von Orelli is hindered by his method, he nevertheless arrives at the conclusion that *the Semitic concept of time is closely coincident with that of its content* without which time would be quite impossible. The quantity of duration completely recedes behind the characteristic feature that enters with time or advances in it.[1] Johannes Pedersen comes to the same conclusion[2] when he distinguishes sharply between the Semitic understanding of time and ours. According to him, time is for us an abstraction since we distinguish time from the events that occur in time. The ancient Semites did not do this; for them time is determined by its content. Time is the notion of the occurrence; it is the stream of events.

[1] *Ibid.*, p. 27.
[2] Johannes Pedersen, 'Gammeltestamentlig Skepticisme', *Edda*, IV (1915), 302 ff.

When we try to insinuate ourselves into the Hebraic understanding of time by way of a passage like Eccles. 3.1 ff., it strikes us that occasionally we, too, characterize time by its content. We speak of wartime, peacetime, hard times, time of mourning, feast time, favourable time, office hours, bad year, etc. Therefore it is not so very difficult for us to experience the Hebraic perception of time, but we must allow to stand as a general rule what for us is an exception, and is hardly thought of by us as 'proper' time.

Thus, in part, the chronological times were named and characterized in accordance with their content in the Old Testament; day is the time of light and night is darkness (Gen. 1.5; Ps. 104.20).[1] It is therefore something quite unusual when the day grows dark; Job cursed the day of his birth with the wish that it might become darkness (3.4 f.). When the prophets of judgment wanted to preach with drastic trenchancy that the day of the Lord would bring disaster, they said it would be a day of darkness and gloom, of clouds and thick darkness (Joel 2.2). Amos says: And on that day, says the Lord God, I will make the sun go down at noon, and darken the earth in broad daylight (8.9). Even if the recollection of an eclipse has provided the image for the prophet,[2] the threat lies not in the physical manifestation but in the unusual fact that the good life-giving light is to be changed into unnatural darkness, as the continuation of the oracle shows: I will turn your feasts into mourning, and all your songs into lamentation (8.10). The chronological details of P usually have some deeper meaning; thus the age of men from Adam to Moses (with the chief exception of righteous Noah who achieves the same age as the first man) always diminishes. The manifest intention is to signify the decrease of good fortune and perfection. The tendency of giving meaning and content to the chronology increased in later days; thus the entire book of Jubilees is governed by that tendency.

The time of inner life, like chronological time, followed its course in rhythms, not however in rhythms which are always repeated anew but in rhythms of antitheses which are constantly replacing one another and every pair of which, together with the stages in between, forms a qualitative unity. There is:

A time to be born and a time to die;
A time to plant and a time to pluck up that which is planted;
A time to kill and a time to heal;

[1] This is partly true, at least, in German, e.g. *Herbst* means Autumn. [Harvest, etymologically related to *Herbst*, is an obsolete name for Autumn in English. Tr.]
[2] Cf. Mowinckel, M.M.M., on this passage.

A time to break down and a time to build up;
A time to weep and a time to laugh;
A time to mourn and a time to dance;
A time to cast away stones and a time to gather stones together;
A time to embrace and a time to refrain from embracing;
A time to seek and a time to lose;
A time to keep and a time to cast away;
A time to rend and a time to sew;
A time to keep silence and a time to speak;
A time to love and a time to hate;
A time for war and a time for peace (Eccles. 3.2–8).

So is man's life, thinks the Preacher; he mentions only the extremes, but he has included with them all the stages in between.[1]

c. *The time of history*. While gladly admitting the fundamental truth in our interpretation, Walter Eichrodt doubts that there is a peculiar Hebraic sense of time,[2] such as has been maintained here, by C. H. Ratschow in part,[3] and by John Marsh in a particularly extensive and thorough way.[4] Eichrodt's criticism must be welcomed gratefully, because he puts his finger on a point which was so obvious to us that it was hardly mentioned. Therefore, a clarification of our interpretation should, we believe, contribute to our being able to reach an understanding with Eichrodt, or at least to the clearing up of a few misunderstandings.

What Eichrodt feels to be missing is the appreciation for the necessity of a definite chronological sequence in the story of salvation (*Heilsge-schichte*):

> God's plan of salvation cannot otherwise be spoken of than by reference to definite points in time which by their special significance stand out from the ordinary course of events in bold relief and become landmarks of God's progressive action toward the attainment of his purpose. The delivery from Egypt, the sealing of the Covenant at Sinai, the conquest of the promised land are named at the very beginning of God's relation with Israel as the decisive points in the course of events, to which the people's thinking is to be directed in order to understand the more recent acts of God and to face them in proper readiness. For again and again in the course of history such times and days of Jahveh appear, announced by seer and prophet, expected and lived through in

[1] Correspondingly, the Hebrew can identify an entire country or an area by mentioning its boundaries (*vide infra* 'The Boundary'); on the Hebrew predilection to consider two concepts of opposite content as a unity, cf. n. 1, p. 74.

[2] Walter Eichrodt, 'Heilserfahrung und Zeitverständnis im Alten Testament', *Theologische Zeitschrift*, XII (1956), 103–25.

[3] Carl H. Ratschow, 'Anmerkungen zur theologischen Auffassung des Zeitproblems', *Zeitschrift für Theologie und Kirche*, LI (1954), 36–87.

[4] John Marsh, *The Fulness of Time*.

suspense because God's hidden redemptive will appears and provides a new goal for the work begun.[1]

Obviously we grant that certain events in the life of the people (or of the individual) are more important than others and that some of them stand out as landmarks in the course of events. Secondly, we grant that the course of events remains objective and steadfast and that the place of one event in the time-series can never be exchanged with the place of another. In the life of the individual childhood, youth, manhood, and old age cannot be interchanged, nor in the life of the people can the time of the Patriarchs, the time of Moses, the time of David, etc. What we firmly deny is the assertion that time is a mode of viewing things, a line, most of all something spatial or capable of being represented spatially (whether the line is straight or circular is of no concern in *this* regard). For this reason we need not have spoken at all of a specifically Hebraic sense of time as distinct from one that is European, but only of a clear and exact sense of time as distinct from one that is inconsistent and unclear. In fact, we do maintain that the European sense of time is a confused mixture of time and space. The incontrovertible examples of this are the spatial images (thus not only expressions) that we involuntarily make of time, as, for example, when we say: the future lies before us, the past lies behind us. It should be clear to everyone, however, that time neither lies, stands, nor is, but goes, comes, and becomes. When we admit this and say correctly: the future is coming, then the future vanishes from in front of us and comes after us (cf. g below). This contradiction cannot be dismissed as a curiosity or a joke, but it must be taken earnestly as a sign of a pervasive inner confusion in our entire sense of time. Bergson has shown this clearly. We could also recall Leibniz who very briefly but aptly defined time as an order of succession, and space as an order of coexistence; since the points on any single line are coexistent, it is completely inappropriate to illustrate time as a line. The sense which is plainly made for successive impressions is hearing.[2] We *see* the spatial and *hear* the temporal.

Hebrew images and expressions for time are simple, clear, and without inner contradictions because spatial images have not become entrenched there; instead, spatial images are inappropriate to the Hebrews for representing the correct state of affairs in space (cf. Chapter One, Section A, 5, above).

---

[1] Walter Eichrodt. *Theologische Zeitschrift*, XII (1956), 103. [The rendering is made by the translator.]
[2] Cf. the final chapter, 'Summary', below.

The Hebraic (i.e. Old Testament and, in part also, New Testament) problem of time and history is therefore primarily epistemological in the philosophical sense. For this reason everything theological, every utterance about God, revelation, and the plan of salvation should first of all be held at a distance in order to clarify the epistemological side of the problem. This does not mean that this task is to be performed in a purely philosophical way; for when a man understands in the Hebrew manner, he can solve this problem if, with the help of the language, he insinuates himself sympathetically into Hebrew thinking. Yet this does not mean that the philosophical side of the problem has no theological significance; for if the Hebrew sense of time, in contrast to the Greek-European, is clear and without inner contradictions, the Israelites must have been able to understand more easily and to express better a temporal-historical revelation of God than the Greeks.

There is not room here for us to discuss the details of the time problem; by way of conclusion, we would emphasize that when we admit the significance of chronology, i.e. the successive series of occurrences, in the Old Testament, we do not thereby alter our high regard for contemporaneity nor what we have said previously regarding time. Thus everyone can become contemporaneous with a well-remembered occurrence of his past while he is reliving it once more in his memory without forgetting at that moment the year or the epoch in which it took place and the significance it eventually acquired for the remainder of his life subsequently.

d. *The tenses.* It has wellnigh become a dogma in theology and in Semitics that the Hebrew verb is timeless; but I beg theologians particularly to answer the question how it is possible psychologically that a people, whose language has no expression for the notion of time and whose time-words are timeless, became the people of history, while the contemporary and contiguous Greeks, whose time-words can distinguish past, present, and future with accuracy, who developed delicately shaded expressions for the notion of time, and whose thinkers reflected profoundly on the content of the time-notion, selected space as their thought-form and never evinced any real sense of historical development.[1] It is no answer to the question to say that the ancient Israelites were a primitive people and were therefore unable to construct verb-forms as in Greek; there are even forms which the Greeks do not have and which can express such ideas as were apparently of greater interest to the Israelites than 'time'. If Max Mueller is right in his position that in language there lies

[1] As von Dobschütz (*op. cit.*) pointed out.

a petrified philosophy, here is imbedded an enigmatic problem of folk psychology which in any case should urge a theologian to deeper reflection upon the notion of time.

There is a quite simple solution to the problem—somewhat paradoxical to us at first—if we assume that it is the Hebrews and Semites who have the adequate understanding of time, not the Greeks and we Europeans. We must then ask whether the tenses of Hebrew verbs do not express time more clearly than do our tenses; at all events, they are fundamentally different from ours. The Indo-Germanic framework of three time-spheres (past, present, and future) is quite foreign to the Semitic notion of tense which views what happens principally from the standpoint of completed or incomplete action.[1] We have already indicated above that our distinction between past, present, and future, like the Greek conception of time in general as well as our own, is much more a matter of space than of time. This is in decided agreement with von Dobschütz's thesis that the Greeks employ space as the primary mode of thought, considering it so important that they model the other mode of thought, time, in its image. Thus we are agreed with Bergson's contention that our concept of 'time' is 'spatialized'; he distinguishes between 'spatialized' time which he calls *temps* and real time which he calls *durée*.[2] *Temps* can be translated by the word *time*, but in place of *durée*, 'duration', we prefer the term *occurrence*, i.e. not this or that occurrence, but the occurring in itself;[3] think of everything that can occur or be accomplished in time, leave all concrete content out of account, and we have left the notion of pure occurrence.[4] From the European standpoint it is quite natural to consider this kind of time, this occurring, as timeless because it lacks the 'spatializing' of our 'time'. Judged impartially on epistemological grounds, however, it appears as real time; when, hereafter, we speak of the Semitic notion of time, this sort of time is meant.

[1] Ges.-K., § 47a, n. Harris Birkeland (*Laerebok i hebraisk grammatik* [Oslo, 1950], §§ 647 ff.) thinks that the perfect consecutive expresses the future and the imperfect consecutive the past; the two tense-forms should represent a Canaanite innovation which could have lasted only a few centuries. In the event that Birkeland is right in his assertion, the two consecutive forms do not, in any case, contribute anything toward illuminating the peculiar Israelite *conception of time*.

[2] H. Bergson, *Essai sur les données immédiates*, chap. II. Kant (*Critique of Pure Reason*, p. 82) also makes a distinction similar to Bergson's when he distinguishes 'time itself' as something that 'does not change' from the *content of time*. Compared with Bergson, he evaluates the two 'times' in a totally opposite way, since he considers the region of time or the time-line, that is spatialized time, as the true time.

[3] [The word here translated 'occurring' is *Geschehen*, the infinitive of the verb *geschehen* used substantively or as a gerund. Tr.]

[4] This is substantially the definition of Semitic 'time' given by Pedersen ('Gammeltestamentlig Skepticisme', *Edda*, IV [1915], 302 ff.) and it agrees with the explanation given in Ges.-K., § 74a, n. 1.

According to Gesenius-Kautzsch, the Hebrew perfect serves to express actions, events, or conditions which the *speaker* means to depict as *factually before us*, whether they belong to an already finally closed past, still reach into the present, or although still future are thought of as already before us.[1] In contrast to the perfect, the Hebrew imperfect expresses those actions, events, or conditions which are observed by the *speaker* at any point in time as still continuing, in process of taking place, or as newly emergent. In this regard, it is immaterial whether its emergence is characterized as something to be expected with certainty, or as something only conceived or desired subjectively, and consequently as something only eventual (the modal use of the imperfect). In the light of Babylonian-Assyrian usage, Knudtzon would prefer to describe the imperfect as *fiens* (Latin, present passive participle of *facio*), that is as an expression of the actually or even only internally present. Gesenius-Kautzsch says further that the imperfect 'places the action, etc., in a more direct relation to the judgment or feeling of the *speaker*'.[2]

In these citations from Gesenius-Kautzsch we have allowed ourselves to stress the thrice-repeated 'speaker'; therein lies the heart of the matter. While we, by means of our three tenses, move the actions about in space, while we cling to their falling upon a line, for the Semite it is the judgment of the speaker that is the fixed point to which the actions are oriented. In this case two psychological possibilities exist: the actions could be considered concluded or still in process of development. For us, actions are oriented objectively, impersonally, and spatially; the Hebrews think subjectively, personally, and temporally.

e. *The psychology of the tenses.* Finally we should like to arrive at what there is specifically in the notions of past, present, and future; the terms presuppose that a *man* has entered time, and the whole of time is defined from *his* standpoint. We Europeans think that we are at a given point of the time-line with our faces pointed forward. The point in time where we now stand is the present, today or now, depending upon the precision with which our location is to be defined; before us lies the future and behind us the past. Without man there can be no talk of present, nor consequently of any past or future. To this definition of time from the standpoint of thinking and speaking men we can apply the term 'relative time'. Instead of placing themselves at some point or other on an imaginary time-line, the Hebrews proceed from the time-rhythm of their own life. Relative time is then reckoned from the standpoint of the person speaking since they think of their lives and history as something like a

---

[1] Ges.-K., § 106. [2] Ges.-K., § 107 a; italics my own.

life journey. Therefore, the relative times, present, past, and future, become strictly relative because every connexion with space (time-point, time-line, extent of time) is suppressed, and every movement of time is defined with the aid of our own life movement. One is so accommodated to another series of occurrences that one becomes contemporaneous with it and lives within it. From the standpoint of the one who is speaking there are only two kinds of actions, those which are complete and those which are not.

The Hebrews, therefore, have two *tenses*: complete (perfect, *factum*) and incomplete (imperfect, *fiens*). (In the same way, we have only two tenses, past and future, if we conceive the present as only a point in time separating past from future.) If we compare the term *complete* with the corresponding term *past*, we find that *complete* defines the action from the viewpoint of an experiencing person, but *past* defines it with reference to an impersonal, objective point on the time-line. *Fiens* defines the action as incomplete in relation to the person speaking; *future* defines it as not carried to its effect in relation to our position, or in other, even more spatial, words, as still *lying* before us.

Present means exactly what the word says: 'presence', i.e. we are at the place where the action is taking place, as spectators and witnesses. What is present for the Hebrews? We can get an idea of this if we analyse the terms for *now*:

1. *pa'am* means 'pace, step, time' (from *pa'am*—'impel'). *pa'am* can be emphasized *zoth happa'am*—'this time', *'attah happa'am*—'now this time'.[1] Surely the idea underlying this notion is this: when a common action is to take place simultaneously, such as a march, a journey, or a dance, it begins with the leader deciding and determining the first step perhaps with a preparatory command: *pa'am*—'Step!'

2. The demonstrative pronoun *zeh*— 'this, here, there, now'. The similarity among the first three of these meanings is clear; one points his hand definitely to a person or a place and says: *zeh*—'This! Here! There!' But when an action is to be carried out at a definite moment and the definite movement is made with the hand, it does not designate a given point but strikes in the air like a starting signal and says: *zeh*—'Now!' The origin of the temporal meaning of *zeh* can be thought of as something like that.

3. The third word for *now*, *koh*—'thus', is a demonstrative adverb, and the development of its meaning will have been the same.

The three exact words for the moment 'now' are similar to one another in that they (originally) designate the present moment by an energetic bodily

---

[1] Von Orelli, *op. cit.*, p. 51.

movement. An action which begins now, *happa'am, zeh, koh,* is therefore simultaneous with this movement. The Hebrew term *now* thus signifies *subjective simultaneity* while our term expresses the present.

4. The fourth word for *now*, *'attah,* is really *'eth*— 'time', with its adverbial, originally accusative, declensional ending *-ah.*[1] As *'eth* expresses psychical time, time as content and not chronological time, so it is with *'attah*; therefore, *now* when events are thus and so, e.g. 'Do not lay your hand on the lad or do anything to him; for *now* (seeing you have not withheld your son, your only son, from me) I know that you fear God' (Gen. 22.12). 'For *now* (that we have peace) the Lord has made room for us' (26.22). *'attah* means, therefore, the homogeneity of two time-contents. When *'attah* designates time, the emphasis is not on the moment of time, but on the situation.

We need not exaggerate the contrast, however, and present the Hebrew conception of tense as something unique; in most of the world's languages the original function of the tense-stems of the verb was not that of designating time (present, past, future) but of designating aspect (kind of action).[2] Even the modern Indo-Germanic languages have recognized and expressed the significance of the distinction between complete and incomplete actions; at all three points on the time-line our languages show two verb-forms which define the distinction between complete and incomplete: in the present we have present and perfect, in the future we have future and future perfect, and in the past we have imperfect and pluperfect. Secondly, we are also familiar with the fact that a tense-form can express all three time-spheres, since the present tense means not only present time but also future (e.g. he comes tomorrow) and the past (the historical present). When the past or future event appears particularly vital to the speaker's judgment so that, in a sense, he experiences it, it also becomes present to him. In spite of this, the fundamental distinction between Greek and Hebrew time-conception remains unaltered: Greek developed definite verb-forms which could express the distinction between past, present, and future; Hebrew did not.

f. *Contemporaneity.* The importance of the notion of contemporaneity for the historical understanding of Christianity has been discerned with particular clarity by Sören Kierkegaard and amply presented in his works. To be a true Christian and truly to believe in Christ means, according to him, to leap across and forget the centuries in order to become con-

---

[1] *Ibid.,* p. 50.
[2] P. L. Harriman (ed.), *The Encyclopaedia of Psychology* (New York: Philosophical Library, 1946), p. 846. Cf. F. Blass, *Grammatik des neutestamentlichen Greichisch,* ed. A. Debrunner (4th ed., Göttingen: Vandenhoeck & Ruprecht, 1913), § 318.

temporaneous with Jesus and his disciples as well as his opponents, to see and hear the simple, misunderstood Rabbi, and then in that situation to make with the soul's passion a decision for him, because one believes in him as the Son of God. The idea of contemporaneity, says Kierkegaard, simply and solemnly, 'is for me *the* thought of my life. Therefore I die happy, eternally thankful to Providence that I was allowed to become aware of this thought and to make it known.' He derived the idea itself from the New Testament.[1] That idea of contemporaneity, which we as well as Kierkegaard can form only with great difficulty because we are hindered in our manner of thinking by the three time-spheres, is given without difficulty to the Semites and particularly to the Hebrews in their languages. The contemporaneity of the speaker with the action and the occurring of which he speaks is the simplest and most natural thing he can imagine. If the capacity for experiencing contemporaneity with the action under discussion is the most important precondition for historical understanding, then the Israelites were born a people of history; and if contemporaneity with the decisive revelatory events is the most important condition of faith, the Israelites had the best natural presuppositions to become the people of revelation. We may recall that H. Wheeler Robinson tried to explain the peculiar ability of the Israelites to experience past and future as present by means of the concept of 'corporate personality'.[2] As an example we can cite the ancient poem in Genesis 49, where Jacob-Israel and the names of the twelve sons are at one moment individual persons and at another nations and tribes, and we find ourselves at one moment in the presumptive present and at another in the distant future without a suggestion of any time specification or distinction between time-spheres.

We can approach the problem of contemporaneity from the psychological side as well. A situation or an event from a time long past, which is prodigiously similar to our own, strikes us as modern, indeed present. Not infrequently, for example, a passage from an ancient work presents a situation so closely approaching our own that modern hearers assume some living man or other to be the author. On one occasion Professor Leiv Amundsen read before an audience of philology students in Oslo a passage from a political pamphlet of Isocrates; among those whom the students guessed to be the author of the passage were Roosevelt, Fridtjof Nansen, Churchill, and Trygve Lie. Without realizing it, they had leaped

---

[1] S. Kierkegaard, 'Samtidigheden', *Oieblikket, nr. 8; 11 Sept. 1855 (Samlede Vaerker,* XIV, 309–15).
[2] *See* p. 70, n. 1.

across two millennia to become contemporaneous with the author now long dead. The feeling of contemporaneity arises for us, too, when the psychical content of two periods of time appears identical. Contemporaneity is no assertion about chronological time, i.e. time in our sense, but about psychological time, i.e. time in the Israelite sense. Strict contemporaneity is, therefore, the same as psychological identity since two psychological contents coalesce into one. It corresponds to the geometric congruence of Greek thought which expresses the spatial identity of two quantities.

g. *Before and after.* As shown above, we Indo-Germanic peoples think of time as a line on which we ourselves stand at a point called now; then we have the future lying before us, and the past stretches out behind us. The Israelites use the same expressions 'before' and 'after' but with opposite meanings. *qedhem* means 'what is before' (Ps. 139.5), therefore, 'remote antiquity', *past.* '*ahar* means 'back', 'behind', and of the time 'after'; '*aharith* means 'hindermost side', and then 'end of an age', *future*:

> 'For I know the plans I have for you, says the Lord, plans for welfare and not for evil, to give you a future ('*aharith*) and a hope' (Jer. 29.11). 'Know that wisdom is such to your soul; if you find it, there will be a future ('*aharith*), and your hope will not be cut off' (Prov. 24.14). (Note how the future is here defined qualitatively and not in the first place chronologically.)

It is not hard for us, however, to understand the Hebrew mode of expression; for we also think and speak in the same way, once we stop thinking of time as something spatial, statically definable, almost visible, and instead appreciate time as the transcendental design of history, human as well as cosmic (cf. the use of the term *toledhoth*, Gen. 2.4). Then we have to think of ourselves as *living men who are on a journey from the cradle to the grave and who stand in living association with humanity which is also journeying ceaselessly forward.* Then the generation of the past are our *progenitors*, at least our *forebears*, who have existed *before us*, because they have *gone* on *before us*, and we follow *after* them. In that case, we call the past *foretime.* According to this mode of thinking, the future generation are our *descendants*, at least our *successors*, who therefore come *after* us. They belong to the *after-age, posterity*; they are the *latter growth.* From this viewpoint the future in the Nordic languages is called 'eftertid' (after-time) and the future generation 'efterslekt' (posterity). Thus we express our notion of time in two quite different, if not altogether opposite, ways according to whether we have in mind physical-astronomical time or psychological-historical time: the future *lies* before us but *comes* after us.

From the psychological viewpoint it is absurd to say that we have the future before us and the past behind us, as though the future were visible to us and the past occluded. Quite the reverse is true. What our forebears have accomplished lies before us as their completed works; the house we see, the meadows and fields, the culture and political system are congealed expressions of the deeds of our fathers. The same is true of everything they have done, lived, or suffered; it lies before us as completed facts, and we could unroll their genesis individually as much as we want, just as in a motion picture. The present and the future are, on the contrary, still in process of coming and becoming.

h. *The verbal origin of the concept of time.* Among psychologists of language spatial images are considered to be more original than temporal images. This is correct to the extent that what *we Europeans* consider as time is a late achievement; as shown above, this notion is shot through with spatial images. We need not identify time in itself with this mixed product; linguistic expressions of real time are as original as those of space, at least in Hebrew. It is completely false that temporal adverbs and prepositions were in all languages—so far as etymology can be found —originally spatial expressions.[1] Even in Hebrew space and time are frequently expressed by the same adverbs and prepositions, but both concepts are usually founded upon action. Thus the fundamental meaning of the preposition *min*—severance or separation—gives rise to the spatial meaning *out of, away from, before,* and to the temporal meaning *since, from* (that time) *on.* The basic meaning of the preposition *'adh* is continuance or endurance, from which is derived the meaning *until, up to,* spatially as well as temporally. The verb *'aḥar* means hesitate, be behind, whence is derived *'aḥar* as an adverb 1, behind; 2, of time: after this, after that; as a preposition 1, of place: behind; 2, of time: after. In these cases, the adverbs and the prepositions are really verbal substantives.

Time can also be expressed by a verb. *shakham* (only in the *Hiph'il* in the Old Testament) means 'load on the backs of beasts of burden', something nomads do early in the morning; hence its derived meaning is 'rise up early, be active early'. The infinitive absolute (*hiph.*) appears at I Sam. 17.16, with the meaning 'early, in the morning'.

Psychologists of language as well as semanticists should be familiar with the idea that the Hebrew language, like Israelite thought in general,

[1] As maintained by Harriman, 'Semantics', *Encyclopaedia of Psychology*, p. 846, col. 2.

is dynamic through and through. As is well known, Hebrew words generally have a triliteral form in whose three consonants inhere the root meaning; by insertion of different vowels and by means of prefixes and suffixes a variety of words of different classes and a great number of different forms of single words can be constructed. As a general rule the verb stem is considered by etymologists to be the basic form, ample evidence of which is supplied by a look at any lexicon. Obviously, etymology is often difficult to establish; many verbs have been constructed from nouns, but the cases in which etymology can establish a verb stem as the root-form are so imposingly numerous that they can be cited as a proof for the verbal thinking of the Hebrews. Action, however, the content of the verb, has more to do with time than with space, a fact of which we have spoken sufficiently above.

i. *Endless time.* Our notion of eternity inherited from Plato (Section A above) is at base the same thing as the divine beyond (*Jenseits*), and is therefore rather more something spatial than something temporal. The Hebrew language has no word for the same notion; Hebrew equivalents for eternity are temporal to the extent that they do not signify things beyond but things pertaining to this life. Because our idea of eternity is religiously coloured, it is advisable to avoid this term when we want to translate the Hebrew equivalents into our language and to translate them by means of the notion of 'boundless time'.

The commonest word for boundless time is '*ôlam*; according to the most widespread and likeliest explanation the word is derived from '*alam* meaning 'hide, conceal'.[1] In the term '*ôlam* is contained a designation of time extending so far that it is lost to our sight and comprehension in darkness and invisibility. It is characteristic of the nature of this term that it can be used of hoary antiquity as well as of the unbounded future; thus, '*ôlam* is not an endlessly long time but simply a boundless time. When '*ôlam* refers to the past, it can mean eternity: . . . a great and powerful people; their like has never been from of old ('*ôlam*), nor will be again after them through the years of all generations (Joel 2.2). Wisdom says: Ages ago ('*ôlam*) I was set up, at the first, before the beginning of the earth (Prov. 8.23). Used of the future '*ôlam* can mean boundless time to come; the rainbow is to appear as a token of an everlasting covenant (*berîth* '*ôlam*) between God and the world (Gen. 9.16). Von Orelli maintains correctly, 'When Hebrew antiquity's ability to form the concept of boundless time is disputed, it is the result of a prejudice.'[2]

Even when '*ôlam* is used of God, it suggests only unbounded time and

[1] Von Orelli, *op. cit.*, p. 69. [2] *Ibid.*, p. 72.

does not refer to his being beyond time or to his transcendence, although the Hebrews used the expression that Jahveh was enthroned in heaven. For his transcendence other expressions had to be used:

Lord, thou hast been our dwelling place in all generations.
Before the mountains were brought forth,
  or ever thou hadst formed the earth and the world,
  from everlasting to everlasting thou art God (Ps. 90.1 f.).

Thy kingdom is an everlasting kingdom,
  and thy dominion endures throughout all generations (Ps. 145.13).

. . . I heard him swear by him (God) who lives for ever . . . (Dan. 12.7).

The Lord is the everlasting God,
  the Creator of the ends of the earth (Isa. 40.28).

Trust in the Lord for ever,
  for the Lord God
  is an everlasting rock (Isa. 26.4).

Since 'ôlam means only an unbounded time, in certain contexts it can encompass a period relatively short according to our objective way of thinking; thus a bondman is one who can never obtain his freedom: 'ebhedh 'ôlam (Deut. 15.17), or again he serves his master for ever: le'ôlam (Ex. 21.6; Lev. 25.46). King Achish believed that David would become to him 'ebhedh 'ôlam (I Sam. 27.12), which obviously means that he would serve him only for the rest of his life. Hannah tells her husband that she would bring the child Samuel after his weaning to Shiloh, in order that he might appear before the Lord and remain there 'adh 'ôlam, i.e. always (I Sam. 1.22). Bathsheba's wish 'May my lord King David live le'ôlam' (I Kings 1.31) means no more than life until a time now lost to sight.

Although in the Old Testament 'ôlam always means time which is boundless in a certain respect, nothing is said therein of the objective duration of astronomical time; it is always the concern of exegesis to ask in each case how far the author's gaze pursued time. The poet and even the prophet could speak of 'ôlam with greater freedom than others:

Behold, these are the wicked;
  always at ease, they increase in riches (Ps. 73.12).

The duration of the wicked ones' good fortune is short, viewed *objectively*, for they will come to a horrible end (vv. 17 ff.); but as long as they are able to triumph, they themselves believe that their good fortune will last for an unbounded time, and for the pious the delay is intolerably long. We, too, can say in such cases that a short time endures for an eternity.

Moreover, it is appropriate here to recall that *'ôlam*, like all time designations, is filled with a content. When *'ôlam* defines a psychical property, it can approach a definition of quality without losing its character as endless time; this is true when God's everlasting love (Jer. 31.3) is spoken of or his everlasting mercy (Isa. 54.8).

The Hebrew language knew no word that compassed more than *'ôlam*, but there is in the genius of Hebrew an impulse toward emphasis and repetition by way of synonym; hence *'ôlam* was emphasized in various ways. This tendency may have been helped also by the fact that this very frequently used word became threadbare. Already in the hymn of the Exodus (Ex. 15.18) we find the combination *le'ôlam wa'edh* used to express as strongly as possible Jahveh's eternal lordship: Jahveh is king for ever and ever; the LXX and Vulgate found in the second word a longer period going beyond eternity, which is pure nonsense. The expression *me'ôlam 'adh 'ôlam*, from eternity to eternity, demonstrates that the endlessness of time stretches backward as well as forward (Pss. 90.2; 103.17; Jer. 7.7; 25.5). In doxologies (I Chron. 29.10; Dan. 2.20) this expression leads easily to the erroneous idea that a succession of eternities is being spoken of; the same effect is produced by the plural form *'ôlamîm* which must have been chosen in ceremonial language to express the ineffable. The form is to be understood here and elsewhere as intensive plural.[1]

The other words for indicating endless time, *'adh* and *tamîdh*,[2] contribute nothing essentially new toward clarification of the idea and can, therefore, be omitted here.

If von Dobschütz is right in maintaining that the Israelites think temporally and the Greeks spatially, then the ἄπειρον of Anaximander corresponds to the Hebrew *'ôlam*. Anaximander called τὸ ἄπειρον the Infinite or more correctly the boundless, 'the undefined, eternal, and immutable first cause of all things whence they all arise and whither they return'.[3] Thus the Greeks mean to define by τὸ ἄπειρον the first cause of all *things*, and the Israelites by *'ôlam* mean to define the beginning and end of all *becoming* or *having become*: τὸ ἄπειρον is the spatially extended boundless, but *'ôlam* is the temporally extending unbounded. For the Greeks the content of the world was eminently spatial, for the Israelites it was principally temporal. The ordinary Hebrew designation

---

[1] Not 'plural of local extension' as Ges.-K., § 124b, thinks, working from our spatial conception of time.

[2] Von Orelli, *op, cit.*. pp. 86 ff.

[3] H. Schmidt, *Philosophisches Wörterbuch* (9th ed.), p. 32; G. Rudberg, *Ur Hellas liv*, pp. 21 ff.

for the universe is 'heaven and earth', *hashshamayim weha'arets*; but even these are thought of temporally since he knows their beginning (Creation) and their history (Gen. 2.4). Hence, it was very easy for a Jew, when in the Hellenistic age he had to find a Hebrew word for κόσμος, to translate it by *'ôlam*; in all the Old Testament writings, however, *'ôlam* has only a temporal meaning. A start toward the transition from the temporal sphere to the spatial sphere is offered by *ḥeledh*—duration of life, e.g. Ps. 39.6 where 'my life' is parallel to and synonymous with 'my days'; after a thorough examination von Orelli comes to the conclusion that *ḥeledh* does not represent time as something moving but signifies *duration*.[1] This term, which is incontestably temporal, did achieve the spatial meaning 'world': *yoshebhe ḥeledh*—inhabitants of the world (Ps. 49.1). It is more than likely that the spatial meaning of *ḥeledh* in this Psalm is to be traced to Hellenistic influence.

C. SPACE

1. *Form*

The question of space and time leads further to the question of form in general. Kant is undoubtedly right in maintaining that according to our way of thinking space and time are *forms* of intuition or *forms* of thought; that is to say, we distinguish between the content of space (or of time) and space (or time) in itself. For example, we can think of empty space and empty time; therefore, space and time must be, in some way or other, *forms*. It is not only true that the Hebrew language lacked words for space and time in our 'abstract' sense, but there is also lacking in Israelite thought the inner necessity to form such terms. The Hebrews simply think of the matter in an entirely different way.

We shall indicate this peculiarity in material objects of space; according to the Greek and general European viewpoint, an object consists of form and matter. If we could abstract the form of the object, formless matter would be left over.[2] We further think of the form of the object as its outline or contours. If we take no account of the empirical content in objects, there are left, according to Kant, empty forms which represent space intuitively; with the help of such pure forms (points, lines, triangles, etc.) geometry defines the properties of space. According to Kant, the given point of departure for all thinking is *sense experience*, and from that is abstracted the intuition of space which should possess even

---

[1] Von Orelli, *op. cit.*, p. 45.
[2] Matter without form is unthinkable; cf. the author's essay, 'Begrepet ordning', NTT, XLI (1940), 177 ff.

greater validity than the experience, because according to Kant's (erroneous) opinion the theorems of Euclidean geometry have clearly established validity. The logical necessity of geometry is founded upon the fact that geometric theorems do not stem from experience but only from simple intuition of space.[1]

The basis of Plato's thinking is the eternal or transcendent world of which our world of experience is only an image; this image is in itself beautiful and glorious, but the glory of the world is nothing compared to the glory of eternity. That in our world which most nearly approaches the beauty of the transcendent world is the beauty of geometry. (One has to be fascinated by geometry in order to be able to enter into Plato's experience and to understand him.) For Plato, then, geometry is more a sublime art than a serviceable, interesting science. This does not mean that he would detract from geometry's strict regularity (the true artist is convinced that even the most exalted art is subject to strict laws); the emphasis, however, does not lie in that direction. It is a matter of self-evident characteristics with which students of geometry have great difficulty but which do not bother the master because they have come to him in flesh and blood. Hence, for Plato geometry is a sensible image of invisible eternity. It belongs to the world of experience, to be sure, but it has laid aside its sensuousness as much as any visible object is able. Platonic eternity is therefore something in being, at rest, and (according to our way of thinking) spatial. Here is to be seen the similarity and the difference in the evaluation of pure form in Plato and in Kant. Sensible form is for both of them the greatest significance, but for Plato the form is a means of approaching and apprehending eternity, while for Kant the form is a means of experiencing and understanding the sensible world.

An analogous similarity and difference can be noticed in the way both thinkers assess the pure *thought*-forms; for both of them the thought-forms are of decisive significance. For Kant they are aprioristic and transcendental, that is to say they form the highest pinnacle attainable by human thought so far as it is concerned with the world of experience; as transcendental, the thought-forms do not belong to the world of experience but bear upon it only in and through experience.[2] According to Plato, the Ideas do not belong to the world of experience but to eternity, although originally experience does awaken in us a presentiment of them; when one thinks of the Ideas intuitively, one has union with eternity.

It is characteristic of the Hebrews that form was an indifferent matter

[1] Kant, *Critique of Pure Reason*, pp. 70 f.   [2] *Ibid.*, pp. 92 ff.

for them to the extent that they constructed no word for form or for its synonyms, like outline or contour. To be sure, they have a variety of words which can be translated 'configuration (*Gestalt*)', but none which signifies the *form* of the object. Israelites were interested in shape only as appearance or something inconclusively expressed: the *content* of the shape. The expression is inconclusive to the extent that it presupposes a distinction between form and content, a distinction that the Israelites did not make; to the extent that it is affirmed that the Israelites had interest at least in form, it is conclusive. *demuth* is image, model, pattern, and then shape, appearance. *tsûrah* is an infrequently used word (like the related *tsir*) and appears only twice: in Ezek. 43.11, it means the external appearance of the new Temple where it is involved with arrangements and proper use; in Ps. 49.14 where the text is corrupt, it means that the figure of the godless (is destined) for destruction (on the part?) of the underworld. *qetsebh* can mean cut or shape, as at I Kings 6.25, where it is a question of making two carved cherubim; the idea underlying the notion is, therefore, dynamic—the word is probably added at I Kings 7.37 from 6.25.[1] *temûnah* is used at Deut. 4.16, 23, 25; 5.8 of a human image of this appearance, thus of an idol. From the verb *ra'ah* is formed *mar'eh*—sight, appearance, also human appearance and its form (Gen. 24.16; 26.7; Isa. 53.2, etc.). At Isa. 53.2, *mar'eh* is synonymous with *to'ar*, another ordinary word for human appearance and characteristically also synonymous with *hadhar*—splendour, glory. As indicated in the previous chapter, the beauty of human appearance is not in the form of the body or parts of the body, but in the peculiar properties appearance betrays in various ways. Even *'ayin* can mean aspect, appearance, and form.

Consequently, the Hebrew language formed no specific expressions for designating the outline or contour of objects and did not even need them. We shall first of all try to feel with the Israelites how they could experience the world visually and still get along without the notion of outline, form, or contour. When we draw a tree-trunk, we first of all draw the outline with two vertical lines; we believe that we can even see the contour. We are really in error, however, for when we go up to the tree and go around it, we can see only bark and wood, but no kind of strokes, lines, or contours. Thus, these are only auxiliary lines which we introduce involuntarily into what we see in order to make a representation of the visual impression; form and shape in the sense of outline and con-

---

[1] A. Kamphausen, *Die Heilige Schrift des Alten Testaments*, ed. E. Kautzsch, I, 473, n.e.

tour, therefore, are in our drawings but not in reality. According to certain techniques we can suppress our natural tendency and see, draw, and paint the object without contours. This is precisely what the Israelites do by nature. They see objects as they are with their colour and shadow, experience their hardness and their temperature with their hands, but they do not see contours, and therefore they employ no words to express this notion. The significance of the outline and form of objects increases to the extent to which all perception is disregarded as the Greek ideal requires or as the Kantian ideal requires still more.

2. *The Boundary*

Perhaps the most important line in our conceptions is the boundary line; it separates two areas from one another or divides an area into two parts. It is characteristic of the boundary line, therefore, that it lies *between* two areas while itself having no breadth. This is especially clear in Latin: *finis* comes from *findo*—'split'; if a piece of wood is split into two parts and they are put back together, there is a boundary line between the two pieces, a line which takes up no space. The Hebrew idea of *gebhûl* is something different in principle; it never designates a mathematical line but a thing, frequently a mountain or mountain ridge which separates one area from another. Etymologically, *gebhûl* is related to *gebhal*—'mountain'. Stones and fences are boundaries that are set by men (Prov. 22.28; cf. 23.10). The sands are the boundary of the sea (Jer. 5.22), the sea is the boundary of the land (Num. 34.6). When sea, lake, or river are designated as boundaries, a part of the water belongs to the area being bounded; quite by accident we hear that Sihon, king of the Amorites, ruled over half of the river Arnon (Josh. 12.2). As the Israelites established natural time-units by means of their ends and boundaries, they did the same things with the natural units of area: the lands, the isles, the world.[1] All the borders of Egypt signifies the whole land of Egypt (Ex. 10.14); all the borders of Israel means the whole land of Israel (I Kings 1.3). The borders of darkness is the area of darkness (Job 38.20); the 'boundary round about the people of Judah' means 'their entire land' (Josh. 15.12); the field of Ephron 'throughout its whole area' means 'within its borders on every side' (Gen. 23.17); when Saul had fallen, the Philistines sent messengers 'round about', that is in every direction (I Sam. 31.9). *sabhîbh*—round about, is synonymous with 'border'

---

[1] The fact that *fines* can also mean 'land' in Latin need not lead to the false conclusion that the Romans had therefore the same concept of boundary as the Hebrews. When *fines* means 'land' in Latin, the word is used metonymously: boundary line in place of the land enclosed by the boundary.

for the word really means 'a circle'. When the Israelites have established the circle, the whole field is thus defined. It is not hard to understand that *'i* (pl. *'iyyîm*), which properly means 'coastlands', also signifies the notion 'island', for when the coasts are named, the land that lies inside them is included with them; the homeland of the Philistines is *'i kaphtôr* (Jer. 47.4), the island of Caphtor, Crete or Carpathus.[1]

When an Israelite wants to describe the situation in the whole land, he needs to mention only the circumstances in the farthest outlying regions:

> They lift up their voices, they sing for joy;
>   over the majesty of the Lord they shout from the west.
> Therefore in the east give glory to the Lord;
>   in the coastlands of the sea,
>   to the name of the Lord,
>   the God of Israel,
> From the ends of the earth we hear songs of praise,
>   of glory to the Righteous One (Isa. 24.14 ff.; cf. Job 37.3; 38.13).

Deutero-Isaiah is fond of the expression *'iyyîm* (40.15; 41.1, 5; 42.4, 10, 12; 49.1; 51.5); we translate it by 'isles', 'coasts', or 'shores', but we obviously do not plumb its deepest meaning for, since according to the Israelite understanding the world-continent was surrounded by water,[2] the continent that lies between is included in the mention of the coasts, *'iyyîm* should therefore be translated by 'world' or some similar expression:

> He will not fail or be discouraged
>   till he has established justice in the earth;
> And the *whole world* waits for his law (Isa. 42.4).

No greater liberty is taken by translating *'iyyîm* as 'world' than by translating *gebhûl* as 'land'. Mowinckel translates *'iyyîm* as a 'circle of coasts' (Isa. 40.15) and means thus to designate the whole world. In Isa. 41.5, *'iyyîm* stands parallel with *qetsoth ha'arets*—'the ends of the earth', that is the earth itself; in 40.28, this is the only possible translation, for Jahveh is not the creator of the ends of the earth but of the whole earth. *qetsoth* is the plural of *qatseh*; the ordinary word for 'end' is *qatseh*. At another place *miqtseh ha'arets* designates the whole circuit of the earth:

> Sing to the Lord a new song,
>   his praise from the ends of the earth! (Isa. 42.10)

qatseh can be combined with *gebhûl* to designate the uttermost part of a boundary area (Gen. 47.21; Num. 20.16; 22.16); in such cases and in

---

[1] M.M.M. *in loc.*   [2] Mowinckel (M.M.M.) on Deut. 4.18.

similar ones, we can translate *gebhûl* by 'border' (borderline). The Hebrew concept is something that is, however, different in principle; it designates a part of an area or a thing to which it belongs. It may be that this part is only the rim of it, like the rim of the altar (Ezek. 43.13, 17, 20).

It is of decisive importance that *gebhûl* together with its synonyms never means a dividing line between two areas, and thus, in principle, it is not the same as our term boundary. This is no shortcoming in the language and conceptual world of the Hebrews, for the boundary line is not a datum of nature or of the physical world. It is a pure product of our (European) mind, an imaginary line that *we* have necessarily in order to govern the world practically and theoretically from our presuppositions. With the help of boundary lines we make representations of our visual perceptions and arrange them in an orderly way; with the aid of abstract boundary lines we also make abstract representations which we can also define (definition of *fines*) and compare with one another. It is in such acts as these that Greek, Indo-European logical thinking consists.

We are so conscious of the advantages of this way of thinking that we naïvely assume that it is the only way to think clearly and profoundly; we are not generally aware of the disadvantages of this way of thinking, and only keen minds like Kant's have generally become cognizant of them. The disadvantages are related to the fact that the boundary is an auxiliary line that we, so to speak, draw into the picture. An auxiliary line ought to be erased after its job is done, that is, one should not found in reality something of which no account can or should be taken ultimately in representing and in thinking. These things, however, are least possible of accomplishment. The Israelites have to do without the advantages of our way of thinking, but they are also exempt from its disadvantages.

3. *The Boundless or the Infinite*

We shall try to illustrate these properties and distinctions by starting from the concept of a boundless quantity. The concept is, first of all, impossible for us to form since the fact that it is bounded is already inherent for us in the notion 'quantity'. The notion 'boundless quantity' contains for the European, therefore, a *contradictio in adjecto*. The two most important boundless quantities that we know are boundless time (eternity) and boundless space (the universe); we have further abstracted both of these quantities in the idea of infinity, an idea that has occupied European thinkers far too much. The one who has reflected most basically upon this idea is certainly Immanuel Kant;[1] he experienced most pain-fully the antinomies contained in the notion of infinity.[2] These antino-mies led him to his doctrine of the 'thing in itself' (*Ding an sich*) which is to be distinguished sharply from the thing as an empirical phenomenon. This is no solution of the problem, however, but only a dismissal of the problem of infinity; according to Kant all experience is finite, and so infinity does not belong within the range of our experience.[3]

Other philosophers and mathematicians like Newton, Trendelenburg, and Herman Cohen explain infinity by means of motion; an infinitely large quantity can be viewed as one that is constantly increasing, and an infinitely small one as one in the process of disappearing. This is quite correct; yet this is no help to us, for, as we have shown earlier, motion is as inexplicable as infinity. As Descartes and Herman Cohen point out, motion needs to be explained with the aid of the concept of infinity;[4] infinity and motion are conceptual correlatives, i.e. one concept is explained in terms of the other.

There is a simple solution to the problem if we take as our point of departure the concept that is difficult for us; thus we could define the static as zero motion (motion = o) and explain the finite as a part of the infinite (or better: of the boundless). The boundless may very well be experienced and even thought about as follows: *Every* visual perception is at its sharpest and then diminishes in clarity in all directions until it ends in imperceptibility. There is to be found no trace of a boundary surrounding the field of vision like a circle; the boundless is not the diffi-cult, problematic notion but the natural, the primary, and the always newly given thing. The boundaries which have been formed by us and intrude into the perceptions can be dispensed with, as the Semites prove.

Eivind Berggrav has tried to replace the concept of infinity or bound-lessness with the term 'boundary-exceeding tendency' (*grenzüber-schreitende Tendenz*);[5] this new term is only a new and psychologically very good name for the infinity impulse, for infinity can be defined as a quantity growing beyond every finite quantity and so beyond every

---

[1] Closer observation reveals that Infinity and its problems are the main theme in the division of the *Critique of Pure Reason* entitled 'The Transcendental Dialectic', occupy-ing (in the German edition) 384 out of 884 pages.
[2] Kant, *Critique of Pure Reason*, pp. 299 f.
[3] *Ibid.*, pp. 448 f. Max Mueller says very well: 'The Infinite is hidden from the senses, it is denied by Reason, but it is perceived by Faith.' *Lectures on the Science of Language*, *II*, p. 598.
[4] Kurt Geisler, *Die Grundzüge und das Wesen des Unendlichen in der Mathematik und Philosophie*, pp. 297 ff.
[5] Eivind Berggrav, *Der Durchbruch der Religion im menschlichen Seelenleben*. The title of this book in the Norsk, *Religionens terskel*, means 'The Threshold of Religion'.

boundary. Yet the peculiarity of European man is not that he exceeds, but, as we have shown, that he *forms* boundaries. In order to form a boundary in general, he must, in his imagination, already have been 'on the other side', since a boundary is a dividing line between two areas or, what amounts to the same thing, a line separating an area into two parts. When a man sets himself boundaries, he sets problems for himself which he can solve in terms of his strength and time; 'by bounding, he shows himself master'. Berggrav is doubtlessly right in saying that a religious man will not come to rest within boundaries set by himself or by another man; involuntarily he aspires beyond them. The *born* religious man lives in the infinite and eternal world as his home (Phil. 3.20). It is no accident, therefore, that the Semites who can live without boundaries have been responsible for three world-religions; for them infinity or boundlessness is no problem.

Excursus : Biblical Faithfulness to Reality

Oscar Cullmann has subjected the biblical conception of time to a fundamental analysis;[1] while the amplification of his basic idea is, without doubt, an accomplishment of lasting value, his representation of the biblical conception of time is incomplete and misleading. Had he corrected it, his basic idea would have been even clearer and more convincing. His basic idea is this: According to the New Testament God has revealed himself neither in supra-temporal ideas nor in an eschatological (literally, end-time) event, but exhaustively and finally in the history (*Geschichte*) of Jesus Christ. The New Testament also draws the conclusion that God reveals himself *only* in history, since it draws a line from Jesus Christ backward through history to the Creation and forward from Jesus Christ to the eschaton. On this 'straight line of an ordinary process in time God here reveals himself, and from that line he controls not only the whole of history, but also that which happens in nature'.[2] This historical redemptive and revelatory line he calls the Christ-line;[3] Jesus Christ's historical act of redemption is thus the middle or the centre of this line.[4] The adequate symbol of the Christ-line is 'our manner of reckoning time, which numbers the year of Christ's birth as the year 1 and lets the previous period move with steadily *decreasing* numbers down to this year, while the subsequent period proceeds with steadily *increasing* numbers from this starting year'.[5]

What Cullmann apparently means to emphasize is that according to

---

[1] O. Cullmann, *Christ and Time*, trans. F. V. Filson.   [2] *Ibid*., p. 23.
[3] *Ibid*., pp. 107 ff.   [4] *Ibid*., pp. 121–76.   [5] *Ibid*., p. 118.

the Bible God has revealed himself and will reveal himself in actuality—
and indeed especially in the historical person of Jesus of Nazareth. For
this reason we believe that Cullmann's intention becomes legitimate if we
expand his argument to say that the New Testament underscores not
only the decisive significance of the time of Christ but also that of his
spatial location. He was born in Bethlehem of Judea (Matt. 2.4 ff.),
grew up in Nazareth (Matt. 2.23; John 1.45; cf. Luke 4.16 ff.), taught in
Galilee (Matt. 3.13 ff.). He had to die in Jerusalem since it was not possible
for a prophet to die outside Jerusalem (Luke 13.33). He lived in the land
of the Jews from whom salvation comes (John 4.22, etc.). As important
as it is to underscore that the Word, the Logos, is he through whom God
acts, still the divine *being* of the Logos may not be forgotten. In the
beginning *was* the Word (John 1.1, 2, 4); in the Logos become flesh the
disciples *saw* the divine glory (v. 14), indeed God himself (1.18; 14.19).
In Jesus Christ God is not only audible but also *visible* and tangible
(I John 1.1). In the revelation of God in Christ there is not only a divine
Now but also a divine *Here*; together they form the hard reality. It is
one-sided to designate the revelation of God only as historical (*geschicht-
lich*); just as characteristic of God's revelation in Christ is that it unfolded
in the material world spatially, visibly, and palpably, even though for
obvious reasons the last moment recedes sharply among the Hebraically
thinking disciples. Yet even in the New Testament this viewpoint is
sufficiently attested by the Johannine literature.

As a result of the above arguments, Cullmann is wrong if he thinks
that the difference between the biblical and Greek conceptions of time
consists in the fact that the biblical as linear and the Greek cyclic, and that,
for that reason, the Greek has to experience 'the fact that man is bound
to time . . . as an enslavement, as a curse.'[1] As we said above, our grammatical tense- or time-conception is always what Cullmann designates
by the misleading expression *linear,* while objective, astronomical time
is always cyclic. The element of truth in this view lies in the fact that
the Bible knows of one *goal* of history; Jesus signifies the embodiment
of the Old Testament revelation and of the Messianic hope; and ultimately the return of Christ and the coming of the Kingdom of God is
the final goal (*telos*). The quality of pressing toward a goal, characteristic
of biblical time, is given of itself if one recalls that time never knows of
a 'backwards' but only of a 'forward'.

If what Cullmann cites from von Dobschütz and agrees with is correct,
'the Greek conception of blessedness is . . . spatial . . . determined by

[1] *Ibid.* p. 52.

the contrast between this world and the timeless Beyond',[1] then the Hebraically conditioned conception of the revelation of God in *time* corresponds to a Greek-conditioned conception of the revelation of the invisible God of the timeless Beyond in the *visible* and *palpable* '*this world*', as it is said, 'That . . . which we have seen with our eyes, which we have looked upon and touched with our hands, concerning the word of life' (I John 1.1.) From this viewpoint Logos is not God in his revelatory *action*[2] but the likeness or image of the invisible God (Col. 1.15; II Cor. 4.4; Heb. 1.3). The Greek's flight from this wretched world into the blessed timeless Beyond corresponds to the Jewish flight from time's necessity into the hope of a glorious future coming in the final age. Over against both stands the Christian proclamation of God's revelation in the *reality* of the present world and of time, that is to say, the proclamation concerning Jesus of Nazareth.

Eschatology and belief in the timeless Beyond are not two forms of the Christian hope that are mutually exclusive, but they are equally necessary thought-forms enjoying equal privileges and complementing one another. The Bible knows not only of a glory that is coming but also of a glory that belongs to the timeless Beyond. The cessation of all conflict and of all history, when God is everything in the universe and in all (I Cor. 15.28), corresponds to the becoming visible of the invisible world of the New Jerusalem which John saw in the Spirit. We cannot go further into the matter of how Hebrew and Greek thinking cross in the New Testament and still more in the history of dogma; that would demand an inquiry of its own.

D. QUANTITY AND NUMBER: SPATIALLY QUANTITATIVE AND DYNAMICALLY QUALITATIVE QUANTITIES

Ernst Cassirer has penetratingly and brilliantly examined the linguistic development of the concept of number;[3] yet from the beginning he bars the way to full understanding of peoples' conception of quantity because he has in view only arithmetical quantity, number. Especially if the mathematical ideas of the Greeks are to be comprehended, geometry must be brought into the inquiry. Because space perception was the given thought-form of the Greeks and because the visible form of things occupied their attention, geometry had to become for them the most important branch of mathematics. The Greeks, including Euclid (Books 7–11),

[1] *Ibid.*   [2] *Ibid.*, p. 24.   [3] *The Philosophy of Symbolic Forms*, I, 226–49.

thought geometrically even when they dealt with numbers. The square afforded a visual representation of the second power and the cube of the third; they knew square numbers (4, 9, 16 . . .) and cubic numbers (8, 27, 64 . . .) and illustrated geometrically such arithmetic problems as irrational quantities. Hence for the Greeks the concept *large, quantity* (largeness) was pre-eminently a spatial idea.

The Israelites developed no mathematical science; it is interesting, however, to emphasize that among the neighbouring Phoenicians, who were related to them, arithmetic flourished and that among the Babylonians algebra achieved a stage never reached in Greece, a stage achieved only at the beginning of the more recent history of our own mathematics. From all that can be gathered from ancient texts, the development of a proper mathematics is connected with the semitizing of Babylonia. The different talents of Greek and Semite become apparent even in mathematics; while the Greeks solve algebraic problems geometrically, the Babylonians inversely reduce geometric problems to algebraic formulae.[1]

The Hebrew language has no expressions for the simplest geometric figures such as the triangle, quadrilateral, or square, not for the corresponding adjectives. The passive participles *rabhûaʿ* and *merubbaʿ*, formed from the verb stem *rbʿ*, we translate as *four-cornered*, but they have nothing whatever to do with angles and visual representations. They mean simply what has been made into a quadruple quantity. The word *meḥûghah* is translated as 'compass' (Isa. 44.13), but what is meant is not a circular form but an artisan's tool. The other words, too, which we can frequently translate as 'circle', refer to concrete things: *kikkar*— environs, a round object made of bread or lead, measure of weight, talent; *pelekh*—district round about, spindle; *ṣôdh*—circle of men, assembly.

Obviously the Israelites know things that are spatially large such as the depth of the sea (Gen. 7.11), a great space in between (I Sam. 26.13), a large territory (Amos 6.2), or a great journey (I Kings 19.7). The adjective used in each of these cases is *rabh*, derived from the verb *rabhabh* which ordinarily means 'be or become many'; the principal meaning of *rabh* is generally 'many, numerous'. The fundamental meaning of *rabhabh* is to 'become thick or dense'. Another word for great, *rabhah*—be or become many, has the precise meaning 'to grow'. A third word for great is *gadhol*; Nineveh was a great city (Jonah 1.2). This word comes from

[1] Edmund Hoppe, *Mathematik und Astronomie im klassischen Altertum*, p. 8; O. Neugebauer, *Vorlesungen über die Geschichte der antiken mathematischen Wissenschaften* (Berlin, 1934), pp. 2 f., 172, 206, 212.

gadhal—become great, grow up. Other words having a similar meaning include *'addîr* from *'adhar*—be glorious; *kabbîr* from *kabhar*—become great or many (originally meaning to plait or weave). Small, *me'aṭ*, is related to the Assyrian verb, *maṭu*—diminish;[1] *qaṭon*, small, comes from *qaṭan*—be or become small or less, etc. The concept of greatness has, therefore, arisen in the Old Testament not by way of a spatial mode of viewing things but through dynamic conceptions and actions.

The 'more' of the comparative degree is expressed by the preposition *min*—from, away from; thus Saul was a head taller than (tall away from) the entire people, i.e., he towered over all the others.[2] The image is thus dynamic, but like us, the Greeks conceive visually and spatially the concept 'greater': e.g. we put two people alongside one another and discover that one is much larger than the other.

As Cassirer correctly maintains, the most important number for an understanding of the concept of number is the number 2; some primitive people, like the Bushmen and the aborigines of Victoria, have developed no numerical words beyond two, while among others numerical words exist for only 1, 2 and 3. Cassirer thinks that he can establish as a fact that the act of numbering has originally to do with the conception of the I, thou, and he. A common etymological root for the expressions *you* (*thou*) and *two* appears to have been established especially for the Indo-European languages.[3] It is now very interesting to be able to establish that the Hebrew expression for *two* has nothing at all to do with *thou*, or with any other person; nor is there behind it any other perception of visible objects such as two eyes, two ears, two fingers, etc. *shenayim* comes from the verb *shanah*—double, repeat, do for the second time. Thus the Hebrews form the concept of number not as we do through visual perception but through frequent repetition of the same motion; naturally only the movements of the members of the human body are taken into account. The idea of 'times' in enumeration is expressed in Hebrew by *pa'am*—pace or step, *reghel*—foot or tread, *yadh*—hand, 'units which are adapted to being multiplied to plurality by identical *repetition*, i.e. to form a number', as von Orelli already saw.[4] Number or quantitative variety is thus not something spatial and quantitative but dynamic and qualitative. The twice-done movement is a duplicate, the thrice-done a

---

[1] The meanings are drawn from F. Buhl, *Wilhelm Gesenius' hebräisches und aramäisches Handwörterbuch über das Alte Testament*, 16th ed.

[2] Ges.-K., § 133b.

[3] E. Cassirer, *The Philosophy of Symbolic Forms*, I, 244; cf. the references made by Cassirer at this point.

[4] Von Orelli, *op. cit.*, p. 51, n. 3; italics my own.

triplicate, etc. We, too, are familiar with such units or repetition and designate them as rhythms; a rhythm is a definite number or unit of repetitions. We perceive immediately that rhythms, e.g. verse rhythms, are distinguished qualitatively by different lengths. The number seven is, therefore, a rhythm of actions or natural events, such as days, repeated seven times. Numbers are distinguished qualitatively as rhythms, each with its own peculiarity.

This interpretation is confirmed by the peculiar form and syntax of the Hebrews numbers two to ten; in origin they are abstract substantives meaning two-ness, three-ness, etc., and are combined as such with the pertinent substantive.[1] If we disregard the possibility that the Israelites were particularly adept at abstract thinking, there remains only the hypothesis that the smallest and basic numbers were thought of as qualitatively different totalities.[2] Even the words for the larger numerical units were conceived and employed as expressions of different qualities:

> Saul has slain his thousands
> And David his ten thousands (I Sam. 18.7).

The qualitative conception of numbers is not something peculiar to the Hebrews but must be considered as a possibility which is psychologically natural to man, as Cassirer observes:

Even where actual counting has not progressed beyond the first meagre beginnings, the differentiation of such groups can be highly developed —for this requires only that each specific group be recognized by some general qualitative characteristic, and not that the group itself be articulated and quantitatively defined as a 'sum of units'. The Abipones, whose faculty of counting was only partially developed, are reported to have been extremely expert at distinguishing concrete groups. If a single member of the large packs of dogs which they took with them on hunting expeditions were lacking, it was noticed at once, and likewise the owner of a herd of four to five hundred cattle could recognize even at a distance whether any were missing and which ones. Here individual groups are recognized and differentiated by some individual characteristic: in so far as one can speak of 'number', it appears not in the form of a specified measured magnitude, but as a kind of concrete *numerical gestalt*, an intuitive quality adhering to a totally unarticulated general impression of quantity.[3]

---

[1] Ges.-K., § 134a.

[2] From there it was but a step further to the conception of holy numbers.

[3] *Op. cit.*, pp. 232 f.; cf. Max Wertheimer, 'Das Denken der Naturvölker', *Zeitschrift für Psychologie*, LX (1912), 321 ff. It would be more correct here to speak of numerical *content*; it should be clear that primitive peoples, whose ability at abstraction is poorly developed but whose memory has not been weakened, remember their possessions and especially their domestic animals in a way similar to that in which we recall our friends

We can elucidate the intrinsic coherence between 'sum of units' and quantity as quality by an illustration from physics. Three candles, each with a short wick, are burning before us; we light a new candle with a wick of such length that the light from it is just as intense as that from the other three candles. If we disregard the visual conception and concentrate our attention upon the intensity of light, the light from the larger wick is identical with that from the three smaller ones; the triple quantity and the corresponding intensity have the same net effect. For men accustomed to notice the qualitative peculiarities of things, it would be natural to use the same grammatical form for quantity and intensity. This is just the case in Hebrew; the Hebrew endings *-îm* (masculine) and *-ôth* (feminine) designate plurality as well as intensity. The most important intensive forms are as follows:[1]

1. The *surface*-plural for designating local extension, *shamayim*—'heaven', *mayim*—'water':
2. The *abstract* plurals
a. For summing up the conditions inherent in the idea of the stem: *hayyîm*—'life'; *sanwerim*—'blindness';
b. For intensifying the characteristics inherent in the stem (amplificatory plural) :*'ônîm*—'might', *'emûnîm*—'faithfulness', *de'îm (de'ôth)*-'thorough knowledge', *ye'orîm*—'great river';
c. For summing up the several parts of an action: *ḥanuṭîm*—'the embalming', *kippurîm*—'atonement';
3. The plural of excellence or majesty (which perhaps are to be construed rather as abstract plurals): *'elohîm*—'god-head, God', *'adhonîm*—'lord', *be'alîm*—'the owner (lord)'.

After what has been detailed above we should perhaps come nearer to the Hebrew way of thinking if in our analysis of the meanings of the endings *-îm* and *-ôth* we took the intensive as our point of departure. The Hebrew plural should then preferably be designated as intensive. That the 'plural' was felt by the Hebrews as a kind of intensity is betrayed by the repetition of a word whereby we, and particularly the Hebrews, evoke the feeling of intensity (cf. II Kings 25.15) to convey the notion 'each, every': *yôm yôm*—'every day', *shanah shanah*—'year by year'.[2] The notion

and relatives who are certainly not numbers and figures to us but individuals. There is no individual characteristic inhering in the *totality* of the animals, but there is a characteristic which belongs to each single animal, and these peoples' memories are so unimpaired that they can recall all these characteristics and from far off can see which animals are missing. Strictly speaking there is no number here nor a numerical *gestalt*, but only its primitive first stage. From this standpoint, it is also easy to understand why, when, and how number must arise, namely as an abstraction of individualities when life becomes so rich that the memory can no longer maintain simultaneously the individual characteristics.

[1] Ges.-K., § 124.   [2] Ges.-K., § 123c.

every includes for us the conception of a complete collection of the individual instances of a particular kind; this word is therefore in the plural. The ordinary Hebrew word for the corresponding idea (*kol*) is a substantive which means 'sum total' or 'totality' and never appears in the plural. The sum total of a kind or class is no multiplication of individual instances, as we most naturally conceive the relation. Israelite thinking goes in the opposite direction; the sum total is the given and the individual person or thing is the derived notion. *Mo'abh* is the people, the genus of Moabites; *mo'abhi*—Moabite is a particular instance of the genus of Moabites. Even the Hebrew superlative is an intensive or qualitative form which is expressed simply by means of the definite article.[1] We can express ourselves similarly. No one is ever in doubt of the fact that we have superlatives in mind when we say, Shakespeare is *the* English poet', or 'God is not only good, he is *the* Good'.

E. HISTORY AND NATURE

1. *Historical understanding among Greeks and Israelites*

When we examine the way in which the feeling for history developed among the Greeks and among the Israelites, we are immediately confronted with a riddle. On the one hand it is maintained that the Greeks and only the Greeks understood what history is; on the other hand, it is maintained with equal vigour that the Israelites and only the Israelites developed a historical sense. The former viewpoint is represented both by scholars of history and by writers of history. A representative of this position is the famous German expert in antiquities, Wilamovitz.[2] According to his interpretation, Herodotus properly bears the distinction he has borne since ancient times, 'the father of history'. At his side stands the younger and even more significant historian, Thucydides. Wilamovitz's judgment is categorical: 'All our historical writing rests on foundations laid by the Greeks as absolutely as does all our natural science.'[3] To prove this he cast his eye over the ancient world from India to the west. In the Old Testament and among the Arabs after Mohammed he finds isolated historical descriptions of exceptional value, as in the stories of Abimelech (Judges 9), of David, and of Ahab (I Kings 16.29—22.40). Yet the Semites lack precisely that quality whereby the Greeks made historical writing into a conscious art: 'they have historical writing,

---

[1] Ges.-K., § 133g.
[2] Ulrich von Wilamowitz-Moellendorff, *Greek Historical Writing and Apollo*, pp. 3–26.
[3] *Ibid.*, p. 5.

but they have no historian.'[1] The judgment of the famous English historian, Lord Macaulay, is just as categorical; in his diary under the date of 27th February 1835, he wrote: 'This day I finished Thucydides. He is the greatest historian that ever lived.'[2] Max Pohlenz[3] and Werner Jaeger[4] make similar judgments.

On the opposite side stand the philosophers of history, the historians of ideas, and the theologians among whom we may name Rickert, Windelband, Simmel, Skard, Spengler, Mowinckel and Reinhold Niebuhr. Rickert finds that the unique, that which occurs only once, is the proper category for history, while the natural sciences disregard differences and inquire only into what is repeated again and again without change. It is thus a mental impoverishment when historical science, too, is made into a kind of natural science; the problem appropriate to history, the new in history, the unique, origin and growth, all disappear in such a case. Even nature changes; it is not precisely the same this year as it was last and will not again in the future appear exactly the same. The temporality of the world with reference to being, however, comprises a great problem, one of the most difficult and most insoluble of those problems we meet at the ultimate boundary of our thinking about the world. Becoming must have its ground in being; then either the same thing is always happening, or else becoming is something other than previous being. The former is the scientific-mechanical notion founded upon the law of the conservation of energy, in consequence of which nothing new ever happens; the latter is the typically religious conception.[5] We should also like to permit a modern theologian to express himself; Reinhold Niebuhr writes, 'The classical culture, elaborated by Plato, Aristotle and the Stoics, is a western and intellectual version of a universal type of ahistorical spirituality.'[6]

It is obvious that the two groups are talking about different things since they see history from different viewpoints. It is thus necessary to clarify the concepts in order to be clear as to what each group means when it speaks of history. For the writer of history, History is past events seen in their connexion as a totality; the task of the historical scholar is,

[1] *Ibid.*, p. 6.

[2] G. O. Trevelyan, *The Life and Letters of Lord Macaulay* (London: Longmans [1876]), I, p. 467.

[3] Max Pohlenz, *Der hellenische Mensch*, pp. 190 ff., 215 ff.

[4] W. Jaeger, *Paideia*, I, 379 ff.

[5] Heinrich Rickert, *Die Grenzen der naturwissenschaftlichen Begriffsbildung: Eine logische Einleitung in die historischen Wissenschaften*, pp. 441 ff.

[6] Reinhold Niebuhr, *Faith and History: A Comparison of Christian and Modern Views of History* (New York: Scribner's, 1949), pp. 16 f.

first of all, to discover and present what actually took place and then, when possible, to explain these historical facts as the effects of previous causes and circumstances. As it can be seen, the historian avoids the difficult problem of becoming which was posed by Rickert because, on principle, he concerns himself only with facts and attempts to explain them only *en masse* since they can be explained from other historical facts. He is conscious of the fact that his explanations are never exact and complete, and so he needs to have nothing to do with the philosophical problem of history. Philosophers and theologians, on the other hand, observe historical events as intentional, consciously purposeful, human actions which are in full swing and are developing. When the action is concluded, or when it is observed as a completed fact, there is no longer any action; it is gone, it is dead.

Now we can put the two conceptions opposite one another and allow each to illuminate the other. The one thinks causally and consequently in terms of natural science; the other thinks finally or teleologically. The one puts itself outside the events and looks backwards; the other puts itself into the events and thinks itself 'into' the psychic life of the man involved and how they directed themselves forward in thought and will. The one concerns itself with the past, the other with the present and future. It cannot be said that the one way of observing is more correct than the other; both are possible and necessary, and each in its own field works out best; causal thinking in science, final or teleological thinking in ethics and religion. The former is Greek, and the latter is Israelite. The Greeks have given to the world the science of history; the Israelites gave to the world historical religion. In contrast to all their neighbours, both peoples knew what history is; this is no consequence of their mental giftedness, however, for there is another reason. Through mighty events both peoples experienced what history is, and by the investment of their lives they made history. The peculiar mental capacity of each of the two peoples comes to the fore in the way in which they experience history and express it. For both peoples history was a source of present and future knowledge. Thucydides wrote his history because what happened would, according to human ways, surely happen again in the future in the same or a similar way. This was conceived in a genuinely Greek way, for history is an eternal repetition; nothing new happens under the sun. Even in the stream of eternally changing events the Greeks sought the unalterable, the regular occurrence. Thus they employed the same method with regard to history as with regard to nature because history was a piece of nature. For this reason their mental life can justifiably be called non-historical.

If God is to be found, he must be sought in the unalterable, in mental being, in the Ideas.

God revealed himself to the Israelites in history and not in Ideas; he revealed himself when he acted and created. His being was not learned through propositions but known in actions. The majority of Old Testament books are historical, and those that are not (Song of Solomon, Proverbs, Job, Ecclesiastes, for example) have concrete human life as their subject; they are not systematic presentations. History is a movement toward a goal which is set by God; with his promise or his blessing he gets the movement under way, supervises it, and actively intervenes when he finds it necessary. The people's past, present, and future is a continuous whole where everything lives. Forefathers and those who are now living are a unity; what God did to the Patriarchs, he did to us: the Lord brought you (us) out of Egypt (Ex. 13.9, 16).[1] Analogous to the life of an individual man, the people's life is experienced as a whole; as in individual lives past events and deeds are effective and vital in the present, so for the Hebrews was this true in the nation's life. The nation is a person; if we bear this constantly in mind, it is not difficult to understand and participate in the Hebrew conception of history. We also mention again what was said above (B, 2) about the Israelite conception of time. Here it should be particularly emphasized that history leads to a goal, as all actions that are valuable in a religious-ethical way are consciously pursuing a goal. If God reveals himself to the nation Israel and to humanity in religious-moral actions through which he leads them consciously toward a purpose, the life of humanity must have a final great end in which God's highest thoughts and purposes are to be worked out. Hence, in the framework of Hebrew piety eschatology is just as necessary a conclusion as immutable eternity is for the Greeks who think religiously.

It now becomes clear how necessary it is to keep the two conceptions separate and distinct; if they are mixed, both are corrupted. In modern times this has happened twice: in Hegelianism and in Evolutionism, i.e. the modern belief in progress promulgated as a science. The flaw is the same in both systems: historians will carry out their enterprise as a science, but they will not be satisfied with the historical facts of the past and understand them, as well as possible, as causal effects of earlier events; instead, they suppose that they can construct scientifically a favourable future as the goal of past historical facts.

[1] Ludwig Köhler, *Hebrew Man*, pp. 139 ff.

2. The Proclamation of Creation in the Old Testament and the Doctrine of Creation in Plato

In the Old Testament, the creation of the world is a historical event; thus it does not belong to any sort of a (natural) scientific category. It represents no primitive explanation of the world (i.e., cosmogony); it is the beginning of history. Theologians have long seen that the Jahvist's creation story (Genesis 2) represents the beginning of his historical account. In most recent times, Old Testament scholars have perceived that the Priestly writer's account of creation serves the same purpose: 'The priestly code, together with the laws which are to be reckoned with it, is a great presentation of history. It begins with the creation, and runs through the revelation to Abraham to the revelation to Moses, and the proclamation of the law of God by Moses. The remainder is the fulfilment of the promise to Abraham, the taking of the promised land'.[1] The idea that God created the world became known only in later times; it is not an axiom of the Old Testament but a conclusion drawn from it. The creation of the world by God, in the Old Testament, is not an absolute fact important in itself; rather, creation is thought of as the inauguration of history.[2] If we would understand the biblical faith in creation, we must discover the centre of the Old Testament revelation out of which the belief in creation arose as its final conclusion. That centre is God's mighty and merciful leading of the people out of Egypt through Moses, particularly the miraculous delivery of the people at the Red Sea. Although these events observed from the point of view of world history might be quite insignificant, through them Israel experienced Jahveh's unlimited power over the might of the Egyptians as well as over nature, and they experienced it so trenchantly and convincingly that this event became the starting point, source and foundation of all later religious faith in Israel. Through his power and goodness Jahveh changed the hopeless situation of his people unexpectedly and, in human terms, inconceivably into a favourable one. It was therefore a creative act. For Israel the supreme actions of Jahveh were always of the same sort: almighty grace for the obedient and wrath for his enemies. Originally Jahveh had to do only with Israel, but later the horizon extended; Jahveh's power then extended over neighbouring peoples, over the great nations, over humanity and over nature, from the time of Moses, from the time of Abraham, from the beginning, and on back into eternity. Religious

[1] *Ibid.*, pp. 143 f.
[2] Ludwig Köhler, *Old Testament Theology*, pp. 85 ff.

universalism and belief in creation are thus correlates both of which come to full expression simultaneously in Deutero-Isaiah. In this work, for that reason, we can also best study what conceptions are connected with Israelite belief in creation. The creator has unconditioned power over nature (40.12), over the heavens (40.22), over the host of heaven (40.26), over the nations (40.15, 17), over the princes and rulers of the earth (40.23 f.), over the gods of the heathen (40.18 ff.); the transformation of the desert into a fruitful field is Jahveh's creative work (41.20), and the same work, to be sure with mention also of the negative side, is viewed as Jahveh's battle (42.10–17; 51.9; cf. Pss. 74.13–17; 89.10–13). Jahveh, the creator of the people and of the individuals (43.1, 7), is their redeemer and possessor (43.1; cf. Pss. 24.1 f.; 95.5), their keeper and defender in great perils (43.2), their god and saviour (43.3), their holy one and king (43.15). All these names are explanatory synonyms for creator. In this same chapter (43.15–21), we learn the way in which Jahveh has created formerly; it was through the miraculous deliverance at the Red Sea, and now he intends to create something new, i.e., he will accomplish the same miracle anew when he gives water and fertility to the desert. The creation of the world, the deliverance at the Red Sea, and the repatriation of the exiles from Babylon are one and the same creative act of Jahveh; the same three moments of the work of creation are juxtaposed several times by this poet (44.24, 26 f.; 45.9–13; 51.9 f., 12–14; 54.5). In the 104th Psalm, creation and preservation pass imperceptibly into one another, just as in Deutero-Isaiah creation and election are also intimately related concepts (54.5–10; cf. 44.1 f.).

God's creative activity is thus not limited to the genesis of the world, as it is for us, but creation is a collective concept which expresses all the positive saving actions of God at all times, and once even his negative action (Isa. 45.7). So for the Second Isaiah the knowledge of the creation of the world by Jahveh is a true message of joy, a comforting gospel of the same kind as the tradition of the Exodus; it is a source of praise (Pss. 8; 89.12; 104.1 ff.; 136.3 ff.), of joy (Prov. 8.27 ff.), and of trust (Ps. 121.2). Something of this tone is still very evident in the learned presentation of the creation of the world in Genesis 1, particularly at v. 31. The creator loves his people as a married man loves the bride of his youth (Isa. 54.1–7), or as a father (Isa. 64.8; Mal. 2.10; cf. 1.6; Ps. 103.13 f.; Deut. 32.6). Here we have a transition to New Testament usage where the designation father replaces that of creator; here and there we can establish directly that God the Father has taken over the functions of the Old Testament creator (I Cor. 8.6; Matt. 11.25). The richness of the Old Testament idea has not disappeared in the New; we must, however, look for it in other expressions (e.g. Rom. 4.17; II Cor. 4.6).

If we would grasp the biblical idea of creation in a purely philosophical way, we can learn a great deal from Henri Bergson's *Creative Evolution* to the extent that he has understood that creation is a historical concept which does not deal with the origin of things. We can get an idea of what creation is, he says, when we analyse the creative beginning of human actions.[1]

The question of the origin of the world concerned Greek philosophy from the time of Anaximander and Anaximenes. With them it was, however, a problem of natural science which consequently had to be solved in accordance with the scheme of cause and effect, and it had necessarily to be concluded that in some way or other the world was eternal, even though its manifestations might change. For that reason, all Greek philosophers taught the eternity of the world, and this quite well agreed also with their timeless, static thinking. The question is whether Plato in the creation myth reproduced in the *Timaeus* constitutes an exception; this question has been answered differently in the course of history from ancient times until the present. Aristotle answered affirmatively and contested his interpretation; scholars and disciples of Plato answered the question negatively. Archer-Hind offers the solution to this controversy in a remark in which he dismisses one of Aristotle's objections to Plato as groundless: '. . . the truth is, as not rarely happens when Aristotle is at cross purposes with Plato, that Aristotle is treating from a physical point of view a subject which Plato deals with metaphysically.'[2] The notion of creation in Plato's *Timaeus* belongs not to the field of physics and natural science but to that of metaphysics and religion, where it is a matter of the relation of the world and man to God. Therefore, Plato begins his inquiry with a prayer, in which he calls upon the gods for their assistance that, so to speak, it might be pleasing to them, and consequently in a way that is fitting for man to begin such an inquiry. It is obvious that the biblical notion of creation is, generally speaking, comparable only with the Platonic; here we have a classic example of why, in this book, we have had to cite Plato so often as indicative of Greek thinking. The myth in Plato's *Timaeus*, like Plato's myths in general, is to be understood as a pictorial expression of an idea which he is incapable of expressing conceptually.

---

[1] H. Bergson, *Creative Evolution*, pp. 192, 243.
[2] R. D. Archer-Hind, *The Timaeus of Plato*, p. 118.

We need not enter into the Platonic myth in detail; a few features are sufficient to compare it with the biblical idea of creation. Its religious character appears in the fact that the perfect God is referred to frequently as creator and father,[1] that before creation the four basic elements were in the state which must be inevitable when God is far from them,[2] and that the world and men are created good and beautiful. The problem on which Plato ruminated was this: what is the relation between the sensible world and the supra-sensible world? Now in his thinking he had found that the sensible world was transitory, and the supra-sensible was everlastingly wonderful, beautiful, and divine. If however, the sensible world is trans-itory, it must have had an origin and apparently will also pass away. The most natural explanation of this fact is that the world and men are created by God, and consequently some sort of creation myth is made necessary. What the myth is to explain, therefore, is not the origin of the world but its peculiarity in relation to the supra-sensible world; in other words, the myth is to explain the relation between the being of the sensible world and that of the supra-sensible world. For that reason the chron-ology and the sequence of the act of creation play no rôle in the *Timaeus*. Thus he sees himself compelled to report the creation of the celestial bodies before the world-soul, although he knows that this sequence is quite incorrect,[3] and later he begins anew to describe the origin of the world[4] in order to be able to express new ideas and qualities.

When we come from the biblical idea of creation to the Platonic, it is obvious that in spite of all their religious-moral similarity they are quite different; the former speaks of the becoming and the latter of the being of the world and of man, but by the former as well as by the latter the essence of the world and of man is expressed. Both ideas therefore have a great deal of actuality. According to Plato man achieves his acme when he absorbs and realizes in himself as much of the eternal world as possible; according to the Bible man achieves his acme when he becomes as he was in the beginning, i.e. at creation (Matt. 19.8). These two viewpoints and series of ideas must be kept distinct from each other; if they are confused with one another, there arise insoluble and unnecessary difficulties for our thinking.

3. *Functional Cosmology* versus *Visual Cosmology*

For us Europeans it is self-evident that a cosmology must be visual; the Greeks' cosmology was such, and therefore the Hebrews' cosmological

---

[1] Plato *Timaeus*, pp. 28, 37, 41.
[3] *Ibid.*, p. 35.
[2] *Ibid.*, p. 51.
[4] *Ibid.*, p. 53.

ideas must have been such. There is simply no other possibility. Consequently, out of various expressions in the Old Testament something on the lines of the following cosmology of the ancient Hebrews is formulated: the earth is an orb that is surrounded by water; over it arches the firmament like a bell glass which is equipped with apertures (channels, windows); above the firmament lies a portion of the primeval sea or the original waters of chaos; there, also, are the storage places for snow and hail as well as for light and darkness; there, too, God dwells in his palace surrounded by numerous heavenly beings; beneath the earth is Sheol and the primeval sea out of which the springs bubble up; when it rains, it means that God opens up the lattice-work of the firmament so that the water up there can flow down.

When we have recognized that the Hebrews have offered us no visual image either of a man, a building, or an object, it is a uniquely pleasant surprise to us that they have given us so visual an image of the universe. This cannot possibly be correct; moreover, it can soon be proved that it is not the case.

Even in the most ancient times the Israelites knew that rain comes from the clouds. This is not remarkable in itself for every man can easily establish the fact through personal observation, and the ancient Israelites lived much nearer to nature than we do and in their daily life were dependent upon correct observations of nature. So already in the very ancient Song of Deborah:

> . . . the earth trembled,
> and the heavens dropped,
> yea, the clouds dropped water (Judg. 5.4).

They knew that the clouds bring with them rain from the sea. Elijah's servant said to the prophet:

> 'Behold, a little cloud like a man's hand is rising out of the sea.' And he said, 'Go up, say to Ahab, "Prepare your chariot and go down, lest the rain stop you".' And in a little while the heavens grew black with clouds and wind, and there was a great rain (I Kings 18.44 ff.).

Had it ever been in place to relate that God opened the windows in heaven and let it rain, this would have been the instance, for the rain is surely to be traced to Jahveh's direct interference; yet Jahveh lets the rain come from the clouds. Isaiah also knew that the rain fell from the clouds:

> I will also command the clouds
> that they rain no rain upon it (Isa. 5.6. Cf. Ps. 77.17; Prov. 3.19 f.; 16.15, *et passim*).

How then shall we explain the mythological expressions for cosmography that occur in the Old Testament? The account of the flood is illuminating in this regard. The oldest source, J, relates that the flood was caused by a heavy rainstorm; the source of the Priestly document, more recent by several centuries, is the first to relate that all of the springs of the great abyss burst and the sluices of heaven opened (Gen. 7.11; 8.2). Now it is generally recognized that the mythological interpretations of the universe belong to the ancient times and the more naturalistic ones to a more recent epoch, especially when, as here, the ancient narrator is naïve and the more recent one reflective. Yet the situation here is quite the reverse. There is a parallel phenomenon in Plato's philosophy where in certain instances the philosopher resorts to mythological concepts. The same is true here; when the Priestly document resorts to mythological expressions, it asserts that it is speaking of an eschatological event: the chaos which is always threatening the universe once broke in upon the human world and destroyed it because of men's sins.

The second place where the 'heavenly windows' are mentioned is in the late, so-called Isaiah Apocalypse, where we undoubtedly have to do with eschatological events:

> For the windows of heaven are opened,
>   and the foundations of the earth tremble.
> The earth is utterly broken,
>   the earth is rent asunder,
>   the earth is violently shaken (Isa. 24.18 f.).

In both the other places where the *'arubboth hashshamayim* occurs (II Kings 7.2, 19; Mal. 3.10), it is a religious term; 'windows' is an expression for Jahveh's direct intervention:

> thereby put me to the test, says the Lord of hosts, if I will not open the windows of heaven for you and pour down for you an overflowing blessing (Mal. 3.10).

Compare also the following:

> Yet he commanded the skies above,
>   and opened the doors of heaven;
> and he rained down upon them manna to eat
>   (Ps. 78.23 f.).

The Hebrew word for 'firmament', *raqia'*, betrays its individuality by the fact that it occurs only in religious expressions (Genesis 1; Pss. 19.2; 150.1; Dan. 12.3; Ezek. 1.22 f., 25 f.; 10.1). It is therefore completely inappropriate for use as evidence of a profane cosmological concept. The very frequent association of heaven and clouds in the Old Testament is, in our opinion, testimony of the fact that the Hebrews, when they spoke and thought 'naturalistically' about these things, identified heaven with the clouds, as is the case already in the Song of Deborah. Perhaps we have here the psychological explanation of the frequently occurring idea that Jahveh dwelt in the clouds and revealed himself from them. We too use the term 'heaven' in a naturalistic sense and in a religious sense which coalesce, however, in a rather indefinite way into one concept.

It should not surprise us that religious poets and preachers in Israel, as among all other peoples, use mythological concepts as images. No one can contest the fact that we have an example of this in the ancient satire upon the king of Babel:

> 'How you are fallen from heaven, O Day Star, son of Dawn!
> How you are cut down to the ground,
>   you who laid the nations low!
> You said in your heart, "I will ascend to heaven;
> above the stars of God I will set my throne on high;
> I will sit on the mount of assembly in the far north" '
>   (Isa. 14.12 f.).[1]

The book of Job is most enlightening for a study of Hebrew cosmological concepts. Here sober, unaffected interpretations of nature stand alongside colourful mythological expressions; but even the normal phenomena of nature are to the author great miracles of God:

> He binds up the waters in his thick clouds,
>   and the cloud is not rent under them (26.8).
> Can you lift up your voice to the clouds,
>   that a flood of waters may cover you? (38.34)
> Who can number the clouds by wisdom?
> Or who can tilt the waterskins of the heavens (38.37).

How can drops of water be suspended in the clouds without breaking them? And what causes them to fall down? The poet has studied nature; he knows the life of the wild animals (38.39–39.30), and he knows the constellations (38.31 f.). He knows that the course of the stars is regular:

> Do you know the ordinances of the heavens?
> Can you establish their rule on the earth? (38.33).

He also knows that the earth is suspended in space:

> He stretches out the north over the void,
>   and hangs the earth upon nothing (26.7).

---

[1] By this we do not deny that there were also in Israel people who took the metaphysical images literally; such a one was, perhaps, the poet of Psalm 104 (cf. vv, 3, 13). We should hope that a less prosaic interpretation were also possible. Failing this we can maintain thankfully that a literalistic understanding of metaphysical-mythological images is an exception in the Old Testament.

For the poet this is all one miracle after another and reveals God's greatness and his glory. He cannot refer to Jahveh's revelation in history because Job, as a non-Israelite, does not know of it. In the poem, nature in itself holds no interest; it is a question of penetrating through nature to its creator and sustainer. From a religious viewpoint there is no distinction between the 'scientific' description of nature and the mythological; the distinction is a stylistic one. When he wants to disclose the secret of creation, he resorts to mythological images:

Where were you when I laid the foundation of the earth?
    Tell me, if you have understanding.
Who determined its measurements—surely you know!
    Or who stretched the line upon it?
On what were its bases sunk, or who laid its cornerstone,
    when the morning stars sang together, and all the sons of God
        shouted for joy? (38.4–7)
Or who shut in the sea with doors, when it burst forth from the
    womb;
    when I made clouds its garment, and thick darkness its swaddling
        band (38.8. f.). . .
Have you commanded the morning since your days began,
    and caused the dawn to know its place (38.12). . .
Have you entered into the springs of the sea,
    or walked in the recesses of the deep?
Have the gates of death been revealed to you,
    or have you seen the gates of deep darkness? (38.16 f.)
Where is the way to the dwelling of light,
    and where is the place of darkness,
that you may take it to its territory (38.19 f.). . . . ?

When God uses snow and hail as weapons in war, they are supernatural powers and must be described correspondingly:

Have you entered the storehouses of the snow,
    or have you seen the storehouses of the hail,
which I have reserved for the time of trouble,
    for the day of battle and war? (38.22 f.).

When God changes the desert into a fruitful land by abundant rains, it is an act of creation in accordance with the Israelite view and consequently must be expressed mythologically:

Who has cleft a channel for the torrents of rain,
    and a way for the thunderbolt,
to bring rain on a land where no man is,
    on the desert in which there is no man;
to satisfy the waste and desolate land,
    and to make the ground put forth grass? (38.25–27).

In place of creator, the poet can call God father, and instead of creating he can speak of begetting and bearing:

> Has the rain a father,
>   or who has begotten the drops of dew?
> From whose womb did the ice come forth,
>   and who has given birth to the hoarfrost of heaven?
>   (38.28 f.).

When a man is familiar with the most diverse natural phenomena and can explain them in naturalistic ways, it is psychologically impossible to assume that he means the mythological expressions literally; they are images which the poet uses for reasons of style. It is also then quite readily explained that the *ancient* narrators, poets, and authors, in order not to be taken literally, avoided using mythology. In later eras this danger no longer existed, and for this reason mythological images abound in that period.

It is easy for theologians to forget that the Babylonians produced not only crude mythology but also scientific astronomy; the connexion between these two has scarcely been examined. It was the same priestly circle that pursued both, and the one could hardly be had without the other. There apparently existed a tension which became more and more intolerable with the growth of astronomical knowledge and made urgently necessary a 'demythologizing' which, however, the Babylonians themselves could not carry out. It came about in a twofold manner, with the Greeks and with Jews. Thales turned the Babylonian creation myth into natural philosophy; the peculiar basic idea of his philosophy, that everything arose out of water, is easiest to explain in this way. Thales had also acquired considerable astronomical knowledge from Babylonia. In Judea, profound religious minds appropriated the Babylonian creation myth for their faith in Jahveh and changed it into history by incorporating it, as the first part, in God's redemptive-historical revelation. Apparently they must have learned some astronomy besides; however, they could find as little application for it in their theology as Thales did in his philosophy.

Nature and history are correlative terms, like being and motion, space and time. Existence can be experienced as both. Nature is then existence construed as something that exists, while history is existence construed as development and continuous happening. Nature is the content of space, and history is the content of time.

For us existence is nature as well as history. Something else took place in Hellas and Israel when each of these highly gifted nations realized one-sidedly the two possible conceptions of existence. For the Greeks, existence was nature, as W. F. Otto correctly observes: 'Here we perceive the spiritual tendency of the people destined to teach mankind to investigate nature—both within and around man; the Greek approach, that is to say, first gave mankind the idea of nature which is so familiar to modern man.'[1] The Greek historians, chiefly Thucydides, attempted to understand history also from the viewpoint of nature, especially human nature. Consequently, history itself became a part of nature: what happened once will surely happen again that way or similarly. Thereby the ground was laid for understanding history as science in the sense of natural science.

In Palestine, intellectual development followed quite another course. After centuries of endeavour, Hebrew thinkers succeeded in representing nature as history in that they first conceived of the world as the habitation of man (cf. Isa. 45.18) and then conceived of creation as the establishment of this habitation. The numerous expressions for cosmology drawn from domestic architecture are relevant here: such expressions as door-post, cornerstone, gate, door, window, foundation, tent, etc. When we have understood how to read the creation narrative in the Priestly document in this way, it is easy to see that the Jahvist was already striving to represent the creation of the world as a great building operation. Both narratives begin with Chaos, P with the Chaos-water (Gen. 1.2), J with the lifeless desert (Gen. 2.5); then they relate how God changed the original Chaos into the habitable world (German, *Menschenland*). It is usually held that the two creation accounts contradict each other and are irreconcilable. That is true if we interpret them visually, but when we have perceived that they are to be interpreted functionally, they agree very well. Then we have an example of the familiar Hebraic tendency to express an idea in two different ways. As an analogy, we can cite the destiny of the lost in the New Testament. In Matt. 25.30, Christ describes it as darkness (= Gen. 1.2), in v. 41, as fire (cf. Gen. 2.5); visually the expressions are irreconcilable, functionally they are identical.

All the details in chapter 1 of Genesis must be interpreted functionally, even the mention of sun, moon, and stars (vv. 14–18); this P does repeatedly. Yet the desperate attempt is made to reconcile this functional interpretation with the visual in such a way that P is said to have imagined how God fastened sun, moon, and stars as greater and lesser balls in the celestial vault (cf. vv. 14, 17). Everyone would have seen through the untenability of such an idea even then, for sun, moon, and stars accomplish entirely different movements in the heavens and therefore, could

[1] W. F. Otto, *The Homeric Gods*, p. 7.

not possibly be nailed up in one and the same vault. This fact also warns us to make images of the firmament that are not too primitive or gross. In Psalm 19, where the word *raqia'* (v. 1) also occurs, the sun is likened to a bridegroom who comes out of his chamber and like a strong man traverses his course from one end of the heavens to the other (vv. 5 f.). Moreover, God has prepared a tent for the sun (v. 4); but where this tent is to be pitched is a very difficult problem for those who always postulate visual images, for tent is elsewhere a designation for the firmament.

When we interpret the creation narrative functionally, it is ingenious that the creation of the light is put at the beginning of the narrative, for nothing expresses the biblical idea of creation so clearly as the displacement of the darkness by salvation-bestowing light, a point that the Apostle rightly saw (II Cor. 4.6). Creation and salvation are almost identical terms in the Old Testament, particularly in Deutero-Isaiah (Isa. 41.18–20; 40.12–31; 42.5–9; 43.1–7, 15–21; 44.1–4; 45.12 f.).

The impossibility of writing a Hebrew cosmography dawns upon one when one attempts to determine God's dwelling place in the universe. He dwells everywhere (Ps. 139.7 ff.) and nowhere (I Kings 8.27). The many different particulars of God's dwelling in the Old Testament are not to be interpreted geographically but either historically or theologically, for every detail of a divine dwelling place has a meaning which is generally easy to guess. When Jahveh's transcendence and numinous character are to be indicated, heaven is designated as his dwelling place:

> God is in heaven, and you upon earth;
>   therefore let your words be few (Eccles. 5.2).

This means: there is a distinction between God and you that is as wide as the heavens; therefore, be humble (cf. Ps. 115.16). For a Hebrew, it is possible for a man to set himself in heaven, but this means making himself equal to the Most High (Isa. 14.12 ff.). The ungodly raise their voices against heaven (Ps. 73.9) or build a tower whose pinnacle reaches to the very heavens (Gen. 11.4). The destruction of Judah was a fall from heaven to earth (Lam. 2.1 f.). He who is enthroned in heaven laughs at the kings of the earth (Ps. 2.2 ff.). The humble man prays:

> To thee I lift up my eyes,
>   O thou who art enthroned in the heavens! (Ps. 123.1; cf. 121.1)

When Jahveh says,

> Heaven is my throne
>   and the earth is my footstool (Isa. 66.1),

it does not mean that Jahveh sits in heaven with his feet upon the earth, but that the whole earth has no more value for him than a footstool for an earthly king.

If we would understand the modest rôle played in the Old Testament by heaven as the dwelling place of Jahveh, we must bear in mind that for the Hebrew heaven is not identical with the divine world, and therefore, it is not, as it is for us, a name for the divine transcendence, for heaven is one of the works of Jahveh's creation just as much as the earth (Gen. 1.1; 2.4; Pss. 8.3; 33.6) and one day will be scattered with the earth like smoke (Isa. 51.6). Jahveh exists as independently of heaven as of the earth (I Kings 8.27). Divine transcendence is not spatial as it is in Greece, even for Plato (cf. *Symposium*), but it is temporal. He is the first and the last (Isa. 44.6; 43.10; 41.4); before the universe was, he existed (Gen. 2.4; 1.1).

When it says that Jahveh will dwell in the midst of his people, this is an expression of his religious proximity:

And I will dwell among the people of Israel, and will be their God. And they shall know that I am the Lord their God, who brought them forth out of the land of Egypt that I might dwell among them; I am the Lord their God (Ex. 29.45 f.).

When it says, Jahveh is in his holy temple, Jahveh whose throne is in heaven (Ps. 11.4), it means, on the analogy of Isa. 66.1, that the highly exalted god of the universe is in the Temple, near and gracious; the sense is therefore the same as in Ps. 134.3. In I Kings, chapter 8, we have a whole theology of Jahveh's place of sojourning. When the name of Jahveh is used in connexion with definite places, it has a historical meaning; as God of Sinai (Judg. 5.4 f.; Deut. 33.2–4) or Horeb (I Kings 19.8 ff.) he is designated as Israel's covenant god.

The childishly naïve details of the divine dwelling place in the Jahvist have the same meaning: and Jahveh came down to see the city and the tower which the sons of men had built (Gen. 11.5). By this the narrator means to say that the highly exalted god would no longer permit the goings on of insolent men to take place. For the tower builders, Jahveh was religiously distant, and he came to punish them. For Adam and Eve in the garden he was religiously near like a father to his children (3.8 ff); after their disobedience he was religiously far away (3.23 f.).

In short, what we call the cosmological ideas of the Bible are virtually the cosmological ideas of the Middle Ages; they are neither Hebrew nor Greek, but a naïve mixture of both.

4

Symbolism and Instrumentalism

A. THE HEBREW CONCEPTION OF THE *thing*

THE DISTINCTION between Greek and Israelite thinking can be seen from yet another viewpoint, one to which Canon Oliver Quick first called attention.[1] If we take as our point of departure the concept of the *thing*, we find that the Israelites really had no such word. Frants Buhl, to be sure, contends that *dabhar* renders the Greek concept of *thing* as well as our own,[2] just as in other Semitic languages expressions for *word* can also mean *thing*. Now it is to be noted that our word 'thing' is ambiguous; it means 'matter', e.g. 'subject of a request', as well as 'object'. It is correct that *dabhar*, and its equivalents in the other Semitic languages, can mean 'matter' but not 'object'. *dabhar*—'the word in spoken form', hence 'efficacious fact', is for the Semites the great reality of existence, with the result that *lo'-dabhar* ('no word, no deed, no affair') signifies the corresponding nothingness, nothing, no thing. When the Hebrews represent *dabhar* as the great reality of existence, they show their dynamic conception of reality.

The Hebrews have a second word for 'thing' which more nearly approaches our notion 'object', to which Prof. Mowinckel once called my attention; this word is *keli*—'utensil, implement, instrument', whence a variety of other meanings can be derived:

implement for playing and singing, i.e., musical instrument (Ps. 71.22; Amos 6.5; II Chron. 34.12),

implement for hunting and battle, i.e., a weapon (Gen. 27.3; II Kings 7.15),

utensil for storing and carrying liquids, i.e., vessel (I Kings 17.10; II Kings 4.3 ff.),

implement for adorning, i.e., ornament (Gen. 24.53), and thing in general, i.e., object (Gen. 31.37; Num. 19.18; Jonah 1.5).

[1] O. C. Quick, *The Gospel of Divine Action.*
[2] Frants Buhl, 'Über die Ausdrücke für: Ding, Sache u.ä. im Semitischen', *Festschrift Vilhelm Thomsen zur Vollendung des siebzigsten Lebensjahres am 25. Januar 1912 dargebracht von Freunden und Schülern*, pp. 32 ff.

The basic meaning that hovers in the background of all these meanings is 'implement, utensil'; it is always a question of an object that is used for some purpose or other. Consequently, *kelî* is also related intrinsically to the Hebrew dynamic conception of reality, as we have previously developed it, although the emphasis in this word is upon use for some sort of activity, i.e. upon its function.

A third word for 'thing', also organically related to the Hebrew conception of reality and expressing a third side of it, is *ḥephets*, which signifies the delight one has in something (Ps. 1.2). In addition, it can mean 'matter, request, affair', but it can also designate concrete things which one desires or values highly: King Solomon gave the Queen of Sheba all her *ḥephets* that she asked, i.e. everything for which she had a fancy and for which she asked (I Kings 10.13). Wisdom is said to be better than jewels and all *ḥaphatsîm*, i.e., precious things and gems do not compare with it (Prov. 8.11=3.15). Thus, *ḥephets* does not mean 'object in itself' but 'object' as the expression of a definite quality: what is desired, what is treasured. Things as expressions of qualities is a detail discussed above *in extenso* (cf. the discussion on the Song of Solomon); the new facet of the Hebraic conception of things and of reality that is here particularly underlined is the instrumental.

B. THE GREEK CONCEPTION OF THE *thing*

Canon Quick may correctly translate the Greek conception of the thing and of reality when he asserts that the thing is a means of knowing. The one who seeks to know is not attempting to alter something or other in his environment, but he is trying only to observe how it really is and to reflect upon the true being or order of things and upon what is behind the phenomena. Quick expresses it more Platonically: the thinking personality is seeking 'to reflect in its own consciousness the true being or order of what exists beyond the environment or some part of it'.[1]

The two attitudes are inseparable in life; one cannot exist without the other. Knowledge as perception is an activity of our minds and includes, in any case, the endeavours to remove an inner ignorance. In general, man can scarcely live without any activity whatsoever; on the other hand, consciously purposeful activity is impossible without knowledge of some kind or other. We must know, up to a certain point, what effects will follow upon our movements, and for this reason we must have an inkling

[1] Quick, *op. cit.*, p. 11.

of a firm order existing in the world and ruling it. Reflex actions seem to presuppose a certain unconscious knowledge since they are distinguished from purely mechanical movements by the fact that they are to a certain degree appropriate. The conduct of the lowest forms of animal life remains hidden from us because it seems to be appropriate without our being able to presuppose conscious thinking on the part of these animals. The movements of lower animals can be designated neither as activity nor as thinking, but they belong to a previous stage where undeveloped activity and thinking coalesce. Although knowing and doing are inseparable, yet they remain radically different once each becomes truly itself. Activity is not knowledge nor is knowledge activity, despite all the sophisms of Behaviourism and Pragmatism.

Knowledge and activity each has its own special way of seeing and dealing with the external things that our senses perceive. In relation to our knowledge they are signs or symbols; in relation to our activity they are instruments or *implements*. The negative relation of a thing to our knowledge is called riddle, and in relation to our activity it is known as hindrance. Everything in the world is potentially a sign as well as an implement for us, just as it is potentially a riddle or a hindrance. The sun may be for me a sign of direction, a sign of astronomical reality, or a sign of the goodness of God; it can also be an instrument whereby I am warmed or by means of which I read a book. The inventive mind of man is able artistically to create signs as well as instruments. A musical score is a system of signs, but it is also a means for playing music; a violin is in the first place a musical instrument, but it is also a sign having profound meaning for a musician's feelings. Yet we do distinguish signs from instruments (means or implements); we call that a sign by which primarily we know a thing, but that through which we accomplish an act we call an instrument.

Thus far everything is clear and simple; however, a mystery is opened before us when we perceive that this distinction between the two attitudes of man toward his environment corresponds to a distinction in reality itself. It is characteristic of reality that in part it affects us and in part tells us something; every sense perception is the result of our physical environment influencing us. All our senses have developed from the primitive sense of touch, even those which mediate perception of remote objects, such as hearing and seeing. We can neither see nor hear unless invisible and inaudible vibrations come into relation with our eyes and ears. Without external, tactual stimuli there would be no internal, psychical knowledge. On the contrary, however, even the simplest conception cannot be considered merely as a product of pressure and contact; vibrations on my sense-organs are not conceptions, and it is not even possible to imagine how mere vibrations could produce conceptions. Yet air and sound waves do produce such conceptions in us because our consciousness interprets the vibrations as meaningful. The next question is whether our consciousness intrudes something into the vibrations that was not there before. This is impossible; our consciousness can find no meaning in meaningless waves. The waves coming from the outside must originally have had a meaning which, by means of the waves, we sense in our sense-organs. The sense-organs, then, function somewhat similarly to our radio receivers which also can reproduce only the meaningful waves which they have previously sensed.

When we examine external reality without regard to its action upon us, we discover in it two strictly separate but mysteriously connected orders. The necessary connexion of an occurrence with a succeeding occurrence we call *cause*; the necessary connexion of a single event with a totality of events we call *reason*. We can take a commonplace as an illustration. When an airplane starts and becomes airborne, we observe a series of apparently very remarkable occurrences all of which can be explained, however, as causes and effects; yet our mind poses a series of quite different questions, too. Why has man invented such a thing as an airplane? What purpose has the airplane today? The connexion of cause and effect is an unbroken series continuing to infinity, a series, however, which cannot be reversed. In the connexion reason-inference, the reason can be considered as the first cause of a series of occurrences: the man wanted to fly, and so the machine was set in motion; this is so without the reason necessarily being a cause in the physical sense. The reason can also be designated the *end* of the series of occurrences: e.g. the pilot wanted to reach a certain destination quickly. The reason cannot be established at a point any more nearly localized; it cannot be said to happen itself at all. Its connexion with the causal chain is not itself causal; the reason is *expressed* through the occurrences. Thus the series of occurrences is *causative* and *instrumental* when we view it in connexion with its intended result; observed in connexion with its reason, the series is *expressive* and *significant*, and it expresses something that exists through it generally. Following this, Canon Quick demonstrates how the distinction between instrumentalism and symbolism in connexion with theology corresponds roughly with the distinction between the Israelite manner of thinking in the Old Testament and the Greek manner of thinking in Platonism.

Thus far the distinguished English scholar goes. Undoubtedly, the distinction detected by him between Greek and Hebrew thinking is essential and characteristic; yet I believe that this distinction can be worked out more clearly and acutely. First of all, physical and metaphysical thinking cannot be compared with one another, as Canon Quick does even more clearly in his subsequent argument; they belong to two distinct and incommensurable spheres. The physical chain of causes must be compared with the logical chain of reason and inference; both are objective and impersonal. Like must always be compared with like. The antithesis found by Quick is surely universal and can be proved even in the purely physical realm, since every atom, observed from one viewpoint has wave structure and viewed from another has quantum structure. The dynamic and static forms of the atom are mutually exclusive to our way of thinking; in order to be true to reality, however, they must at the same time be maintained as mutually complementary. Into physics, however, we may intrude neither psychological nor metaphysical observations. It is sufficient for us that physics for its part is free from metaphysical observations of a materialistic variety.

The antithesis, which Canon Quick designates as the antithesis between symbolism and instrumentalism, is not easy to establish univocally in concepts; it must be elucidated, as Canon Quick has so well done, by means of examples. The individual concepts very frequently have the same ambiguity and can be explained in a twofold way. If, for example, instrument signifies means, instrumentalism can describe not only the Hebraic kind of thinking but the Greek kind as well. In the case of the Hebrews, the instrument is a means of action; in the case of the Greeks, things and events are conceived as a means of understanding and perceiving. The antithesis remains unresolved but is expressed by the same word since the antithesis now lies within the concept. Also, if symbol means both *sign* and *symbol*, Hebrew thinking can just as well be characterized as symbolism, for it was typical of the Jews, as St Paul testifies, that they looked for signs; as we have already developed, things could be symbols for the Israelites too. The antithesis still remains but has been intruded into the concepts, since signs are two entirely different things in Hebrew and in Greek. An Israelite *sign* is an expression of the divine will and power; a Greek symbol is an image of eternal truth or divine essence. If a thing is a symbol for an Israelite, it expresses a dynamic property, while symbol for the Greek expresses a meaning or true being. As we have already shown, not only the Greeks but the Israelites as well knew true being; yet this alters nothing, for 'being' to the Israelite is a dynamic, powerful, effective being, while for the Greek 'being' is immutable, at rest, and harmonious. That antithesis is always there, but it does not lie in any word or in a circumscribed viewpoint; yet it extends throughout the whole to every detail. Although Quick is fairer to the Greek way of thinking than other theologians who have dealt with the same subject, even he comes finally to the conclusion that the Israelite's dynamic way of thinking is more valuable and more necessary for religious thinking than the Greek. The reason for this is surely that in spite of everything he has not recognized this antithesis clearly enough in its uniqueness; hence, it is not quite correct to say that Jahveh is exclusively a god of action in opposition to the god of Plato who is exclusively a god of being. For just as Jahveh is *in being*—to be sure it is a dynamic and power-laden being—so also there proceeds from Plato's god a great effect, except that this effect is not active and invasive but attracting, or one might even call it magnetic. Plato's highest Idea awakes in man an irresistible love which gives him the power to overcome all hindrances along the way to God. Despite his static idea of God, even Aristotle knew a divine activity or power which he described as the eternal ἐνέργεια ἀκινησίας.[1]

I believe, therefore, that we shall be just as fair to the *intentions* of the discerning Englishman with the following arguments, although they can be but brief and suggestive. Our simplest sense-perceptions are possible only because a sensible order pervades the whole of reality. What I conceive as a tree cannot be *only* my *conception* for no tree exists therein; the tree must be objective. If, on the other hand, I assume that the world of nature is inaccessible to our conceptual faculties, it is quite evident that neither the perceived tree nor something similar to it can exist in the world of perception. If we discard as inadequate a purely subjective idealism, there is only one alternative left, namely, that what we conceive as a tree really is a tree, i.e., that reality is at least as meaningful as our perceptions of it. Perception has therefore not only a physical cause but also corresponds to a reasonable meaning in nature which can be expressed rationally. In this case, perception of a material object presupposes an objective and rational order of nature. Finally we come to the conclusion that there are to be recognized in our ordinary physical perceptions a reason and an activity which do not stem from us, and what is more, are recognized through physical nature which are their symbol and instrument. Therefore, I perceive from the simple physical perceptions even to the reflective observations of world history the unfolding

[1] Aristotle *Metaphysics* xi. 7, 1072a. 24 f.

and accomplishment of a purpose-conscious divine will and the revelation of a reasonable world order.

In summary we can say that God can be thought of as an active personality who, through appropriate acts, is leading the world and especially mankind to a goal; God can also be thought of as a reasonable being who is disclosing himself to men through the world as a system of symbols. In the former instance, God's power is experienced and felt; in the latter instance, the being of God is perceived. It is not correct to say, in the former case, that God has caused the occurrences since the immanent causes and effects remain as they were, but we think of God by way of an analogy with a human personality who employs the lawful order of the world in order to accomplish his will. It is even more absurd, however, to say that God is bound or hindered by that lawful order. The former case is best expressed thus: we discover in the occurrences and in the course of the world a divine will. We could also have said that we perceive a divine meaning, but that would approach the latter viewpoint. In the latter case, it is not correct to say that the reason which we can establish, for example, in mathematics, in logic, or in the physical world order, is religious in itself, but the systems of order mentioned are themselves only symbols which permit us to intimate a divine wisdom standing back of them. Thus in both cases there stands behind the world a divinity who uses the world as a means partly for action and partly for self-disclosure.

EXCURSUS: THE TRANSPARENCE OF GOD

Ever since ancient times, God's overall relation to the world has been designated simultaneously as that of *transcendence* and *immanence*; in the two notions, God's being as well as his activity have been brought into prominence.[1] God's relationship to the world, however, is represented by these two concepts neither clearly nor exhaustively.[2] One gets the impression that something is lacking, so that dogmatic theologians have had to subsume under either transcendence or immanence motifs which have little to do with these concepts. What has been lacking up until now

---

[1] C. E. Luthardt, *Kompendium der Dogmatik*, ed. Robert Jelke, p. 186; Th. Steinmann, 'Immanenz und Transzendenz Gottes', RGG¹, III, 440 ff.; A. C. McGiffert, 'Immanence', ERE, VII, 163 ff.

[2] Steinmann's article (*op. cit.*) may be cited as evidence. The concepts immanence and transcendence are oriented to space and thus are formed by the Greek mind. Hebraically expressed the concepts of God's eternity and temporality mean the same thing, i.e. God is exempt from all temporal vincula, he is before, after, and independent of every occurrence, of all time (Ps. 90.1-4), and at the same time he is active in everything that occurs (Amos 3.6).

in the doctrine of God's relation to the world is a third term of relationship or a third dimension in the relation. God is not only above the world and in the world, but he is also *through* the world; as the Apostle has already said: ὁ ἐπὶ πάντων καὶ διὰ πάντων καὶ ἐν πᾶσιν (Eph. 4.6). God's being *through* the world is a separate category which expresses what is most characteristic of God's relation to the world in Greek as well as in Israelite terms. God reveals his *essence* through the world which then must be seen as a system of symbols, and he reveals his *will* through the circumstances and occurrences of the world which then appears as a system of action-mediations. With the category of God's being *through* the world we can do more justice to the religious content of polytheism than is customary, for it is characteristic of polytheism that the divinity is revealed through sensible objects, or what amounts to the same thing, that he can appear as a human personality. Obviously, then, the divinity is not identical with the human being concerned, for the human body of the divinity in the theophany disappears and vanishes. It is thus only a manifestation of the divine personality, even when the corporeity is sufficiently conceivable realistically. In polytheism as much as in Platonism the single sensible object and the world as a whole are the symbol of God through which we observe and perceive the one who truly is, the divine.

In Israelite religion the world and its content form an instrument in God's hand whereby in consciousness of purpose he performs his acts. Accordingly, God's relation to the world could be called God's *instrumentality*, which best expresses the Hebrew kind of thinking. God reveals himself to men in the world through his deeds, which are accomplished naturally by means of things in the world (Rom. 1.20). This same relationship could be rendered in the Greek manner by means of the concept of God's *transparence*. God's transparence thus asserts that God is known through the world as the one who really is. Things operate as symbols: 'Alles Vergängliche ist nur ein Gleichnis.'[1]

We have found, therefore, that the overall relationship between God and the world is three-sided, or perhaps better, it is triadic, which is precisely what we should have expected in a trinitarian religion.[2] Perhaps

---

[1] The opening lines of the final ode of *Faust*, sung by the Chorus Mysticus (Part II, Act V); a translation of these lines:

> All that is transitory
> Is only a symbol.

Bayard Taylor (trans.), *Faust, A Tragedy* (2 vols. in 1; New York: Houghton, Mifflin and Company, 1899), II, 462.

[2] Luther recognized the three dimensions in the overall relationship between God and the world. After creation God is *intra, extra et super omnes creaturas* (*Genesis-Vorlesung, D. Martin Luthers Werke* [Weimar: Hermann Böhlhaus Nachfolger, 1883-]).

this throws some light on the doctrine of the Trinity and particularly on Christology, for as the First Person of the Trinity corresponds to the transcendence and the Third Person to the immanence, so the Second Person of the Trinity corresponds to the transparence. That God was in the Person Jesus Christ and revealed his essence through him is conceived in a Greek way; that he sent his Son and through him actualized his will is conceived in an Israelite way. For Greek as well as for Hebrew thinking, the peculiar *scandalon* of Christology does not lie so much in the transparence of God in itself, but partly in the fact that both ways of thinking were confused with one another. So, for example, St Paul preached the transparence of God in Christ chiefly as a divine act; in this mode it was presented to the Greeks in a form that was foreign to them and therefore difficult of access.[1] In part also, and obviously principally, the *scandalon* of Christology consists in the fact that the man Jesus of Nazareth was designated as the highest expression of God's transparence, Jesus who was externally unimposing and whose earthly fate, viewed in terms of ordinary experience, was shocking. On the other hand, in the very confusion of the ways of thinking lay one of the most important preconditions of Christianity's victory in the world of that day: first, because when the complementary method of thinking was first carried out, it was much more effective than the long known and now exhausted method (cf. I Cor. 2.13; 1.17), and second, because the Hellenistic culture of that period was not pure Greek but was suffused with oriental elements, a condition which became more pronounced in succeeding ages. Thus it is easily explained how the Apostle Paul achieved truly great results in the harbour cities of Greece and Macedonia, while, on the contrary, he achieved no enduring results in Athens, the principal seat of ancient Greek culture. Even in the harbour cities, the genuinely Greek circles were uncordial to his preaching; it was surely not only in Athens that he made the discoveries which he mentions in I Cor. 1.17, and 2.13.

XLII, 9, 25 ff.). Here, God's being *extra omnes creaturas* corresponds to what we have called the third dimension in the relation of God to the world, for as one who is *extra* God is neither immanent nor transcendent.

[1] Anders Nygren, *Die Versöhnung als Gottestat* ('Studien der Luther-Akademie', 5).

5

Logical Thinking and Psychological Understanding

THERE ARE two ways to approach reality and its appearances intellectually and to grasp them; we call these two ways logical thinking and psychological understanding. When we think logically we place ourselves objectively and impersonally outside the matter and ask what is the strict truth about it; when we would understand a matter psychologically, we familiarize ourselves with it and through sympathetic pursuit of its development we try to grasp it as a necessity.

In our psychic life, thinking and understanding are inseparable. For example, we cannot admit the truth of a mathematical proposition without understanding the argumentation employed in its proof; however, when we have understood the argument, the proposition strikes us as true in itself, and its truth is in no way at all dependent upon us and our act of thinking. We must assert that even if there were no one who could understand the proof, the truth of the proposition would undoubtedly still stand. On the other hand, even if we would understand a matter psychologically, we think more or less consciously in accordance with logical laws of thinking. Without some sort of logic, even though it be primitive, no understanding is possible. Logical truth, in this case, is not the goal of intellectual activity but the aid to genuine psychological understanding, as inversely the psychological acts of thinking were an aid to the discernment of logical truth.

Although logic and psychology are not to be separated, they are certainly to be distinguished rather than to be confused one with the other, as so often happened during the first decade of this century in the intense conflict over the question of the proper epistemological method. The transcendentalists thought that epistemology was a purely logical affair (in Kant's sense) which examines the presuppositions of all knowledge. For them epistemology was a kind of self-consciousness of all scientific knowledge in its rudiments. With Kant, the transcendentalists began from mathematics, more precisely from geometry, as the ideal science and asked under what conditions it was possible. The claim of psychology to be able to say something fundamental to the problem of knowledge was rejected on the grounds that that science was a science like all the rest whose presuppositions and validity had first to be examined by epistemology. Against this the psychologists could have urged, as Hegel had already done from his own presuppositions, that epistemology as science is already a cognition; it could reasonably have been maintained that this activity has first to be examined psychologically.

B. THE WARRANT FOR THE TWO VIEWPOINTS

We cannot enter more deeply into this controversy with its partly unpleasant sides;[1] we likewise forgo a detailed debate with the conflicting schools since it would lead us too far afield. It can be said, however, as is so often the case, that the disputants were right in their positive assertions and wrong in their negative ones. An epistemology which presented a synthesis of the two tendencies, let us say of the philosophies of Kant and Bergson, among several, would be just about what is wanted.

With the transcendentalists[2] we must maintain that logical truth is a scientific value *sui generis*, which has nothing to do with psychology even if the discovery of it is psychological in kind. The transcendentalists' error is that they believe that this exhausts the meaning of psychology for epistemology. This is not the case, however, for there are still large segments of reality not to be grasped by formal, logical thinking, but to the sound investigation of which the predicate science must be applied. Kant's thesis, that an inquiry deserves the predicate science only to the extent that mathematical method may be used in it, has certainly tempted the ambition if not the scruples of scholars, engaged in the fields in question, to stretch their sciences upon the Procrustean bed of mathematics. For this reason we must greet joyfully the reaction of psychology against that fatal bias.

Logical thinking and psychological understanding are not only different in kind, but they have different segments of reality as their *specific* fields of inquiry. Platonic-Aristotelian logic is a science of spatial cate-

---

[1] For example, the personal animosity between H. Rickert and William James, *Kant-Studien*, XIV (1909), 173, n. 1.

[2] H. Rickert, 'Zwei Wege der Erkenntnistheorie', *Kant-Studien*, XIV (1909), 169–228; Max Scheler, *Die transzendentale und die psychologische Methode*.

gories, and it has for its presupposition 'that which is' or 'the objective and unalterable'. It seeks after *truth* which becomes known through some sort of intuition to the one doing the thinking. There is, however, another science of time-categories which has as its object 'becoming' or 'that which is becoming'; it seeks for *certainty* to which the thinker is led through recollection. As an example of such a science we have mentioned the philosophy of Henri Bergson. It too encompasses the whole of reality and advocates the view that the universe is a dynamic reality which is to be understood by analogy with life; life is the fundamental fact of existence, and it is manifested in creative activity which is to be grasped not in concepts and logical thinking but through intuition. Aside from a certain disposition toward mysticism, which comes to the fore particularly in his doctrine of time, the weakness of Bergson's philosophy lies in his depreciation of the mind or the intellect as an organ for apprehending the essence of reality. In direct opposition to Kant, he grants to mathematical-physical science only a practical but no epistemological significance. His onesidedness must be understood as a consequence of the way in which the problem was posed by the transcendentalists who also held that only a single and onesided solution to the epistemological problem was possible. One could have agreed with Bergson, had he confined himself to positive tenets and left open the possibility that reality could also be viewed from a static aspect which is to be apprehended intellectually. When we speak hereinafter of psychological understanding and logical thinking, we mean the two different ways of thinking by means of which the reflecting man is able mentally to appropriate reality; formally speaking they are mutually exclusive, but speaking materially they are complementary.

It is not difficult to see that Israelite mental life belongs to the former type and Greek mental life to the latter. It is hardly necessary to demonstrate that Greek thinking is of the logical sort after all that we have already particularized upon the subject and taking into consideration what is otherwise familiar to us. It is considerably more necessary to penetrate the peculiarity of Israelite thinking, first because the psychological kind of thinking is, in general, more foreign to us than the logical, and second because the singular value of Israelite thinking is misconstrued by a majority of scholars and mistaken for primitive thinking as though it were prelogical. Israelite thinking is prelogical to the extent that it stands closer to natural life than the subtle, lifeless, unimaginative, and almost fossilized abstractions of our highly scientific thinking; this also applies to Greek thinking, however, and not only to that of a Socrates or a Plato but also to that of an Aristotle. To be sure, Greek mental life bears a more advanced stamp than the Israelite, but it must be recalled that Israelite mental life is by and large significantly older than the Greek, although it cannot be classified as primitive.[1]

In a simple and unadorned language the Hebrew writers have given expression to profound and meaningful truths; occasionally we hear from a biblical writer that the simplicity of his language was a conscious renunciation of the terminology and style of rhetorical and philosophical language which was in his day highly esteemed but today is unpalatable.[2] Moreover, not all thinkers are systematists with an inclination and capacity for broad and comprehensive presentation, for developments of ideas in all their details, and for the architecturally beautiful structure of a system. There are also analytic thinkers whose significance consists in the acuteness and penetrating profundity of their ideas, the extent of whose works may be extremely modest. For a long time Leibniz has been recognized as one of Europe's most original thinkers, although he wrote only two longer monographs.[3] The extensive works of his systematically-minded successor, Christian Wolff, have not only aroused the admiration of a broad stratum of the educated people of many a decade, but they also achieved Kant's highest approbation,[4] whose assessment of Leibniz was quite unenthusiastic. In this instance, Kant is merely expressing the customary European judgment that only the systematists are real thinkers. Whoever is of this opinion will find no thinkers in the Old Testament, for the Israelites were truly no systematizers, even less logicians; yet, he is hardly right in his opinion.

As the Greeks have made the greatest achievements in the fields of philosophy and science in our cultural province and in the civilized world generally, so the Israelites have achieved the most in the field of religion and morals. The antithesis need not be exaggerated since Greek philosophy did achieve its zenith in morals and religion (Socrates and Plato), while Israel produced minds which made religious problems the object of profoundest existential thinking. Along with the difference in fields of inquiry goes likewise a difference in method of inquiry; in philosophy and science,

---

[1] *Vide supra*, pp. 21 ff.   [2] I Cor. 1.17.

[3] *Theodicy, Essays on the Goodness of God, the Freedom of Man and the Origin of Evil*, Eng. trans. (London: Routledge & Kegan Paul, 1952), first published in 1710; *New Essays concerning Human Understanding*, trans. A. G. Langley (3rd ed.; LaSalle, Ill.: Open Court Publishing Co., 1949, first published in 1765. The *Theodicy* is, in form, only a commentary on a work by Pierre Bayle, and the *Essays* is a discussion with John Locke 'composed in spare time'.

[4] '. . . . in the future system of metaphysics, we have therefore to follow the strict method of the celebrated Wolff, the greatest of all dogmatic philosophers'. *Critique of Pure Reason*, p. 33.

logic is the agreed mode of thinking, but in religion and morals, whose locale is most prominently in the innermost depths of man, it is psychology.

C. THE INDEPENDENCE OF THE ISRAELITE THINKER

To estimate fairly the achievements of Israelite thinkers it must be borne in mind that their originality did not lie in the discovery of new ideas or new material; the claim to this kind of originality is really that of new evidence. In Greek antiquity the discovery of new material was the business of the poet only to a limited degree;[1] even Shakespeare used without hesitation already existent material in his dramas. Nor did the originality of the Israelite thinker lie in *stylistic* reworking of material. Even in this field the Hebrews were apparently devoid of ambition; so far as the form was materially useful they allowed the words and expressions of the authors to remain undisturbed. If those words and expressions came into conflict with Israelite religion, morality, or kind of thinking, the material was partly reworked, partly expurgated, partly expanded, and partly reshaped. In the clarity with which this was seen and in the rigour with which it was carried out lies one of the most essential accomplishments of Israelite thinkers and writers. It must be added that in the field of religion and morals originality is not highly regarded; on the contrary, all the great religious minds, even the most original, come forth with the claim to be preaching the old religion. Moses came with a message from the God of the Patriarchs; the prophets appealed to Moses and the ancient morality; Christ would not destroy the Law and the Prophets but fulfil them; Paul would preach none other than Christ; Luther would bring Christian doctrine back into full agreement with ancient Christianity in Holy Scripture and the ancient Church. The Catholic Church will recognize as religious truth only that 'which has been believed always, everywhere, and by all'.[2] Seen against this background, the conscious use of moral-religious material out of other religions and still more its recasting in the Israelite mind is already a sign of spiritual independence, boldness, and creativity.[3] Independent assimilation and revision of foreign material

---

[1] Bruno Snell, *Entdeckung des Geistes*, p. 285; M. Nilsson, *The Mycenean Origin of Greek Mythology*, p. 2.

[2] 'In ipsa catholica ecclesia magnopere curandum est, ut id teneamus, quod ubique, quod semper, quod ab omnibus creditum est.' Vincentius Lirinensis, *Commonitorium Primum, Patrologia Latina*, ed. J. P. Migne, 50, 641.

[3] We find the same attitude among the Greeks who were much more tolerant of foreign religions than the Romans, and who understood, nevertheless, how to assimilate foreign elements so that the Greek culture kept itself pure right into Christian era, while Rome, when opposition to the foreign finally had to cease, was overrun by foreign religions. *Tiele-Söderblom Kompendium*, p. 350.

was taking place during the ancient period, perhaps even during the time of Solomon's reign. The wisdom teaching of Amen-em-ope was taken over almost verbatim, but all polytheistic traces and all references to the judgment of the dead were carefully expurgated.[1] Another example from the ancient period is the above-mentioned Jahvistic transformation, in Israelite spirit, of the Egyptian narrative of creation.

An example of an astounding religious-psychological insight and of a good insight into human character is the Jahvistic account of the Fall (Genesis 3). If it is correct that the Jahvist wrote the history of Israel from the Creation to the division of the Kingdom,[2] then he was not only a great writer but also a significant historian. It is possible and probable that he belonged to the Temple establishment, but in any case he is an independently thinking, creative personality of the first rank in the ancient royal period. Beyond the shadow of a doubt, he belongs among the thinkers of Israel.

Another great thinker is the author of the Priestly Code (P), who gave us among other things the account of Creation which now stands first (Gen. 1.1–2.4a) and forged the above-mentioned concept of the *Imago Dei*. Among the thinking personalities we number further the man or the school who produced Deuteronomy. It is quite correct in general that we have to reckon not only with thinking personalities but with whole circles or schools of spiritually advanced men who stand behind the great positive values that we have in the Pentateuch and the other Old Testament books. In Isa. 53.1 ff., one such circle adopts the very word, and what is more in a poetic cycle which otherwise clearly bears the stamp of a single author (cf. John 21.24).

In our opinion it is mistaken to count as thinkers only the Wisdom teachers in the narrower sense; all those who ever strove with spiritual problems, found in their struggles tenable solutions, and mediated them to posterity deserve to be counted with them as well. These heroes of the battlefield of the inner struggle are not only anonymous, but they have vanished entirely behind their work. Yet they have bestowed this upon us: to them we owe the entire Old Testament which, next to the New Testament wherein we are addressed almost exclusively by Jews, represents the highest achievement in the field of religion and morals. National leaders acted, kings acted, prophets spoke, wise men and thinkers recounted, taught, and wrote; they made independent contributions to the

---

[1] H. Gressmann, 'Die neugefundene Lehre des Amen-em-ope . . .', ZAW, I, 272–96; Paul Humbert, *Recherches sur les sources Égyptiennes de la littérature sapientiale d'Israël.*

[2] G. Hölscher, *Die Anfänge der hebräischen Geschichtsschreibung*, pp. 6, 99 ff.; M.M.M., II, 302.

development and maintenance of Israelite religion, and they were surely conscious of them. We do not perhaps think, in this connexion, of the lyric to the glorification of Wisdom:

> Jahveh created me as the beginning of his way,
>   As the first of his works, long ago.
> From eternity have I been established,
>   at the very beginning since the foundation of the earth
>   (Prov. 8.22 f. Kautzsch).

If Schencke is right in his contention that in this and similar cases, a previously existent form of the poem regarded Wisdom as a separate deity,[1] in any case all traces of it are expunged consistently in the Old Testament; under no circumstances is there justification for expecting polytheistic inclinations of the post-Exilic writer and admirer of Wisdom. To that extent his independence and ability at transformation have been sufficiently great in the face of the foreign original. Real thinkers would scarcely have praised Wisdom and with it their own wisdom to the degree it is done in Proverbs 8, but this poem can be evidence of how highly certain circles in late Judaism regarded the earlier Wise Men. They have now approached a place alongside the prophets as bearers of revelation.

As an example of a thinker who is creative and self-conscious in the better sense, we can offer the poet who has given us the book of Job. With Steuernagel,[2] and others, we consider the book as a unity with the exception of Elihu's speech (chs. 32–37) and certain other sections (e.g. ch. 28). It is psychologically impossible to write so forceful a book without having fought one's way victoriously through the most trying inner conflicts and temptations; Job's problems were doubtless the problems of the poet's own life.[3] With exemplary keenness, precariously bordering on blasphemy, he contests the Jewish dogma that severe and enduring misfortune is always to be considered God's punishment. So universalistic is his view of God and so humble his faith that he can set up a non-Jew as an unrivalled pattern of piety. So exalted a universalism decidedly calls into question the necessity of a religion of special revelation, or in any case endangers it; under any circumstances his universalism is not to be excelled from a standpoint of revelation. In the New Testament, similar scandal-causing utterances come only from the mouth of Jesus (Luke 4.25 ff.; 8.11 f.). If it is correct that the dualism in the narrative

---

[1] W. Schencke, *Die Chokma (Sophia) in der jüdischen Hypostasenspekulation*; W. F. Albright (*op. cit.*, p. 284) is of the same opinion. Cf. G. Boström, *Die Weisheit und das fremde Weib in Spr. 1–9* ('Acta Univ. Lundensis'); the same interpretation is to be found already in W. Bousset, *Die Religion des Judentums im neutestamentlichen Zeitalter*, p. 592.
[2] Kautzsch, II, 293 ff.   [3] S. Mowinckel, *Diktet om Ijob*, pp. 37 ff.

portions and the monism in the four men's speeches present the two sides of the author's view of God or his faith in God,[1] then he has understood that monism and dualism do not have to exclude one another mutually; in the God of Israel, who is at once God of the world as well as the God of the heathen who know him and pray to him not under the name Jahveh, both are right. At this point the author is already at the New Testament level. Like the author of the book of Jonah, he has in the names of God a delicate instrument for expressing his ideas about God, since he calls the unfathomable deity Elohim, El, Eloah, etc., and the divinity as God revealed for the Israelites he calls Jahveh.[2] This instrument was certainly formed in that intellectually advanced epoch of post-Exilic Judaism.

Deutero-Isaiah, who thinks every bit as universalistically about the God of Israel, knew only monism and employs only the one name of God, Jahveh. Although Deutero-Isaiah wrestles with difficult religious problems, he still belongs to the prophets, the practically working preachers. The authors of the books of Job and Jonah are of the more reflective type and temperament; they are already teachers of wisdom. Obviously we cannot essay an exposition or a rigorous analysis of the problem of Job; such an inquiry would lead us too far afield. Our purpose was only to call attention to the fact that to the poet of the book of Job belongs a place of honour in the succession of the world's great religious thinkers. Undoubtedly, the Preacher of Ecclesiastes is also a great thinker; no one before him achieved to such a degree the unity of profound and consistent pessimism with peace of mind and fear of God.

D. THE FORMAL PECULIARITY OF EACH KIND OF THINKING

First, we would sketch with a few strokes the visual kind of the Greeks' thinking; against this background the Israelites' peculiar kind of thinking stands out so much more clearly. It is astounding how far clear thinking depended for the Greeks upon the visual faculty. As evidence we may cite not only Euclid's Geometry, Aristotle's Logic, and Plato's Doctrine of Ideas, but we should also recall the quite metaphysical significance that Plato accords to the study of geometry—through geometry the highest earthly being is perceived, and true being, i.e. divine being, is betokened. Bruno Snell calls the Greeks 'men of eyes' (*Augenmenschen*)

---

[1] Th. Boman, 'Jobsproblemet', NTT, XLVI (1945), 92 ff.
[2] Th. Boman, 'Jahve og Elohim i Jonaboken', NTT, XXXVII (1936), 159–68, together with Mowinckel's remarks.

and finds the significance of sight for Greek knowledge confirmed by the fact that the expressions for 'know' are derived, in ancient Greek, mostly from the stem, Fιδ—'see', and this meaning is still present in the words in question. Yet even where this is not the case, most of the Greek words for knowing and knowledge are related to the visual faculty, thus γιγνώσκω, γνώμη, γνῶσις, ἱστορία.[1] Gunnar Rudberg says of Plato that he

> is a man of sight, of seeing. His thinking is a thinking with the eyes, proceeding from what is seen. His highest flight of thought—in his doctrine of Ideas—is in many ways tied to vision. In this he is not alone in Hellas; on the contrary, it is a Hellenic characteristic which we can still follow through art, cultus, poetry, and literature—epic, lyric, drama—philosophy and history, in part even in Thucydides' abstract and often onerously approached reflexions and speeches (e.g. the funeral oration of Pericles, ii, 35 ff.).[2]

The meaning of sight for the Greeks is even deeper:

> One had also to see what is invisible to the eye and inaccessible to the senses. This too is sight, viewing, *theoria*. This is comprehended in Plato's works and philosophy. It is later worked out more clearly by Aristotle who knows and glorifies cosmic observation, who also in his later works allowed the action of thinking as well as its result to be visible: *theoria*.[3]

Quite as decided in the Old Testament is the emphasis upon the significance of *hearing* and of the *word in its being spoken*,[4] a fact to which we have already quite frequently referred. The Greek element in Philo's thinking achieves expression not least in the fact that where in his Bible he comes to an expression where God speaks to the ear of man, he is immediately very careful to eliminate God's speaking and to replace the hearing with a seeing, and what is more with a seeing through the eyes of the soul. The change of ears into eyes and further into eyes of the soul is a motif that appears frequently in Philo.[5]

Perhaps we can better understand the formal difference in the thinking of the two peoples if we try to answer the questions: what do they mean by truth? For the Greeks truth, negatively expressed, is that

[1] Bruno Snell, *Die Ausdrücke für den Begriff des Wissens* ('Philologische Unter-suchungen, XXIX'), pp. 1 ff., 20 ff., 59 ff., 69.

[2] Gunnar Rudberg, *Platon*, pp. 231 f.

[3] *Ibid.*, p. 234.

[4] Rudolf Bultmann, 'Der Begriff des Wortes Gottes', in E. Lohmeyer (ed.), *Vom Worte Gottes*, pp. 14 ff.

[5] H. Leisegang, *Der Heilige Geist. I, i: Die vorgeschichtliche Anschauungen und Lehren vom πνεῦμα und der mystisch-intuitiven Erkenntnis*, p. 219.

which is unveiled (ἀληθής=α—privative+ληθης='hidden'; cf. λανθάνω),[1] therefore, that which is revealed, clear, evident, or that which is to be seen clearly. The positive expression for 'true' is connected in Indo-European languages with the notion of being:

> the primitive German form *santha from IE *sont, present participle of the root *es—'be' (Greek ἐών, ὤν— 'being' from *esont, cf. Sanskrit sant—'being (adj.), good, true'), AS soth; in the Nordic languages the root is well attested: sann—'true'; the German word for 'true' (wahr) is one which made its way up from the south and replaced in Anglo-Saxon the older soth.[2]

Even though the positive expression for 'true' does not occur in Greek, the *concept* of truth in Sanskrit is typically Greek: 'that which is' is the true and to that extent is also the good. This is certainly the Platonic doctrine of Ideas *in nuce*; therefore, some light is thrown upon the mysterious sway that Plato has held over the minds of men in the West for two thousand years. Plato made it possible to give expression to the unconscious and therefore most profound thoughts of the Indo-European peoples on the nature of reality.

The corresponding Hebrew concept of truth is expressed by means of derivatives of the verb 'aman—'to be steady, faithful': 'amen—'verily, surely'; 'omen—'faithfulness'; 'umnam—'really'; 'emeth—'constancy, trustworthiness, certainty, fidelity to reported facts, truth'; cf. 'omenah— 'pillar, door-post'. In short, the Hebrews really do not ask what is true in the objective sense but what is subjectively certain, what is faithful in the existential sense; therefore, it is not what is in agreement with impersonal objective being that interests them, but what is in agreement with the facts that are meaningful for them. This shows that Hebrew thought is directed toward events, living, and history in which the question of truth is of another sort than in natural science. In such matters the true is the completely certain, sure, steady, faithful.

Moreover, when we compare the Greeks' act of thinking with that of the Hebrews, the antithesis is simply stated; synthetic *versus* analytic. It is significant that λόγος—'reason' is derived from λέγω—'gather': the points to be taken into consideration are sought, gathered, and arranged according to definite rules into a pleasing whole, and in that way the truth is demonstrated. Israelite thinking is analytic;[3] *bin* meaning 'understand'

---

[1] E. Boisacq, *Dictionnaire étymologique de la langue Grecque, s.v.*

[2] Alf Torp, *Nynorsk etymologisk ordbok*; Friedr. Kluge, *Etymologisches Wörterbuch der deutschen Sprache.*

[3] When Aubrey Johnson calls Israelite thinking synthetic, he really means 'holistic, in totality': '. . . . Israelite thinking . . . is predominantly synthetic. It is characterized by what has been called the grasping of a totality. Phenomena . . . participate in some

really means 'to dismember, separate'; from it comes *binah*—'understanding, comprehension, discernment, insight'. The Hebrew separates the non-essential and external from the essential and important in order to find the heart of the matter, and in order, once having found it, to express it as briefly and pointedly as possible. Once the point has been discovered there is no purpose in setting forth a detailed demonstration with an extensive development of ideas.

When it is the intention to convince hearers, it is appropriate to circumvent the psychic fortifications which every man involuntarily erects in his innermost self; this is achieved by a good parable whose validity the hearers cannot contest. If the parable is cogent, i.e., completely parallel to an event in the life of the hearer, its persuasive power can be very great. One need but recall the well-known parable of the prophet Nathan and its effect upon King David (II Samuel 12) or the parables of Jesus and their effect upon his opponents (Matt. 21.45 f.). When the psychic defences have to be overcome in open conflict, the normal method is that of repetition whereby the appropriate point is constantly hammered. An example of this is to be found in Ecclesiastes whose principal intention it is to hammer home but a single point announced at the very beginning:

> Vanity of vanities, says the Preacher,
> Vanity of vanities, all is vanity.

The familiar *parallelismus membrorum* is an example of Hebrew preference for repetition:

> Blessed is the man that walketh not
>   in the counsel of the ungodly,
> nor standeth in the way of sinners,
> nor sitteth in the seat of the scornful (Ps. 1.1 AV).

The same tendency appears grammatically when a verbal idea is sharpened by appending an infinitive absolute to a finite verb of the same stem. The Hebrew thinkers' and poets' art of composition is not like that in architecture where everything is built step by step, but it is more similar to music wherein the theme is set forth at the beginning and returns later in constantly new variations.

sort of whole. . . . the mental activity of the Israelites as predominantly synthetic, the awareness of totality . . . is the 'Open Sesame' which unlocks the secrets of the Hebrew language and reveals the riches of the Israelite mind' (*op. cit.*, pp. 7 f.). This grasping of a totality or participating in a whole is not the same thing as synthetic thinking. The Greeks, especially Plato, as well as the Israelites consider 'wholes' as fundamental. But Plato starts from the individual concrete thing, always thinking more generally, more abstractly, and more mentally, and mounting ever higher until he sees the protoptyes of all appearances, the Ideas. For the Israelite, the point of departure was the universal of which concrete persons and things appeared as parts or manifestations.

The other expressions for the function of thinking (*yadha'*—'know', *ra'ah*—'see', *shama'*—'hear') likewise have the purpose of finding a point rather than of furnishing a proof. Of these expressions, *ra'ah*—'see' is particularly interesting since, as we indicated above, seeing is characteristic of Greek thinking. When an Israelite uses the word with this meaning, however, he combines with it an image other than that of the Greeks. Visible things become signs for the Israelite disclosing to him the qualities of their possessor or creator. When one has discovered these, he has seen things correctly. Everything that King Solomon had made testified of his wisdom; it is rightly said of the Queen of Sheba that she not only heard his wisdom but also saw it (I Kings 10.4). She would not believe the reports of his wisdom until she had come and seen with her own eyes (v. 7). Of course, the Israelite also knew of an external seeing which discovered only the surface of things, but not until one had plumbed the depths and seen the inside of things, their true content and their centre, did he really understand the matter. The Israelite coined separate expressions for the two kinds of observation: to see the surface or appearance, and to see the heart, i.e. the true essence (I Sam. 16.7). Through Isaiah, God utters the reproach against Israel that they see without understanding (Isa. 6.9). Inversely, religion is 'correctly learning by sight, seeing with open eyes how God carries out his purpose in life and in history. The great seer Isaiah considers as his real purpose in life this seeing and learning by sight.'[1] A seer, *ro'eh*, is a man of God who sees what is hidden from other men, be it runaway domestic animals, hidden sins, or future events. The Wise Man sees deeper than others; when the Preacher says, 'yea, my heart had great experience of wisdom and knowledge' (Eccles. 1.16 AV), it is clear that his observation is of an entirely different kind from the Platonic. Greek thinking is clear logical knowing; Israelite thinking is deep psychological understanding. Both kinds of thinking are equally necessary if one means to be in touch with the whole of reality.

[1] G. Hölscher, *Die Profeten, Untersuchungen zur Religionsgeschichte Israels*, p. 250; S. Mowinckel, *Profeten Jesaja*, p. 90.

Summary and Psychological Foundation of the Differences

FROM THE foregoing exposition, it has emerged clearly that the several features within Hebrew thinking are internally related and that the same thing can be said of Greek thinking. In conclusion we wish to advert expressly to the unitary quality of each of these two so very different kinds of thinking and briefly to demonstrate it.

We are able to appreciate the unitariness of Greek thinking without further explanation because, on the whole, we think in a similar way; however, the unitariness of Hebrew thinking is not difficult to establish against the background of Greek thinking. The matter is outlined in bold relief by two characteristic figures; the thinking Socrates and the praying Orthodox Jew. When Socrates was seized by a problem, he remained immobile for an interminable period of time in deep thought; when Holy Scripture is read aloud in the synagogue, the Orthodox Jew moves his whole body ceaselessly in deep devotion and adoration. The Greek most acutely experiences the world and existence while he stands and reflects, but the Israelite reaches his zenith in ceaseless movement. Rest, harmony, composure, and self-control—this is the Greek way; movement, life, deep emotion, and power—this is the Hebrew way.

According to the Israelite conception, everything is in eternal movement: God and man, nature and the world. The totality of existence, 'ôlam, is time, history, life. The history of heaven and earth (Gen. 2.4) is of the same form as the history of Adam (5.1), Noah (6.9), and Shem (11.10); it is referred to in each case by the same word, tôledhoth. The fact that God created the world and man once and for all implies that God makes history and brings forth life and that he continues them until they achieve their goal. All sources of being are in God, who alone is. However, because, formally speaking, for the Hebrew being is the same as energy, then he who is, the only true one (Jahveh), is identical with the almighty creator, the saviour, and the world perfector, a point that Deutero-Isaiah untiringly reiterates.

As space was the given thought-form for the Greeks, so for the Hebrews it was time. Now, as Kant says, time is 'nothing but the form of inner sense, that is of the intuition of ourselves and of our inner state. It cannot be a determination of outer appearances; it has to do neither with shape nor position, but with the relation of representations in our inner state.'[1] From this it follows that Hebrew thinking necessarily became psychological, since psychology is concerned with us ourselves and our inner states and images. Moreover, it was of equal necessity that Greek thinking should bear the stamp of logic, since logical validity is constructed externally (objectively), independently of our psychical conditions, and for the most part it also permits of demonstration by way of diagrams, at any rate so far as the Greeks evolved it.

For the Hebrew, the decisive reality of the world of experience was the *word*; for the Greek it was the *thing*. Yet the *word* had great significance for the Greek on account of its meaning; on the whole, however, the meaning of the word is independent of the word as spoken or dynamic reality. Likewise, the *thing* had great significance for the Hebrew, not because of form, shape, or appearance, but partly as instrument, i.e. as a means of action, and partly because of its inherent meaning (cf. The Song of Solomon). In the Hebrew environment the *thing* was conceived as a dynamic reality, to the extent that it was an instrument, and as a qualitative unit defined by its content, as the Song of Solomon demonstrates.

From these last arguments, as well as from those before, we can conclude that for the Hebrew the most important of his senses for the experience of truth was his hearing (as well as various kinds of feeling), but for the Greek it had to be his sight; or perhaps inversely, because the Greeks were organized in a predominantly visual way and the Hebrews in a predominantly auditory way, each people's conception of truth was formed in increasingly different ways. The impressions gained by way of hearing or perceived sensually—we are thinking of word, light, warmth, odour, flavour, and so on—have the three aforementioned specifically Hebraic characteristics: they are constantly changing, they are of a dynamic-qualitative sort because they can be expressed in all degrees of intensity and in varying qualities, and they are psychologically meaningful because they can awake every possible mood or feeling. The impressions we gain through sight, the visible things, are static in principle because the eye acts as a camera, and as everyone knows, it can record only momentary or instantaneous pictures, that is to say pictures in which movement is

[1] *Critique of Pure Reason*, p. 77.

at the time so imperceptible as not to be observed. If we observe a body in motion, our eyes follow it so that we retain a relatively static and, at the same time, clear picture of it.[1] When these two conditions are absent, it is impossible clearly to recognize movement as, for example, when we sit in a train and another one passes by. In such a case we can neither see the background of the other train nor establish by perception whether or not *we* are moving. Perception of a moving object takes place at the expense of the clarity of its background which seems vague if we notice it at the same time. Sight impressions must, therefore, chiefly be based upon those images which have form, objectivity, and immutability.[2]

We have pursued the unitariness and the peculiarity of each of these kinds of thinking right back to their physiological or physiologically conditioned presuppositions; farther than this one cannot go. From this vantage point we are able to make a final observation upon our theme. Since both our chief senses, sight and hearing, must pay for their astonishing accomplishments the price of an externally stamped bias, both highly developed peoples of ancient times, Hellas and Israel, could achieve their magnificent contributions to civilization only in virtue of their bias. As their cultural successors and heirs, we can pay them no greater homage than to attend equally to both heritages, to protect them, and, if possible, to find a synthesis between them just as we try in our own lives to make the most of all five senses if we would understand reality and have a thorough grasp of all of it.[3]

Our attempt to represent the unitary Hebraic manner of thinking and the unitary Greek manner of thinking as two possible and equally necessary reactions to one and the same reality can possibly offer a contribution toward illuminating a problem which atomic physics has posed to contemporary epistemology. The Nestor of modern atomic physics, Niels

[1] W. Wundt, *Grundzüge der physiologischen Psychologie*, II, 611.
[2] The sense-physiologists do not seem to be aware of the essential difference between and the incommensurability of optical and acoustical perceptions (cf. Yrjö Renqvist-Reenpää, *Allgemeine Sinnesphysiologie*, p. 59). We are not only in agreement with the Greeks in their high estimate of sight, but we are even advanced farther along the way since we try in various ways to make pictures of invisible phenomena: thermometers, barometers, and other measuring apparatus, graphic presentations, etc.
[3] Oswald Spengler (*Decline of the West*, I, 53–90) has outlined very well the static, geometric, visual, and unhistorical thinking of the Greeks. Obviously he does not know that in Ancient Israel there was a corresponding and complementary kind of thinking, but he rather believes that the dynamic, algebraic, historical thinking which he calls Faustian originated with Western man. Had he been aware of this fact, he certainly would not have seen the adventurous task of the West to be one of developing the dynamic-functional type of civilization as perfectly as possible. Instead he would have seen it as one of finding and presenting a synthesis of both kinds of thinking. The history of Europe in which ever since the Phoenicians Indo-Europeans and Semites have been thrown together lays this task upon us.

Bohr, has continually emphasized that the findings of atomic physics are *complementary*, i.e. they cannot be correctly described without resorting to expressions which are logically irreconcilable. Thus, some experiments show that the atom has wave structure, and others show that it consists of particles (quanta). If both are right, reality possesses opposite properties which complete each other. Bohr calls the unitariness of opposite manifestations of a phenomenon *complementarity*.[1] In that sense, Hebrew and Greek thinking are complementary; the Greeks describe reality as *being*, the Hebrews as *movement*. Reality is, however, both at the same time; this is logically impossible, and yet it is correct.

[1] Niels Bohr, 'Discussion with Einstein on Epistemological Problems in Atomic Physics', *Albert Einstein: Philosopher-Scientist*, ed. Paul Schilpp ('Library of Living Philosophers', vol. 7 [New York, 1951]), pp. 199–241. *Idem*, 'The Unity of Knowledge', *The Unity of Knowledge*, ed. Lewis G. Leary ('Columbia University, Bicentennial Conference Series' [New York, 1955]), pp. 47 ff. An extensive treatment of the problem is to be found also in Niels Bohr, *Atomic Physics and Human Knowledge* (London and New York, 1958); [the last-named title is a continuation of a previous set of papers, Niels Bohr, *Atomic Theory and the Description of Nature* (Cambridge: at the University Press, 1934). Tr.].

BIBLIOGRAPHY

Listing in a systematic arrangement all the works used by the author.

REFERENCE BOOKS

BUHL, FRANTS (ed.) *Wilhelm Gesenius' hebräisches und aramäisches Handwörterbuch über das Alte Testament.* 16th ed., Leipzig: F. C. W. Vogel, 1915.

HARRIMAN, P. L. (ed.) *The Encyclopaedia of Psychology.* New York: Philosophical Library, 1946.

Jüdisches Lexikon, 4 vols. Berlin: Jüdischer Verlag, 1927–30.

KAUTZSCH, E. (ed.) *Die Heilige Schrift des Alten Testaments,* 2 vols. 4th ed., Tübingen: J. C. B. Mohr, 1922–23.

KAUTZSCH, E. (ed.) *Gesenius' Hebrew Grammar.* Translated and revised to German 28th edition by A. E. Cowley. 2nd ed., Oxford: Clarendon Press, 1910.

KITTEL, GERHARD (ed.) *Theologisches Wörterbuch zum Neuen Testament,* in process. Stuttgart: W. Kohlhammer, 1933–.

LUTHARDT, C. E. *Kompendium der Dogmatik,* edited by Prof. Robert Jelke. 14th ed. Leipzig: Dörffling & Franke, 1937.

MICHELET, S., MOWINCKEL, S., and MESSEL, N. *Det Gamle Testamente oversatt.* 4 vols. to date. Oslo: Aschehoug, 1929–.
  i *Loven eller de fem Moseböker,* 1929.
  ii *De tidligere Pro-feter,* 1936.
  iii *De senere profeter,* 1944.
  iv *Skriftene I,* 1955.

Die Religion in Geschichte und Gegenwart, 1st ed., 4 vols. Tübingen: J. C. B. Mohr, 1909–13.
  2nd ed., 5 vols. and index. Tübingen: J. C. B. Mohr, 1927–32.

SCHMIDT, H. *Philosophisches Wörterbuch.* 9th ed., Leipzig: A. Kröner, 1934.

TIELE, C. P., and SÖDERBLOM, N. *Kompendium der Religionsgeschichte.* 6th ed., Berlin: Th. Biller, 1931.

BOOKS, MONOGRAPHS, ETC.

AALL, ANATHON *Der Logos. I Geschichte seiner Entwicklung.* Leipzig: Reislaud, 1896.

ALBRIGHT, W. F. *From the Stone Age to Christianity.* Baltimore: Johns Hopkins Press, 1940.

ARCHER-HIND, R. D. *The Timaeus of Plato,* ed. with Introduction and Notes. London: Macmillan, 1888.

ARISTOTLE *The Physics.* (*See* Wicksteed.)

AUERBACH, ERICH *Mimesis: The Representation of Reality in Western Literature.* Translated by Willard R. Trask. Princeton, N.J.: Princeton University Press, 1953.

BARTH, KARL *Church Dogmatics*, I, II, IV i. Eng. tr. Edinburgh: T. & T. Clark, 1936–.

BAUR, F. C. *Drei Abhandlungen zur Geschichte der alten Philosophie und ihres Verhältnisses zum Christentum*, newly edited by Edward Zeller. Leipzig: Fues, 1876.

BERGGRAV, EIVIND *Der Durchbruch der Religion im menschlichen Seelenleben*. Translated by V. H. Günther. Göttingen: Vandenhoeck & Ruprecht, 1929.

BERGSON, HENRI *Creative Evolution*. Translated by Arthur Mitchell. London: Macmillan, 1911.
Essai sur les données immédiates de la conscience. Paris: F. Alcan, 1889; Geneva: A. Skira, 1945.
La Perception du changement: Conférences faites à l'Université d'Oxford les 26 et 27 Mai 1911. Oxford: Clarendon Press, 1911.

BIRKELAND, HARRIS *Laerebok i hebraisk grammatik*. Oslo: Norli, 1950.
Språk og religion hos jöder og arabere. ('Etnologisk samfunns skrifter utgitt ved Nils Lid', no. iv) Oslo: Norli, 1949.

BJÖRNSON, BJ. *Århundredernes legende. Gjenfortalt efter Victor Hugo 'La légende des siècles'*. 3rd ed., Oslo: Gyldendal, 1927.
Legenden. Translated by Niels Hoyer and Hans von Gumppenberg. Munich: Georg. Müller, 1913.

BLAKE, FRANK R. *The Socalled Intransitive Verbal Forms in the Semitic Languages*. New Haven: Yale Univ. Press, 1903.

BLASS, F. *Grammatik des neutestamentlichen Griechisch*, ed. A. Debrunner. 4th ed., Göttingen: Vandenhoeck & Ruprecht, 1913.

BOHR, NIELS *Atomic Physics and Human Knowledge*. London: Chapman & Hall, Ltd. New York: John Wiley & Sons, Inc., 1958.

BOISACQ, EMILE *Dictionnaire étymologique de la langue Grecque*, 4th ed., Heidelberg: C. Winter, 1950.

BOSTRÖM, GUSTAV *Die Weisheit und das fremde Weib in Spr. 1–9* ('Lunds Universitets Arskrift'). Lund: C. W. K. Gleerup, 1935.

BOUSSET, W. *Die Religion des Judentums im neutestamentlichen Zeitalter*, 2nd ed., Berlin: Reuther & Reichard, 1906.

BUBER, MARTIN *I and Thou*. Translated by R. G. Smith. Edinburgh: T. & T. Clark, 1944.

BÜHLER, KARL *Sprachtheorie*. Jena: Fischer, 1934.

BUHL, FRANTS 'Über die Ausdrücke für: Ding, Sache, u. ä. im Semitischen', *Festschrift. Vilhelm Thomsen, zur Vollendung des siebzigsten Lebensjahres*, ed. E. Kuhn. Leipzig: Otto Harrasowitz, 1912, pp. 30–38.

BULTMANN, R. 'Der Begriff des Wortes Gottes im Neuen Testament'. (*See* Lohmeyer, E.)
Primitive Christianity in its Contemporary Setting, translated by R. H. Fuller. London: Thames & Hudson, 1956.

BURSZTYN, ISRAEL *Vollständige Grammatik der alt- und neuhebräischen Sprache*. Vienna: Gerold & Co., 1929.

CARNAP, RUDOLF *The Logical Syntax of Language*. English translation. London: K. Paul, Trench, Trubner & Co., 1935.

CASSIRER, ERNST *The Philosophy of Symbolic Forms. Vol. I, Language.*

Translated by Ralph Manheim. New Haven: Yale University Press, 1953.

CULLMANN, OSCAR *Christ and Time.* Translated by F. V. Filson. Philadelphia: Westminster Press, 1950; London: SCM Press, 1951.

DALMAN, G. H. *Palästinischer Diwan.* Leipzig: J. C. Hinrichs, 1901.

DELLING, GERHARD *Das Zeitverständnis des neuen Testaments.* Gütersloh: Bertelsmann, 1940.

DRIVER, G. R. *Problems of the Hebrew Verbal System.* Edinburgh: T. & T. Clark, 1936.

DÜRR, LORENZ *Die Wertung des göttlichen Wortes im Alten Testament und im antiken Orient* ('Mitteilungen der vorderasiatisch ägyptischen Gesellschaft', 42, 1). Leipzig: J. C. Hinrichs, 1938.

EICHRODT, W. *Theologie des Alten Testaments I–III*, 2 vols. Leipzig: J. C. Hinrichs, 1933–35; English translation in preparation.

GLOVER, T. R. *The Ancient World: A Beginning.* Cambridge: University Press, 1935.

GEISSLER, KURT *Die Grundzüge und das Wesen des Unendlichen in der Mathematik und Philosophie.* Leipzig: B. G. Teubner, 1902.

GOGARTEN, FRIEDRICH *Ich glaube an den dreieinigen Gott: Eine Untersuchung über Glaube und Geschichte.* Jena: C. Diederichs, 1926.

GRASSLER, R. *Der Sinn der Sprache Beitr. zu. Psychol. d. Erkenntnis.*: Lahr: Schauenburg, 1938.

GRETHER, OSKAR *Name und Wort Gottes im Alten Testament* ('Beihefte zur ZAW', 64). Giessen: A. Töpelmann, 1934.

GRÖNBECH, V. *Vor folkeaet i oldtiden 1–4.* Copenhagen: V. Pio, 1909–12.
  Hellas: Kultur og religion 1–4. Copenhagen: Branner, 1942–44.
  Primitiv religion ('Populära entologiska Skrifter', ed. C. V. Hartmann, 12). Stockholm: Norstedt, 1915.

GUNKEL, HERMANN *Genesis.* 4th ed., Göttingen: Vandenhoeck & Ruprecht, 1917.

GUTHE, H. *Kurzes Bibelwörterbuch.* Tübingen: J. C. B. Mohr, 1903.

HARNACK, A. *History of Dogma.* English translation, 6 vols. London: Williams & Norgate, 1895–1906.

HEIDEGGER, MARTIN *Sein und Zeit.* 2nd ed., Halle: Max Niemeyer, 1929; English translation in preparation.

HEIM, KARL *Glaube und Leben.* Berlin: Furche-Verlag, 1926.

HEINISCH, PAUL *Personifikationen und Hypostasen im Alten Testament und im alten Orient.* Münster i. W.: Aschendorf, 1921.

HEMPEL, J. (ed.) *Werden und Wesen des Alten Testaments* ('Beihefte zur ZAW', 66). Berlin: A. Töpelmann, 1936.
  Altes Testament und Geschichte ('Studien des apologetischen Seminars', 27). Gütersloh: C. Bertelsmann, 1930.

HERDER, J. G. *Vom Geist der ebräischen Poesie* (*Sämmtliche Werke*, ed. B. Suphan, vol. XI. Berlin: Weidmann, 1903).

HERMES, H. *Semiotik: Eine Theorie der Zeichengestalten als Grundlage für Untersuchungen von formalisierten Sprachen.* Leipzig: Hirzel, 1938.

HESSEN, J. *Platonismus und Prophetismus.* Munich: Reinhardt, 1939; 2nd ed., 1955.

HÖLSCHER, G. *Die Anfänge der hebräischen Geschichtsschreibung.* Heidelberg: C. Winter, 1942.
    Die Profeten, Untersuchungen zur Religionsgeschichte Israels. Leipzig: J. C. Hinrichs, 1914.
HÖNIGSWALD, R. *Philosophie und Sprache: Problemkritik und System.* Basle: Haus zum Falken Verlag, 1937.
HOPPE, E. *Mathematik und Astronomie im klassischen Altertum* ('Bibliothek der klassischen Altertumswissenschaft'). Heidelberg: C. Winter, 1911.
HUGO, VICTOR *La légende des siècles,* ed. Paul Berret. Paris: Hachette, 1920–26.
HUMBERT, PAUL *Études sur la récit du Paradis et de la chute dans la Genèse.* Neuchâtel: Secrétariat de l'Université, 1940.
    Recherches sur les sources Égyptiennes de la littérature sapientiale d'Israël. Neuchâtel: Secrétariat de l'Université, 1929.
JACOB, G. *Das Hohelied auf Grund arabischen und andere Parallelen von neuem untersucht.* Berlin: Mayer & Miller, 1902.
JAEGER, W. W. *Aristotle: Fundamentals of the History of his Development.* Translated by R. Robinson. 2nd ed., Oxford: Clarendon Press, 1948.
    Paideia: The Ideals of Greek Culture. Translated by Gilbert Highet. 3 vol . Oxford: B. H. Blackwell, 1939–44.
JOHNSON, AUBREY *The Vitality of the Individual in the Thought of Ancient Israel.* Cardiff: University of Wales Press, 1949.
KAINZ, F. *Psychologie der Sprache. I–II.* Stuttgart: F. Enke, 1941–43.
KERÉNYI, K. *Die Antike Religion.* Amsterdam: Panthéon, 1940.
KELLER, C. *Das Wort OTH als 'Offenbarungszeichen Gottes'.* Basle: Hoenen, 1946.
KLUGE, F. *Etymologisches Wörterbuch der deutschen Sprache.* 14th unaltered ed., Berlin: deGruyter, 1948.
KÖHLER, L. *Hebrew Man.* Translated by P. R. Ackroyd. London: SCM Press, 1956.
    Old Testament Theology. Translated by A. S. Todd. London: Lutterworth Press, 1957.
LEISEGANG, H. *Der Heilige Geist. I i : Die vorgeschichtliche Anschauungen und Lehren vom* πνεῦμα *und der mystisch-intuitiven Erkenntnis.* Leipzig: B. G. Teubner, 1919.
LEROY, O. *La raison primitive. Essai de réfutation de la théorie du prélogisme.* Paris: P. Geuthner, 1927.
LÉVY-BRUHL, L. *Les fonctions mentales dans les sociétés inférieures.* Paris: F. Alcan, 1910.
    How Natives Think. Translated by Lilian A. Clare. London: G. Allen & Unwin, 1926 (translation of previous entry).
    La mentalité primitive. Paris: F. Alcan, 1922.
    Primitive Mentality. Translated by Lilian A. Clare. London: G. Allen & Unwin, 1923 (translation of previous entry).
LITTMANN, ENNO *Neuarabische Volkspoesie.* Berlin: Weidmann, 1902.

LOHMEYER, E. (ed.) *Vom Worte Gottes* ('Deutsche Theologie' III). Göttingen: Vandenhoeck & Ruprecht, 1931.

MARSH, JOHN *The Fulness of Time*. London: Nisbet, 1952.

MORRIS, C. *Signs, Language and Behaviour*. New York: Prentice-Hall, 1946.

MOWINCKEL, S. *Diktet om Ijob og hans tre venner*. Oslo: Aschehoug, 1924. *Dat Gamle Testaments Salmebok*. Oslo: Aschehoug, 1919. *He That Cometh*. Translated by G. W. Anderson. Oxford: B. H. Blackwell; New York: Abingdon Press, 1956. *Profeten Jesaja*. Oslo: Aschehoug, 1925. *Sangenes Sang: Gammelhebraiske kjaerlighetssange*. Oslo: Aschehoug, 1919.

MUELLER, F. MAX *Lectures on the Science of Language, I–II*. London: Scribner's, 1871–72.

MUSIL, ALOIS *Arabia petraea*, publ. by Kaiserliche Akademie der Wissenschaft, 3 vols. Vienna: A. Hölder, 1907–8.

NEUGEBAUER, O. *Vorlesungen über die Geschichte der antiken mathematischen Wissenschaften*. Berlin: J. Springer, 1934.

NIEBUHR, REINHOLD *Faith and History*. London: Nisbet & Co.; New York: Scribner's, 1949.

NILSSON, M. P. *Geschichte der griechischen Religion I*. 2nd ed., Munich: C. H. Beck, 1955. *The Mycenean Origin of Greek Mythology*. Cambridge: University Press, 1932.

NÖLDEKE, TH. *Neue Beiträge zur semitischen Sprachwissenschaft*. Strassburg: K. J. Trübner, 1910.

NYGREN, ANDERS *Agape and Eros*. Translated by A. G. Hebert and P. S. Watson, 3 vols. London: S.P.C.K., 1932–39. *Filosofi och motivforskning*. Stockholm: Diakonistyr, 1940. *Die Versöhnung als Gottestat* ('Studien der Luther-Akademie' no. 5). Gütersloh: C. Bertelsmann, 1932.

ORDING, HANS *Estetikk og kristendom*. Oslo: Aschehoug, 1929.

VON ORELLI, C. *Die hebräischen Synonyma der Zeit und Ewigkeit, genetisch und sprachvergleichend dargestellt*. Leipzig: Lorentz, 1871.

OTTO, WALTER F. *The Homeric Gods: The Spiritual Significance of Greek Religion*. Translated by Moses Hadas. New York: Pantheon, 1954.

PASSOW, FRANZ *Handwörterbuch der griechischen Sprache*. 5th ed., Leipzig: W. Vogel, 1847.

PEAKE, A. S. (ed.) *The People and the Book*. Oxford: Clarendon Press, 1925.

PEDERSEN, JOHANNES *Israel: Its Life and Culture I–II, III–IV*. Translated by Mrs Aslaug Möller, 2 vols. London: Oxford University Press, 1926–47.

POHLENZ, MAX *Der hellenische Mensch*. Göttingen: Vandenhoeck & Ruprecht, 1947.

QUICK, O. C. *The Gospel of Divine Action*. New York: E. P. Dutton, 1933.

RADIN, P. *Primitive Man as a Philosopher*. New York and London: D. Appleton, 1927.

RATSCHOW, C. H. *Werden und Wirken* ('Beihefte zur ZAW', 70). Berlin: Alfred Töpelmann, 1941.

RENQVIST-REENPÄÄ, Y. *Allgemeine Sinnesphysiologie*. Vienna: Springer, 1936.

RICKERT, H. *Die Grenzen der naturwissenschaftlichen Begriffsbildung. Eine logische Einleitung in die historischen Wissenschaften.* Tübingen: J. C. B. Mohr, 1902.

RUDBERG, GUNNAR *Platon*. Lund: C. W. K. Gleerup, 1943.
   Ur Hellas' liv. Stockholm: Diakonistyr, 1934.

SCHELER, MAX *Die transzendentale und die psychologische Methode.* Leipzig: Dürr, 1900.

SCHENCKE, W. *Die Chokma (Sophia) in der jüdischen ·Hypostasenspekulation.* Oslo: J. Dybwad, 1912.

SEIERSTAD, I. P. *Die Offenbarungserlebnisse der Propheten Amos, Jesaja, und Jeremia.* Oslo: J. Dybwad, 1946.

SKINNER, J. *Genesis* ('International Critical Commentary'). 2nd ed., Edinburgh: T. & T. Clark, 1930.

SNELL, BRUNO *Die Ausdrücke für den Begriff des Wissens* ('Philologische Untersuchungen' XXIX). Berlin: Weidmann, 1924.
   Die Entdeckung des Geistes. Hamburg: Claassen, 1948.

SÖDERBLOM, N. *The Living God: basal forms of personal religion* ('Gifford Lectures, 1931'). London: Oxford University Press, 1933.
   Uppenbarelsereligion. 2nd ed., Stockholm: Diakonistyr, 1930.

SPENGLER, OSWALD *The Decline of the West*. Translated by C. F. Atkinson, 2 vols. London: George Allen & Unwin, 1926-28.

STAERK, W. *Lyrik (Psalmen, Hoheslied, und Verwandtes). (Die Schriften des Alten Testaments*, ed. Hugo Gressmann *et. al.*, Vol. III, 1). Göttingen: Vandenhoeck & Ruprecht, 1911.

STENZEL, J. *Philosophie der Sprache*. Munich and Berlin: R. Oldenbourg, 1934.

STURM, W. *Herders Sprachphilosophie in ihrem Entwicklungsgang und ihrer historischen Stellung*. Breslau: Fleischmann, 1917.

SVENDSEN, P. *Gullalderdröm og utviklingstro. En idéhistorisk undersökelse.* Oslo: Gyldendal, 1940.

THOMSEN, VILHELM *Festschrift*. (*See* Buhl, Frants.)

THORNDIKE, E. L. *Studies in the Psychology of Language*. ('Archives of Psychology' no. 231). New York, 1938.

TORP, ALF *Nyorsk etymologisk ordbok*. Oslo: Aschehoug, 1920.

TRESMONTANT, C. *Essai sur la pensée hébraïque* ('Lectio Divina' no. 12). Paris: Éditions du Cerf, 1953.
   Études de metaphysique biblique. Paris: Gabalda, 1955.

URBAN, W. M. *Language and Reality*. London: George Allen & Unwin, 1939.

DEVOGEL, C. J. *Antike Seinsphilosophie und Christentum im Wandel der Jahrhunderte*. Baden-Baden: Grimm, 1958.

WICKSTEED, P. H., and CORNFORD, F. M. (eds.) *Aristotle. The Physics*

('Loeb Classical Library'). London: Wm. Heinemann, Ltd., 1924–1929.

WILAMOVITZ-MOOLLENDORFF, ULRICH VON *Greek Historical Writing, and Apollo.* Translated by Gilbert Murray. Oxford: Clarendon Press, 1908.

WISCHNITZER, RACHEL *The Messianic Theme in the Paintings of the Dura Synagogue.* Chicago: University of Chicago Press, 1948; London: Cambridge University Press, 1949.

WUNDT, WILHELM *Grundzüge der Physiologischen Psychologie.* 3 vols. 6th ed., Leipzig: A. Kröner, 1911.

Völkerpsychologie, Band I. Die Sprache. 3rd ed., Leipzig: A. Kröner, 1911.

PERIODICAL ARTICLES

BOMAN, THORLEIF 'Begrepet ordning', *Norsk Teologisk Tidsskrift*, XLI (1940), 177 ff.

'Israelittiske og greske tankeformer i den eldste kristendom', NTT, XLVIII (1947), 66 ff.

'Jahve og Elohim i Jonaboken', NTT, XXXVII (1936), 159–68.

'Jobsproblemet', NTT, XLVI (1945), 92 ff.

'Den semittiske tenknings egenart', NTT, XXXIV (1933), 1–34.

BULTMANN, R. 'Zur Geschichte der seinem Sein konstituieren', *Philologus*, XCVII (1948), 17.

CARNAP, RUDOLF 'Die physikalische Sprache als Universalsprache der Wissenschaft', *Erkenntnis* (Leipzig), II (1931), 432–65.

'Uberwindung der Metaphysik durch logische Analyse der Sprache', *Erkenntnis*, II (1931), 219–41.

DOBSCHÜTZ, E. VON 'Zeit und Raum im Denken des Urchristentums', *Journal of Biblical Literature*, XLI (1922), 212–23.

EICHRODT, WALTER 'Heilserfahrung und Zeitverständnis im Alten Testament', *Theologische Zeitschrift*, XII (1956), 103–25.

GRESSMANN, HUGO 'Die neugefundene Lehre des Amen-em-ope und die vorexilische Spruchdichtung Israels', *Zeitschrift für die alttestamentliche Wissenschaft*, I (1924), 272–96.

'Farben', RGG¹, II, 827–29.

HEMPEL, J. 'Gott, Mensch, und Tier im Alten Testament', *Zeitschrift für systematische Theologie*, IX (1932), 217 ff.

HJELMSLEV, LOUIS 'Omkring sprogteoriens grundlaeggelse', *University Program* (Copenhagen), 1943, 97.

KIERKEGAARD, S. 'Samtidigheden', *Oieblikket*, no. 8, 11 September 1855. Article to be found in *Samlede Vaerker*, Copenhagen: Gyldendal, 1920–36, XIV, 309–15.

LUND, E. 'Ein Knotenpunkt in der Urgeschichte: Die Quellenfrage Genesis 9.18–19', ZAW, XV (1938), 34–43.

MOWINCKEL, S. 'Hypostasen', RGG², II, 2065–68.

ORDING, H. 'Frelsesoppfatningen hos Platon og i kristendommen', NTT, XXXIII (1932), 261 ff.

PEDERSEN, J. 'Gammeltestamentlig Skepticisme', *Edda* (Oslo), IV (1915), 273–315.

POHLENZ, MAX 'Stoa und Semitismus', *Neue Jahrbucher für Wissenschaft und Jugendbildung*, II (1926), 257–69.

RATSCHOW, C. H. 'Anmerkungen zur theologischen Auffassung des Zeitproblems', *Zeitschrift für Theologie und Kirche*, LI (1954), 360–87.

REGENBOGEN, O. 'Mimesis, Eine Rezension', *Motala* (1949), 11 ff.

RICKERT, H. 'Zwei Wege der Erkenntnistheorie', *Kant-Studien*, XIV (1909), 169–228.

STEINMANN, T. 'Immanenz und Transzendenz Gottes', RGG,[1] III, 440 ff.

WERTHEIMER, MAX 'Über das Denken der Naturvölker. I. Zahlen und Zahlgebilde', *Zeitschrift für Psychologie*, LX (1912), 321–78.

WETZSTEIN, J. G. 'Die syrische Dreschtafel', *Zeitschrift für Ethnologie*, V (1873), 270–302.

INDEX OF AUTHORS

INDEX OF BIBLICAL REFERENCES

SELECT INDEX OF HEBREW WORDS

SELECT INDEX OF GREEK WORDS